281.1
An22
v.15

DATE DUE			

Phillips Library
Bethany College
Bethany, W. Va. 26032

ST. AUGUSTINE
SERMONS
FOR
CHRISTMAS AND EPIPHANY

Ancient Christian Writers

THE WORKS OF THE FATHERS IN TRANSLATION

EDITED BY

JOHANNES QUASTEN, S.T.D. JOSEPH C. PLUMPE, Ph.D.
Professor of Ancient Church History *Professor of Patristic Greek*
and Christian Archaeology *and Ecclesiastical Latin*

The Catholic University of America
Washington, D. C.

No. 15

ST. AUGUSTINE

SERMONS FOR CHRISTMAS AND EPIPHANY

TRANSLATED AND ANNOTATED

BY

THOMAS COMERFORD LAWLER

NEWMAN PRESS

New York, N.Y./Ramsey, N.J.

Nihil Obstat:
　　　　J. Quasten
　　　　　Censor Deputatus

Imprimatur:
　　　　Patricius A. O'Boyle, D.D.
　　　　　Archiepiscopus Washingtonensis
　　　　　　die 21 Feb. 1952

COPYRIGHT 1952
BY
REV. JOHANNES QUASTEN
AND
REV. JOSEPH C. PLUMPE

Library of Congress
Catalog Card Number: 78-62464

ISBN: 0-8091-0137-8

PUBLISHED BY PAULIST PRESS
Editorial Office: 1865 Broadway, New York, N.Y. 10023
Business Office: 545 Island Road, Ramsey, N.J. 07446

PRINTED AND BOUND IN THE UNITED STATES OF AMERICA

CONTENTS

	PAGE
INTRODUCTION	3
TEXT	21
SERMON 1 (Ben. no. 51): AGREEMENT OF THE EVANGELISTS MATTHEW AND LUKE IN THE LORD'S GENEALOGY	21

SERMONS FOR CHRISTMAS

SERM. 2 (184)	71
SERM. 3 (185)	76
SERM. 4 (186)	80
SERM. 5 (187)	85
SERM. 6 (188)	91
SERM. 7 (189)	96
SERM. 8 (190)	101
SERM. 9 (191)	107
SERM. 10 (192)	112
SERM. 11 (193)	117
SERM. 12 (194)	121
SERM. 13 (195)	126
SERM. 14 (196)	129
SERM. 15 (140)	135

SERMONS FOR NEW YEAR'S DAY

SERM. 16 (197)	142
SERM. 17 (198)	149

SERMONS FOR EPIPHANY

SERM. 18 (199)	154
SERM. 19 (200)	159
SERM. 20 (201)	164
SERM. 21 (202)	169
SERM. 22 (203)	174
SERM. 23 (204)	178
NOTES	183
TO THE INTRODUCTION	185
TO THE TEXT	190
INDEX	233

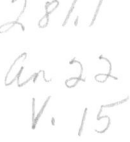

ST. AUGUSTINE

SERMONS
FOR
CHRISTMAS AND EPIPHANY

INTRODUCTION

"Those who read what he has written on divine subjects do so with profit. But I think that they were able to profit more from him whose privilege it was to see and hear him in person as he spoke in the church. . . ."
—*Possidius* [1]

Although the public sermons of Saint Augustine, his *Sermones ad populum,* have never enjoyed the popularity of many of his longer works, it is from the reading of these sermons that one obtains the best portrayal of the brilliant and profoundly spiritual Augustine presenting and interpreting the divine mysteries to the minds of his own people, of his great mind bending down, as it were, to nourish with the truths of God the "little ones in the nest of faith." [2] Here one finds Augustine expounding the Christian creed, exposing the fallacies of the various heresies and schisms, explaining the difficult passages of the Scriptures, resolving the doubts of his listeners—and all this in language that could be understood by his parishioners, by the ordinary layman. Reflected in these words of Augustine one sees the early Christians in their everyday lives,[3] thirsting for truth, tempted by the world around them, and sorely needing the guidance, the encouragement, and even the reprimands that their bishop was so well qualified to give them. In these sermons we also have one of the clearest records of Augustine's own spiritual and intellectual development [4] during his forty years as a priest and bishop.

Augustine's future pre-eminence as a Christian orator was foreshadowed even in his early school days in his native Tagaste and in Madauros: he himself notes that he was acclaimed for his excellence in declamation.[5] Again, for the years 370-373 when at Carthage he studied for the career of a professional rhetorician, he is witness to his own great success.[6] Having taught grammar at Tagaste for a semester or so, he returned to Carthage in the fall of 374 to teach rhetoric. Nine years later he left Carthage to establish a school of rhetoric in Rome. Here his fame increased, and after about a year he successfully applied for the position of municipal professor of rhetoric at Milan, then the seat of the Imperial court. During the two years he taught here, he made the acquaintance of Milan's first citizen, St. Ambrose, and he was attracted more and more to the Christian eloquence and the Christian truth unfolding itself to his soul in the sermons of the great bishop.[7] St. Ambrose baptized him during Easter week of 387.

Augustine, then, had been a noted orator and scholar long before his conversion and ordination. He was a master of every oratorical device.[8] Although preaching and giving religious instruction were at that time, at least in the Western Church, functions generally reserved to bishops, Valerius,[9] Augustine's predecessor as bishop of Hippo Regius, gave these faculties to Augustine while he was still a simple priest. The fruitful results of this action soon led other bishops to allow their priests to preach and instruct.[10]

When Augustine began to speak at Hippo, the people came in crowds to hear him—Catholics, pagans, and schismatic Donatists [11]—and, though by modern standards the diocese of Hippo was not large, his public sermons exerted a widespread influence. He spoke in clear, sure, and forceful language.[12] Augustine lived at a time when heresies and schisms were rampant in the Christian world, when even some of the most vigilant members of the faithful were being led astray by erring ecclesiastics. Though his sermons show his understanding of human weaknesses, his paternal affection and solicitude for the people in his care, they also show his firmness on what must be believed and done to merit salvation. Indefatigable in his pastoral duties, he preached not only on Sundays and feastdays, but on other days as well, especially during the Paschal season. It was not uncommon for him to preach on successive days or to deliver two or three sermons on a single day.

Augustine himself made no effort to edit his sermons after having delivered them, nor did he gather or arrange them in collections. Hence, while the preservation of so much of his spoken word provides us with excellent illustrations of what he preached and how he preached, even in extempore address, many of his sermons have inevitably been lost. Though he probably wrote or dictated some sermons either before or after delivery,[13] so that they could be read by others in his church at Hippo or elsewhere, obviously the survival of so many of his sermons must be credited in very great measure to his effectiveness and popularity as an orator.[14]

Other bishops frequently invited Augustine to come to their cities and instruct their flocks. Thus he was a frequent guest in the metropolitan see of Carthage. In fact, the majority of his popular sermons on the Psalms were given there. People followed him from basilica to basilica, not merely to hear his inspired discourses, but also to preserve the memory of him by preserving his words. In the front of the audience were the *notarii*, stenographers intent upon noting down everything that was said.[15] When the stenographic copy had been transcribed in longhand, a sermon could be read again and again. When a sufficient number of such sermons were available, they were assembled in a volume—codex—until in time there were many such codices. The sermons were generally assembled in the order in which they were copied down or in which they were found, with no effort made to arrange or rearrange them in any special order.

As Augustine's fame spread, the demand for copies of these sermons grew. Copies were made, and in time scattered throughout the Christian West, from city to city, to Italy, Gaul, and Spain. New collections were made, with the sermons taken from various codices. The copyists were often, unfortunately, quite lax in copying the titles, dates, and places where the sermons had been delivered. Sometimes the texts themselves were changed in various ways. Thus in later years a single Augustinian sermon might exist in several versions, each presumed to be a different sermon. Again, in some collections spurious sermons found a place side by side with genuine ones. By the advent of the Middle Ages the contents of a new collection could depend on no more than the whim of the collector.

The Benedictines of St. Maur brought order out of this chaos. In their edition (1683) of the sermons, based on a diligent collation of many manuscripts, they separated the doubtful and spurious sermons from the genuine, divided the sermons into four general classes *(De scrip-*

turis, De tempore, De sanctis, De diversis), and numbered them in an order that survives to-day. They counted 363 sermons as genuine, 33 as doubtful, and 317 as certainly not genuine.[16] Though a new edition, based on the advances of modern textual criticism and including the sermons that have come to light during the long interval, is much to be desired,[17] the Maurist text remains to this day "a masterpiece of human wisdom." [18]

Since the publication of the Maurist edition, a dozen collections of sermons have appeared under the name of Augustine. These total at least 640 discourses, of which 138 are accounted genuine.[19] For an over-all record, as it can be reconstructed to-day, of Augustine's preaching of the *verbum Dei*, we should also add the various groups of sermons or homilies that are found among his exegetical works. Not counting certain discourses that go under the title of treatises,[20] there are 124 *tractatus* on the Gospel of St. John, 54 of which appear to have been sermons actually delivered; the 10 *tractatus* on the First Epistle of St. John; the 205 *enarrationes* on the Psalms, of which at least 119 are sermons delivered.[21] Thus we arrive at a grand total of approximately 1535 known sermons attributed at one time or another to Augustine, of which approximately 685 are genuine. A remarkable record indeed; and new discoveries of Augustinian sermons hitherto unpublished continue in our day.[22]

The sermons included in the present volume are those of the Christmas season: one (Benedictine no. 51) delivered on an unknown date [23] near Christmas; the thirteen (184-196) given on Christmas Day; one (140) possibly delivered on Christmas Day; [24] the two (197-198) on

New Year's Day; and the six (199-204) on the feast of Epiphany.

Augustine makes a clear distinction between the two feasts of Christmas and Epiphany: "Only a few days ago we celebrated the Lord's birthday. To-day we are celebrating with equal solemnity, as is proper, His Manifestation. . . . Let us, therefore, with joy of the spirit hold dear these two days, the Nativity and the Manifestation of our Lord." [25] He gives each of the feasts its traditional date: Christmas, the birthday of Christ, is celebrated on December 25, the feast of Epiphany and the adoration of the Magi, on January 6. He declares these to be the historical dates: "He is said to have been born on the twenty-fifth of December"; [26] "Now, tradition has it that our Lord Jesus Christ, born twelve days ago, was adored by the Magi on this day. That they adored Him is a truth spoken by the Gospel; on what day they did so, is proclaimed by the fact that this glorious feast is observed everywhere." [27]

Augustine derives the date for Christmas from the presupposition that Christ's life on earth began on March 25, the day He was conceived by the Virgin Mary, and that, consequently, allowing for a gestation period of 275 days, He was born on December 25: Augustine mentions the period which is "computed from the twenty-fifth of March —the day on which the Lord is believed to have been conceived, because He also suffered on that same date—to the twenty-fifth of December, the day on which He was born." [28] Actually, however, the date of the feast of the Nativity has an interesting history of very different character. Christmas was not celebrated at all by the earliest Christians, for they regarded the celebration of birthdays as a typically pagan custom.²⁹ Moreover, several documents of the third century indicate that various dates were assigned to the birthday of Christ—March 28, April 2, May 20, and so on.³⁰ Since the Emperor Aurelian (270-275), December 25, the winter solstice of the Julian Calendar, was set aside for the celebration of the *natalis Invicti*, the birthday of the Imperial divinity, the sun-god *Sol Invictus*.³¹ To offset the dominating influence of this pagan anniversary, the Church introduced the feast— to be celebrated on the same date—of the *natalis Christi*, the birthday of Christ, the "Sun of Justice."³² St. Augustine repeatedly reflects this purpose when he urges in his Christmas sermons that not the sun but the Creator of the sun should be the object of adoration: "Not the visible sun, but the sun's invisible Creator gave us this holy day";³³ "Let us . . . keep this day with due solemnity; not, like those who are without faith, on account of the sun, but because of Him who made the sun. For He who was *the Word, was made flesh*, that for our sakes He might be under the sun. Under the sun, to be sure, in His flesh; but in His majesty, over the whole universe in which He made the sun. And now, too, He, incarnate, stands over that sun which is worshipped as God by those who, intellectually blind, do not see the true Sun of Justice."³⁴

Whenever Augustine enumerates the principal feasts of the ecclesiastical year, that is, those of the Passion, the Resurrection, the Ascension, and Pentecost, he does not mention Christmas and Epiphany. This indicates that he did not consider them to be of the same age as the others, but of a later date. We have documentary evidence that at Rome the Church celebrated Christmas on

December 25 in the year 336, and it was thought that the feast was introduced there about the year 330.³⁵ But, as we shall see presently, there is excellent reason for assuming that we should go several decades beyond that date.

The earliest testimony for the celebration of the feast in Augustine's native Africa dates from about the year 360. There, as also at Rome, its observance antedates that of Epiphany, introduced during the Donatist controversies. The Donatists celebrated Christmas, but rejected Epiphany as an innovation of the Oriental Church. Thus Augustine says in an Epiphany sermon delivered probably before the year 412: "With good reason have the heretical Donatists never wished to celebrate this day with us: they neither love unity, nor are they in communion with the Eastern Church where that star appeared."³⁶ Augustine is right: the feast of Epiphany originated in the East and spread to the West, whereas the feast of Christmas on December 25 was created in the West and adopted by the East.

Now, it is argued by Hugo Rahner and others,³⁶ᵃ that after the defection of the Donatists from the mother church in Africa, they would have been no more inclined to follow her in the adoption of a new feast, Christmas, than they were later when Epiphany was introduced. Hence it is quite probable that the feast had already been received in Africa from Rome some time before the rise of the Donatist schism between the years 305 and 312. Rahner would postulate that Christmas had been introduced at Rome, and from there into Africa, some years before the persecution of Diocletian broke out in 302; in other words, before the close of the third century. The feast of the *Sol Invictus*, it will be recalled, had been instituted during the third-last decade of that century.

The testimony for Africa referred to above is a sermon by Optatus of Mileve, delivered around the year 360. This document, the oldest Christmas sermon which has come down to us from Christian antiquity,[37] implies that at that time the feast of Epiphany was unknown in Africa. It speaks in the introduction of the intention to celebrate the mystery of the birth of Christ, and continues treating the intrigues of Herod and the gifts of the Magi in detail, a topic more appropriate for the feast of Epiphany. Not before Epiphany was introduced as an independent feast in the Church of Africa, was the commemoration of the adoration of the Magi separated from the conception of Christmas and made the main theme of the new feast. Augustine's sermons on Epiphany are the best proof of this liturgical development.

Prior to the exchange of these feasts between the East and the West, the "manifestation" of Christ in His birth had been commemorated by the Eastern Church on Epiphany. Henceforth other manifestations of Christ's divinity—theophanies—were commemorated on Epiphany: His "manifestations" to the Magi, at His baptism in the Jordan, and in His first miracle at the marriage in Cana. The first of these, Christ's adoration by the Magi, interpretated as His first "manifestation" to the Gentiles or pagans, became the dominant theme of the feast in the West, as the Epiphany sermons of St. Augustine testify. The Greek name for the feast was rendered *Declaratio, Manifestatio,* and *Apparitio.*[38]

The first sermon in our volume is a long exegetical discourse, apparently delivered on neither feastday nor Sunday: Augustine notes that his audience consists of "only such . . . as desire to hear a sermon" and that he is not speaking "to hearts that are deaf, nor to minds that are bored." [39] The general subject of the sermon is the Lord's genealogy, that is, the agreement of the two lists of His ancestors recorded in the Gospels of Matthew and Luke. The composition of the discourse suggests that Augustine was not following a prepared manuscript, but rather adapting his observations to the reactions of his listeners. At the beginning of the sermon he reminds his audience that he is preaching it in fulfillment of a promise he had made them. He speaks of the evils of the day, and encourages all to be zealous about the salvation of those who prefer the theater to church. He goes on to show why Christ was born of a woman, and proceeds to give a detailed explanation of the apparent inconsistencies of the Gospels in their record of the genealogy of Christ. Other difficult passages in the Bible are explained. He discusses Mary's virginity and Joseph's justice, and insists that Joseph was truly a father—a chaste father just as Mary was a chaste mother—and that the Evangelists rightly traced the Lord's ancestry through him. Augustine shows that both Mary and Jesus gave Joseph the respect due a husband and father; he states that what the Holy Spirit wrought for the one spouse in their virginal marriage He wrought for both.[40] He discourses at length on marriage and its purpose, and warns against adultery and all forms of lust. The sermon also abounds with examples of his love of numbers; in particular, he attaches mystical significance to the numbers in the Scriptural passages he quotes. He concludes by advising his listeners not to be disturbed when they do not yet understand certain parts of the Scriptures, and warns them not to become conceited when they do understand them.

The thirteen sermons that follow were delivered on Christmas Day. Here Augustine emphasizes that this feast should be celebrated with profound joy and gratitude in the hearts of all. He speaks of the wondrous mysteries surrounding the birth of the Savior—not only the birth without a father as the Son of Mary, the Son of man, the Sun of Justice, the Truth sprung out of the earth, [41] but also His birth without a mother as the Son of God from all eternity—for which birth there is no birthday. He insists that Christ was truly God and truly man. He speaks often of the paradox, *infans Verbum*. In Sermon 5 (187) he draws a detailed and beautiful simile between the Word of God and the spoken word. Time and time again in these sermons he reminds his audience of the wonderful mercy of God who for our sakes came into this world without leaving the Father in heaven. He is ever a witness to Mary's perpetual virginity and never tires of extolling a chaste life. He stresses the importance of faith for an understanding of the mysteries. In Sermon 14 (196) he reminds his audience of the lapse of some into certain superstitious practices and warns them not to revert to the celebration of pagan rites on the coming 1st of January —the only note of severity in all the Christmas sermons.

Sermon 15 (140) is primarily a refutation of the Arian heresy, which maintained that Christ was not of the same substance and essence as God the Father. Augustine clearly and forcefully expounds the Church's doctrine that God the Son is one with God the Father. The fact that this sermon is so different from the other sermons for Christmas Day is a strong indication that Augustine did not deliver it on that feast and that it was rather adapted at a later date for use on Christmas.[42]

Sermons 16(197) and 17(198) in this volume are the two extant sermons delivered on the 1st of January—New Year's Day. There is, of course, no reference to the feast of the Circumcision; this feast was probably not celebrated before the sixth century.[43] Both discourses are directed primarily against the pagans and pagan customs and habits. In the first he speaks against evil, or ungodliness, in general, and against idolatry and pride in particular. He exposes the human origin of the pagan gods, and warns his audience against the wiles of pseudo-philosophers. The second is given to a discussion of pagan customs and celebrations, and of what Christians must do to "separate" themselves from unbelievers: they are to show how they differ from them by the difference of their Christian living—in their faith, their hope, their charity.

Our last six sermons were delivered by St. Augustine on the feast of Epiphany. Here he describes the coming of the Magi—the first fruits of the Gentiles—in their search for Christ, the newborn King of the Jews. He calls Christ the Cornerstone uniting two walls coming from different directions, of the Jews (that is, those Jews who, like the shepherds, believed in Him) and of the Gentiles. He sets forth how the Jews who do not believe, bear witness in their own Scriptures to the Christ whom they have refused to recognize, how even the pagan Magi were directed to the birthplace of Christ by unbelieving Jews. Characteristically, Augustine notes the circumstance that these Magi were led by a star in the heavens, and so finds his cue to expose the folly of astrology, the cult of which was so rampant during Imperial times.[44]

In or about the year 405 Augustine wrote his treatise *De catechizandis rudibus*,[45] a manual of practical advice for the religious instruction of the "unlearned"—prospective converts. It is interesting to note how in his sermons to the less learned he followed his own advice: of being well prepared and having a definite objective for each lesson; of adapting instruction to the interests and capacities of the instructed; of giving clear summaries and shunning excessive and unnecessary subtleties; of putting emphasis on wondrous events because they appeal to, and remain in, the minds of people; of avoiding discourses that are too long. If an occasional sermon, for example, the first appearing in the present selection, seems unduly long, it should be remembered that many of his addresses were to people who listened to him with remarkable avidity, who wanted to hear all that he had to say, people who were often disappointed because they thought his homily too short.[46] Bardenhewer's[47] comparison of the great preacher bishop of Hippo with the illustrious orator of the East, John Chrysostom, in which he observes that Augustine often contented himself with a sermon of fifteen minutes, while Chrysostom often required two hours, is certainly borne out for the former as we read his sermons for Christmas and Epiphany; and we agree, too, that Augustine's sole purpose in preaching is to instruct and teach, not to entertain.

But, as Bardenhewer also observes,[48] the élite among Augustine's audience—Roman officials, the better-educated Christians, Donatists, and pagans, and others—did not attend his sermons wholly uncompensated if the spiritual fare they sought also included rhetoric. No-one, for instance, will fail to observe the magnificent artistic effort, involving parallelism and antithesis and a striking use of homoeoteleuton, or rhyme, put forth in the following passage of a sermon for Epiphany—a vivid contrast between the conduct of the Magi and that of the Jews:

In terra eorum isti requirebant,
quem illi in sua non agnoscebant.
Apud eos isti infantem invenerunt,
quem illi apud se docentem negaverunt.
In his terris de longinquo isti peregrini puerum Christum nondum
    verba promentem adoraverunt,
ubi cives illi iuvenem miracula facientem crucifixerunt.
Isti in membris parvis Deum agnoverunt,
illi in factis magnis nec tamquam homini pepercerunt:
quasi plus fuerit videre novam stellam in eius nativitate fulgentem,
quam solem eius in morte lugentem. [49]

It may be, however, that—as has been pointed out recently [50]—rhetorical devices as employed in the passage cited above had a special appeal also to the popular ear. It seems, for example, that the Africans were particularly appreciative of rhyme and all alliteration. So, too, the language of the people favors wordplay, and this device Augustine employs constantly.[51] It is usually quite impossible to reproduce the effect of wordplay in translation, for which reason some of the more notable instances have been set down in the notes. A popular element is also found in numerous cases of repetitious language, which—as is also true of equally frequent instances of extremely concise diction—it is well-nigh impossible to convert into palatable English.

    A word, finally, regarding the use of Scripture in these

Introduction

sermons: Augustine not merely embellishes his teaching of the people with quotations from the Bible; but, as Pope puts it, "It was the Bible all the time. . . . It is the quarry for all his doctrine; it is 'the word of God' that feeds his soul and out of which he 'provides old things and new' for the spiritual needs of his flock." [52] Saturated as his sermons are with material from both the Old and the New Testament, it might be supposed that his audience was extraordinarily well acquainted with the Bible. Such undoubtedly was the case, especially if we consider for comparison popular familiarity with the Bible in our own time. Here we should reflect, however, on the role played in the liturgy of Augustine's time by readings or lessons from the Bible. The available Christian literature, moreover, was still quite circumscribed—it was in largest part the Bible. Again, if it appears that knowledge and love of the Bible were present to a marked degree, it must be remembered that the audiences of St. Augustine owed this particularly to his own incessant efforts and his unremitting application to his office, of which he said: *Nos verba Dei seminamus*—"We are the sowers of God's word." [53]

The fact that during Augustine's lifetime there were many Latin translations of the Bible in use, is also reflected in our group of sermons. In several instances two different versions, apparently including also the Vulgate, are used for the same passage. In part such divergences may be owing to the fact that Augustine quotes from memory. Regarding the Vulgate, it is known, of course, that Augustine was, at least at first, somewhat reluctant and even unwilling to accept the translation, particularly of the Old Testament, made by his contemporary, St.

Jerome.⁵⁴ Further, it is obvious that in a group of sermons dating perhaps—if we follow Kunzelmann's chronology of the sermons ⁵⁵—from more than three decades of Augustine's life, the chances of deviation and variety in Scriptural citation are unusually great. Where significant divergences occur, these receive brief attention in the notes.⁵⁶

⁘ ⁘ ⁘

The text followed in the present translation, except for two of the sermons, is that published by the Benedictines of St. Maur: *Sancti Aurelii Augustini Hipponensis episcopi opera* 5 (Paris 1683) 282-302, 680-82, 881-919, reprinted in Migne's PATROLOGIA LATINA 38 (Paris 1845) 332-54, 773-75, 997-1039. For sermon 2(184) I have used the text furnished by D. C. Lambot, *Sancti Aurelii Augustini sermones selecti duodeviginti*, STROMATA PATRISTICA ET MEDIAEVALIA 1 (Utrecht-Brussels 1950) 74-76; for Sermon 7(189), the text by G. Morin, *Sancti Augustini sermones post Maurinos reperti*, MISCELLANEA AGOSTINIANA 1 (Rome 1930) 209-211.

Two of the sermons here offered, nos. 1(51) and 15(140), have been translated previously by R. G. Macmullen in the collection, A LIBRARY OF FATHERS OF THE HOLY CATHOLIC CHURCH 16: *Sermons on Selected Lessons of the New Testament by S. Augustine, Bishop of Hippo,* 1 (Oxford 1844) 1-32 and 2 (1845) 650-54, reprinted in NICENE AND POST-NICENE FATHERS 6 (New York 1903) 245-59, 529-31. Macmullen is an able translator whom I have consulted with profit.⁵⁷ A French version, which is quite free, of all our sermons is found in M. Raulx, *Oeuvres complètes de S. Augustin* 6 (Bar-le-Duc 1866) 230-46, 372-74; 7 (1868) 151-91. The modern French translation of select sermons made by G. Humeau, *Les plus beaux sermons de S. Augustin*, 3 vols. (Paris 1932-1934), was not available. A recent Dutch version of Sermons 3(185), 5(187), 7(189), 8(190), 17(198), and 19(200) is given by C. Mohrmann, *Sint Augustinus, preken voor het volk*, MONUMENTA CHRISTIANA, 1 reeks 1 (Utrecht-Brussels 1948) 289-310. A free German version of Sermons 2(184), 7(189), 17(198), 18(199), and 20(201) may be found in A. Schmitt, *Augustinus-Predigten, eine Auswahl für Sonn- und Feiertage des Kirchenjahres* (Mannheim 1947) 39-47, 55-69.

1
(Ben. no. 51) [1]

AGREEMENT OF THE EVANGELISTS MATTHEW AND LUKE IN THE LORD'S GENEALOGY

A discussion of the question proposed on Christmas. A day of the shows.

My dear people,[2] may He fulfill your expectation who has awakened it! For though we trust that what we have to say is not our own, but God's, still with far greater reason do we say what the Apostle says humbly: *We have this treasure in earthen vessels, that the excellency may be of the power of God, and not of us.*[3] And so I do not doubt that you remember our promise. We made it in Him through whom we now fulfill it; for when we were making the promise, we petitioned Him; and now as we redeem it, we are really His debtors.

You will recall, too, my dear people, that on Christmas morning we postponed the question which we had proposed to solve; because many, even of those who find the word of God burdensome, were with us to celebrate the festivities usual on that day. But now, I suppose, only such have come here as desire to hear a sermon. We are not, therefore, speaking to hearts that are deaf, nor to minds that are bored; and this your eager expectation is actually a prayer for me.

There is something else: the gladiatorial shows, too, have attracted many away from here; and we exhort you, Brethren, to follow our example and work as diligently as we for their salvation; and do pray earnestly to God for these people whose minds are not yet intent upon the spectacles of truth, but are given up to spectacles of the flesh.[4]

I realize and know full well that at this moment there are among you some who have this day come to despise them; for they are breaking with their inveterate habits. Men change—both for better and for worse. Daily experiences of this sort make us in turn both happy and sad: happy, when men reform; sad, when they become depraved. And this is why, too, the Lord does not say that he who begins will be saved; but He says, *he that shall persevere unto the end, he shall be saved.*[5]

The "Christian shows." Sensual men witness the death of the martyrs in one way, spiritual men in another.

2. But what could our Lord Jesus Christ, the Son of God, who is also the Son of man—for He has seen fit to be this also—grant to us more wonderful, what more magnificent than that He should gather into His fold not only people who attend these frivolous shows, but even a number of those who take part in them? He has actually hounded to their salvation not only men who love the hounding of wild beasts in the arena, but also such as do the hounding.

He himself was made a spectacle. Hear how. He said so Himself, He Himself foretold it before they made Him a spectacle, and in the words of the Prophet predicted as a fact already accomplished what was going to happen, saying in the Psalm: *They have pierced my hands and feet. They have numbered all my bones.*[6] See how He was made a spectacle, so that His bones were numbered! And this spectacle itself He expresses even more clearly— *and they have looked and stared upon me.*[7] He was made a spectacle to be made fun of, made a spectacle by men who certainly did not purpose to favor Him in that spectacle, but to vent their fury on Him.

In this same way He in the beginning caused His martyrs to be made a spectacle, as the Apostle says: *We are made a spectacle to the world, and to angels, and to men.*[8] But two types of men, the one sensual, the other spiritual, are spectators at such spectacles. The sensual spectators look upon the martyrs—those thrown to the beasts, those beheaded, those consumed by fire—as wretched people; they despise and abhor them. But others are spectators even as the holy angels are—paying no attention to the mangling of their bodies, but admiring the unimpaired survival of their faith. A grand spectacle is here offered to the eyes of the heart—a soul unscathed while the body is torn to pieces!

When these things are read in church, you are interested spectators of them with the eyes of your hearts; for if you were not witnessing a spectacle, you would be hearing nothing. You see, then, that you have not passed by the spectacles to-day, but you have made a special choice of them.[9] May God therefore be with you and make attractive the account you will give of these your spectacles to your friends whom you grieved to see running to the amphitheater to-day and unwilling to come to church. Thus they, too, may begin to regard those things as contemptible the attraction to which has made them contemptible; and so they will join you in loving God, to love whom can put no-one to shame, for in Him he will be loving One who cannot be conquered. Together with you let them love Christ, who by that very thing in which He seemed to be conquered, conquered the world. For He has conquered the world, as we see, Brethren: He has subdued all powers, He has subjugated kings, not by a haughty army, but by a derided Cross; not by the fury of the sword, but by hanging on the Wood; by suffering physically, by toiling spiritually. His body was raised up on the Cross, but thus He subjugated souls to the Cross. And then, what gem is there in the diadem of rulers more precious than the Cross on their brow?

In loving Him you are never put to shame. How many are there who return from the amphitheater—beaten because they have been beaten for whom they shout like madmen! And they would be beaten still more, if their favorites were to win. For they would then enslave themselves to vain joy, enslave themselves to the triumph of a perverted desire—they who are already beaten by the impulse which makes them run to that place. Indeed, Brethren, how many do you think were undecided to-day as to whether they should come here or go there? And they who in this moment of hesitation reflected upon Christ and hastened to church, have overcome, not some mere human person, but the devil himself, the most vicious hounder of souls in all the world. Those, on the other hand, who in that hesitation chose rather to run to the amphitheater, have obviously been conquered by him whom the others have conquered—but conquered in Him who says, *Rejoice, because I have overcome the world.*[10]

For this is why the Supreme Commander [11] allowed Himself to be tempted, that He might teach His soldiers to fight.

Why Christ wished to be born of a woman.
Through woman came destruction,
through woman, salvation.

3. Therefore, that our Lord Jesus Christ might do this, He became the Son of man by being born, as we know, of a woman. "But suppose," someone says, "that He had not been born of the Virgin Mary: would that have detracted from what He was? Granted, it was His will to be man: yet He might have been man without being born of a woman. Take the first man He made—He did not make him of woman." Here you have my answer: Why, you say, should He have chosen to be born of a woman? The answer: And why should He shun birth of a woman? Let me concede that I cannot show why He chose to be born of a woman: you show me what there was in woman that He should have shunned.

And here we have stated it, namely, that if He had shunned the womb of woman, this might have been taken as an intimation that He could have been contaminated by her. But the more incapable He was of being defiled because of what He is, the less ought He to have dreaded the womb of woman, as though He could possibly be stained by it; on the contrary, by being born of a woman He could not but show us some great mystery. For of course, Brethren, we, too, admit that if the Lord had wished to become man without being born of woman, this certainly was an easy matter for His sovereign power.

Just as He was able to be born of a woman without a man, so was this possible for Him without the woman.

But here He has shown us that no human being, regardless of sex, should be without hope. The human sexes are male and female. Now then, if He, manifesting Himself as a man—and obviously it was proper for Him to be such—had not been born of a woman, women might have despaired of themselves; they would have been mindful of their first sin, of the fact that it was through woman that the first man was deceived; and they would have thought that they had no hope whatever in Christ. He came, then, as a man to give the male sex special preference; and He was born of a woman to console the female sex. It was as though He addressed them and said: "That you might know that of itself God's creature is not bad, but only an evil desire has perverted it—in the beginning when I made man, I made them male and female. I do not condemn my own creation. See, I have been born a man; see, I have been born of a woman. It is not, therefore, my own creation that I condemn, but the sins which are not my handiwork."

Let each sex see its own honor, let each confess its own guilt, and let them both hope for salvation. When man was about to be deceived, it was through woman that the potion of destruction was administered to him: so, when man is to be restored, let it be through woman that the cup of salvation is presented to him. Let woman make good the sin of man deceived through her, by giving birth to Christ. Hence, too, women were the first to announce the Resurrection of God to the Apostles. The woman in Paradise announced death to her husband; and so, too, the women in the Church announced salvation to the men.

The Apostles were to announce Christ's Resurrection to the nations; women announced it to the Apostles. Therefore, let no one misrepresent the fact that Christ was born of a woman. The Deliverer could not have been defiled by that sex; and as its Creator He could not but show it favor.

The faith of the Gospel has been received in the whole world.

4. "But," say they, "how are we to believe that Christ was born of a woman?" Let me answer—by the Gospel, which has been preached and is still preached to the entire world.

But in their blindness these men, striving to make others blind and failing to see what should be seen, while working to do away with what should be believed, try to call into question what is already an accepted belief the world over. For example, they say by way of reply: "Do not try to silence us by quoting the whole world as authority. Let us look to Scripture itself. You must not act the demagogue. It is only the multitude led astray that favors you."

In the first place, I have this answer to make: I am favored by a multitude led astray? This multitude once was a mere handful. What made this multitude grow, a development which was predicted so long before? Of course, such growth is not apparent where there is no conception of this "multitude" as it was before. And no, I do not say there was a mere handful: there was only one person—Abraham! Consider this, Brethren: at that time Abraham stood alone throughout the entire globe, among all men, among all nations; and to this man it was said,

In thy seed shall all nations be blessed.[12] What this one man believed as a single individual has been presented to many in the multitude of his seed. Then it was not seen, and was believed; now it is seen, and is denied; and what was then said to one person, and believed by one person, is now, when it is professed by many, attacked by some few.

He who made His disciples fishers of men, enclosed within His nets every kind of authority. If it is the multitude that is to be believed, what is better represented everywhere in the world than the Church? If the rich are to be believed, let them note how many rich people He has taken. If the poor are to be believed, let them take notice of the thousands of poor. If it is to be the nobles, almost all the nobility is within; if kings, let them see all of them subjected to Christ; if the leaders among the eloquent, and learned, and experienced, let them behold what great orators, what scholars, what philosophers of this world have been caught by those fishermen, drawn from the deep to their salvation. Let them think of Him who, coming down to heal by the example of His own humility the great evil of the human soul, that is, pride, *chose the weak things of the world that He might confound the strong; chose the foolish things of this world that He might confound the wise*—not those who really were, but those who only seemed to be—*and chose the base things of this world . . . and things that are not, that He might bring to nought things that are.*[13]

*In endeavoring to understand the Gospels, it is safe
to hold that they contain no discrepancies.
The advantage of a hidden meaning.
Curtains hung in a house.*

5. "Say what you wish," they say, "we find that where you read that Christ was born, the Gospels disagree with one another; and two things which disagree cannot both be true."

"When I point out the disagreement," it is said, " I am right in rejecting the faith; or else do you, who accept the faith, show that there is agreement."

"And what disagreement," I ask, "is it that you will point out?"

"A patent one," he replies, "one which no-one can contradict."

How safe you are when you hear all this, because you are the faithful! [14] Listen, dearly beloved, and see what sound advice the Apostle has for us when he says: *As therefore you have received Christ Jesus our Lord, walk ye in Him, rooted and built up in Him, and confirmed in the faith.*[15] With this simple and solid faith we ought to persevere in Him, that He may Himself make known to the faithful what is hidden in Him; for, as the same Apostle says, *in Him are hid all the treasures of wisdom and knowledge.*[16] And regarding these treasures, He does not hide them in order to deny them, but to arouse a desire for them because they are hidden. This is the advantage of something that is secret. Honor in Him what you do not yet understand; and honor it the more, the more numerous the curtains that hide it away. The higher a man's rank, the more is his home hung with curtains. The curtains lend honor to that which is kept secret; but to those who honor it, they are lifted up. Those, however, who jeer at the curtains, are repulsed and kept from even coming near them. Because, therefore, we turn unto Christ, the veil is taken away.[17]

The pious faith of the Scriptures. Augustine's self-deception when he turned to the Divine Scriptures with an impious mind.

6. They marshal their detractions and say, "Matthew is of course an Evangelist?"

We answer "Yes" with pious tongue and devout heart, having no doubts whatsoever; we answer clearly, "Matthew is an Evangelist."

"Do you believe him?" they say.

Who would not answer, as you did just now by the pious murmur of your voices, "Yes, I do"?

Yes, Brethren, if you are securely established in your belief, there is no reason for you to be ashamed. I am speaking to you as one who was once deceived, when in my youth I at first was determined to bring to the Divine Scriptures subtlety for the purpose of discrediting them rather than a pious reverence in consulting them. I myself, by my evil ways, was closing the door of my Lord against myself. When I should have been knocking that it might be opened, I was working to close it all the more. For I in my pride was daring to seek what only a humble person can find.

How much happier you are now! How confidently you

learn, and how safely—all of you who are still little ones in the nest of faith, and receive the spiritual food! But I, wretch that I was, left the nest when I thought I was ready to fly; and instead of flying, I fell. But the merciful Lord, to keep me from being trampled to death by passersby, lifted me up and put me in the nest again. For I was thoroughly perplexed by the things which I am now confidently proposing and explaining to you in the name of the Lord.[18]

How Christ is the Son of Abraham and of David.

7. Wherefore, as I began to say, this is how those people misrepresent things: "Matthew," they say, "is an Evangelist, and you believe him?"

It stands to reason, of course, that if we acknowledge him to be an Evangelist, we necessarily believe him.

"Note the generations of Christ which Matthew has set down: *The book of the generation of Jesus Christ, the Son of David, the Son of Abraham.*[19] How is He the *Son of David,* how the *Son of Abraham?*"

It cannot be shown except through His family lineage. It is quite obvious that when the Lord was born of the Virgin Mary, neither Abraham nor David was in the world.

"And you say that one and the same person is both the Son of David and the Son of Abraham?"

Let us, as it were, say to Matthew: Well then, prove what you say. I am looking for the family lineage of Christ. *Abraham,* he says, *begot Isaac. And Isaac begot Jacob. And Jacob begot Judas and his brethren. And Judas begot Phares and Zara of Thamar. And Phares begot Esron.*

And Esron begot Aram. And Aram begot Aminadab. And Aminadab begot Naasson. And Naasson begot Salmon. And Salmon begot Booz of Rahab. And Booz begot Obed of Ruth. And Obed begot Jesse. And Jesse begot David the king.[20]

Note now how the lineage reaches from David to Christ, who is called the Son of Abraham and the Son of David. *And David, he says, begot Solomon of her that had been the wife of Urias. And Solomon begot Roboam. And Roboam begot Abia. And Abia begot Asa. And Asa begot Josaphat. And Josaphat begot Joram. And Joram begot Ozias. And Ozias begot Joatham. And Joatham begot Achaz. And Achaz begot Ezechias. And Ezechias begot Manasses. And Manasses begot Amon. And Amon begot Josias. And Josias begot Jechonias and his brethren in the transmigration of Bablyon. And after the transmigration of Babylon Jechonias begot Salathiel. And Salathiel begot Zorobabel. And Zorobabel begot Abiud. And Abiud begot Eliacim. And Eliacim begot Azor. And Azor begot Sadoc. And Sadoc begot Achim. And Achim begot Eliud. And Eliud begot Eleazar. And Eleazar begot Mathan. And Mathan begot Jacob. And Jacob begot Joseph the husband of Mary, of whom was born Jesus, who is called Christ.*[21] Thus, then, through the order and succession of parents and ancestors, Christ is found to be the Son of David, the Son of Abraham.

The generations from Abraham to Christ.

8. Against this record drawn up with meticulous care they trump up as their first stricture the fact that the same

Matthew goes on to say: *All the generations, from Abraham to David, are fourteen generations; and from David to the transmigration of Babylon are fourteen generations; and from the transmigration of Babylon to Christ are fourteen generations.*[22] Then, to recount how Christ was born of the Virgin Mary, he said further: *Now the generation of Christ was in this wise. . . .*[23] By setting forth His genealogy, he had told why Christ is called the Son of David, Son of Abraham; and now it was for him to tell how He was born and appeared among men. And so there follows logically the narrative on the basis of which we believe that not only was our Lord Jesus Christ, through whom all things have been made, born of the eternal God, coeternal with Him who was His Begetter before all times, before all creation; but was also born in time by the Holy Spirit of the Virgin Mary—and this we confess as well as the other. You—I am speaking, of course, to my fellow Catholics—you remember and you know that this is our faith, that this we profess and confess. For this faith thousands of martyrs have been slain all over the world.

Christ's conception by the Holy Spirit.
Joseph's justice is sincere, not cruel.

9. Now, as to what follows, those who purpose to discredit the Gospel books wish to laugh at this also; as though this were proof that we were foolhardy to believe what is said in the following: *When as His mother Mary was espoused to Joseph, before they came together, she was found with child, of the Holy Spirit. Whereupon Joseph her husband, being a just man, and not willing publicly to*

expose her, was minded to put her away privately.[24]

To be sure, because he knew that she was not pregnant by him, he drew the logical conclusion, so to say, that she was an adulteress. *Being a just man,* as the Scripture says, *and not willing publicly to expose her,* that is, "to make the matter common knowledge"—and this is also what many codices have [25]—*he was minded to put her away privately.* True, as a husband, he was disturbed; but as a just man, he is not harsh. So great is the justice attributed to this man that he neither wished to have an adulteress in her, nor did he presume to punish her by exposing her. *He was minded,* it says, *to put her away privately*: because he not only did not wish to punish her, but did not wish to betray her. Note the sincerity of his justice! Not because of a desire to have her did he wish to spare her. Love of the flesh induces many to spare their wives involved in adultery; they decide to keep them even if they are adulteresses, so that in them they may have a full enjoyment of carnal lust. But this just man has no wish to keep her, showing that he does not have a carnal love; at the same time he does not wish to punish her, wherefore in his mercy he spares her. How truly just a man is this! He would neither keep an adulteress, nor would he create the impression that he is sparing her because of a lustful love for her; and yet he would neither punish nor betray her. Most deservedly was he chosen for the witness of his wife's virginity. Wherefore in his anxiety, coming to him through human infirmity, he was reassured by an expression of divine authority.

Interpretation of the name Jesus.

10. For the Evangelist continues, saying: *While he thought on these things, behold the angel of the Lord appeared to him in his sleep, saying: Joseph . . . , fear not to take unto thee Mary thy wife, for that which is conceived in her is of the Holy Spirit. And she shall bring forth a Son, and thou shalt call His name Jesus. Why Jesus? For,* he says, *He shall save His people from their sins.*[26] It is seen, then, that "Jesus" in Hebrew means "Savior" in our language.[27] We note this from the present explanation of the name; for as if the question were asked, "Why *Jesus*?" he promptly added by way of explaining the reason of the word, *for He shall save His people from their sins.*

This do we believe conscientiously, this do we hold with all our strength: Christ was born by the Holy Spirit of the Virgin Mary.

The good that comes of heretics. The good that came through the traitor Judas.

11. What, then, is it that these people say?

"If I discover a false statement," says one, "surely you will refuse to believe the whole account."

Find such a case! Let us see it!

"I shall count the generations."

Thus by their misrepresentations those people challenge us and bring us to this. If we but live virtuous lives, if we keep our belief in Christ, if we do not desire to fly from the nest before the time, they actually bring us to this— to the knowledge of mysteries. And so, my dear Christians,²⁸ note the usefulness of heretics—usefulness, of course, in the sense that God makes good use even of bad people. But they themselves are repaid according to what their intentions were, not according to the good that God accomplishes through them. Take the case of Judas: how much good has He done through him! By the Lord's Passion all nations have been saved. But to bring about the Lord's suffering, Judas betrayed Him. And thus God both frees the nations by the Passion of His Son, and punishes Judas for his crime.

Now, as to the mysteries ²⁹ which lie hidden there, no-one who is content to abide by a simple faith, would pry into them; and so, because no-one pried into them, no-one would find them—if it were not for the agitation of these pettifoggers. For when heretics make their false charges, the little ones become very much disturbed; when disturbed, they make search; their search is, to put it that way, a beating of their heads at their mother's breasts that they may give out as much milk as is sufficient for her little ones.³⁰ They, then, because they are disturbed, search; and they who know and have learned these things because they have studied them and God has opened to their knocking, on their part open to those who are disturbed. And thus it happens that while those people practice their sophistries for the purpose of seducing others into error, they actually prove themselves useful for the discovery of truth. For the quest of truth would be conducted less zealously, were it not for the lying adversaries it has. *For,* Scripture says, *there must be also heresies;* and, as though we might ask why this should be so, it immediately adds, *that they who are approved may be made manifest among you.*³¹

If Jechonias is counted twice, three times fourteen generations are found in Matthew.

12. What, then, is it that those people say?

Note that Matthew numbers the generations, and says that from Abraham to David there are fourteen, and from David to the transmigration to Babylon fourteen, and from the transmigration to Babylon to Christ fourteen. Multiply fourteen by three. You get forty-two. But they count the generations, and find forty-one; and they bring up their sophistries, and ridicule and scoff.

Now then, what does this mean—the fact that in the Gospel it is said that there are three times fourteen generations; but when all are counted together there are not forty-two, but forty-one? Without doubt there is a great mystery [32] here. And we rejoice, giving thanks to God, because even through the occasion of people appearing as malignant critics we find something which, the more it was concealed when it had to be studied, gives us so much more satisfaction when it is found. For, as we said by way of introduction, we are producing a spectacle for your minds.

So then, from Abraham to David there are fourteen generations. Then the count begins with Solomon, for David begot Solomon; and beginning with Solomon, the count goes up to Jechonias, during whose life the transmigration to Babylon took place; and here we have another fourteen generations, by including Solomon at the head of the second grouping, and including Jechonias also, to close that count and complete the number fourteen. But the third grouping begins with the same Jechonias.

Why Jechonias is counted twice.

13. My dear Christians, give your thoughts to the delightful mystery there is in this matter. I am sharing with you what my own heart has experienced. I think that when I have revealed this to you and you have the same experience, you will give the same report of it.

Wherefore, give this your attention. Making the count of the third division begin with the same Jechonias, we arrive at fourteen generations up to the Lord Jesus Christ; for this Jechonias is counted twice, as the last of the earlier division and as the first of the division that follows.

"But why," it may be said, "is Jechonias counted twice?"

In time past nothing took place among the people of Israel that was not a mystic symbol [32a] of things to come. As for Jechonias, it is not without good reason that he is taken twice; for, too, if there be a boundary between two fields—a border stone, for example, or some dividing wall—then both he who is on the one side measures full up to that same wall, and he who is on the other side takes his land to extend from the same.

But why this was not done in the first instance where groupings join, where we count fourteen generations from Abraham to David, and another fourteen without repeating David, but starting to count from Solomon, must be explained. The reason for this contains a great mystery. Consider this, my dear Christians. The transmigration to Babylon took place at the time when Jechonias was set up as king to succeed his deceased father. The kingdom was taken away from him, and another appointed in his place. Yet the transmigration to the Gentiles took place during the lifetime of Jechonias.³³ But no guilt of Jechonias is mentioned because of which he was deprived of his kingdom; rather, the sins of those who succeeded him are brought into the case. And so the captivity follows; they go to Babylon. It is not the wicked alone that go; with them go even men who were saints. The captivity included Ezechiel the Prophet. It included Daniel. The three youths were there, made renowned by the flames. They all went in fulfillment of the prophecy of Jeremias the Prophet.

The passing of the Gospel to the Gentiles prefigured by the transmigration to Babylon.

14. Remember that Jechonias, rejected without any fault of his, thenceforth ceased to be king, and passed over to the Gentiles when the transmigration to Babylon took place; and note the prefigurement of things to come in the Lord Jesus Christ. For instance, the Jews did not want our Lord Jesus Christ to be their king; yet they could find no fault in Him. He was rejected in His own person, and rejected in His servants as well; and so they passed over to the Gentiles—into Babylon, as it were. For this also was prophesied by Jeremias—namely, that the Lord was commanding them to go to Babylon;³⁴ and whatever other prophets told the people not to go to Babylon were branded by Jeremias as false prophets. Let those who read the Scriptures remember this with us; and let those who do not, believe what we say.

Jeremias, then, speaking for the Lord, threatened those who would not go to Babylon; but to those who should go there he promised a peaceful life, and a measure of happiness in the cultivation of vineyards, the making of gardens, and the abundance of fruits.

Now then, how does the people of Israel pass over to Babylon—no longer in figure, but in very truth? Whence came the Apostles? Were they not from the race of the Jews? Whence came Paul himself? *For I also,* he says, *am an Israelite of the seed of Abraham, of the tribe of Benjamin.*[35] Many of the Jews, then, believed in the Lord. From them were the Apostles chosen; of their number were the more than five hundred brethren who were privileged to see the Lord after His Resurrection; [36] of them were the one hundred and twenty in the house when the Holy Spirit came.[37] And what does the Apostle say in the Acts of the Apostles when the Jews refused the word of truth? He says: *To you we had been sent; but because you have rejected the word of God, behold we turn to the Gentiles.*[38] Wherefore, here in the spiritual dispensation of the time of the Lord's Incarnation there took place the transmigration into Babylon which was then prefigured in the time of Jeremias.

But what does Jeremias say about the Babylonians to those who were passing over to them? *In their peace shall be your peace.*[39] Therefore, when Israel was again passing to Babylon through Christ and the Apostles, that is, when the Gospel came to the Gentiles, what does the Apostle say, as though using the words of Jeremias of old? *I desire therefore, first of all, that supplications, prayers, intercessions, and thanksgivings be made for all men; for kings, and for those that are in high station, that we may lead a quiet and a peaceful life in all piety and chastity.*[40] Kings were not yet Christians, and he prayed for them.

The prayer, then, of Israel in Babylon has been heard. The entreaties of the Church have been heard—they have become Christians; and you see fulfilled what was spoken in figure, *In their peace shall be your peace.* For they have accepted the peace of Christ and have stopped persecuting Christians, and now, in the security of peace, churches are built, peoples planted in God's husbandry, and all nations bring forth fruit with the faith, hope, and charity which is in Christ.

Jechonias foreshadowed Christ as the Cornerstone between the Jews and Gentiles.

15. The transmigration to Babylon took place at that time through Jechonias, who was not permitted to rule as king in the nation of the Jews; this typified Christ, whom the Jews would not have as their king. Israel passed over to the Gentiles, that is, the preachers of the Gospel passed over to the peoples of the Gentiles. What wonder, then, that Jechonias is counted twice? And, in fact, if he was a figure of Christ passing from the Jews over to the Gentiles, consider what Christ is between the Jews and the Gentiles. Is He not Himself that celebrated Cornerstone? [41] Note that in a corner you have the end of one wall and the beginning of a second wall. It is the same stone to which you measure the one wall, the same from which you measure the second. Therefore the cornerstone which connects both walls is counted twice. Therefore Jechonias, representing the Lord, prefigured Him as the Cornerstone.

And just as Jechonias was not permitted to rule over the Jews, but they went to Babylon, so Christ, *the stone which the builders rejected, is become the head of the corner,*[42] so that the Gospel might come to the Gentiles. Wherefore, do not hesitate to count the head of the corner twice, and the number written suggests itself to you; and thus there are fourteen and fourteen and fourteen; and yet there are not forty-two generations, but forty-one. Because they are like a row of stones: when it runs in a straight line, the stones are all counted but once; but when the row is made to deflect so that an angle results, that stone where the deflection begins must be counted twice, because it belongs both to the row which terminates with it, and to the other which begins from it. So it was with the line of generations: as long as it remained with the Jewish people, it made no angle in the grouping of fourteen; but when the line was deflected and the transmigration to Babylon took place, a sort of angle, as it were, was made at Jechonias. Thus it was necessary to count him twice as the type of that sublime Cornerstone.

Why the genealogy of Christ is traced through Joseph. Joseph, true husband of Mary.

16. They make another malicious charge. "It is through Joseph," they say, "that the generations of Christ are reckoned, and not through Mary."

Give me your attention for a little while, my dear Christians. "It ought not have been through Joseph," they say. Why not through Joseph? Was not Joseph the husband of Mary? "No," they say. Who says so? For Scripture states by the authority of an angel that he was her husband. *Fear not,* it says, *to take unto thee Mary thy wife, for that which is conceived in her, is of the Holy Spirit.*[43] He is also commanded to give the Child a name, even though He was not born of his seed. *She will bring forth a Son, it says, and thou shalt call His name Jesus.* But, of course, Scripture is intent upon showing that He was not born of the seed of Joseph, when he is told in his concern as to how she was with child, that He *is of the Holy Spirit.* And yet his paternal authority is not taken from him, inasmuch as he is commanded to give the Child a name. Then, too, the Virgin Mary herself, knowing full well that she did not conceive Christ as a result of conjugal life with him, yet calls him the father of Christ.

How Joseph is called Christ's father by Mary. Christ does not deny that He is the Son of Joseph.

17. Note the way in which she does this. When the Lord Jesus Christ was twelve years old as man—for as God He is before all time and without time—He stayed behind in the temple as they left; and was debating with the elders, and they were astonished at His learning. But as His parents returned from Jerusalem, they looked for Him in their party, that is to say, among those who were journeying with them; and, not finding Him and filled with anxiety, they returned to Jerusalem; and they found Him in the temple debating with the elders, when He was, as I said, twelve years old. But what wonder? The Word of God is never silent—though it is not always heard.

He is found, then, in the temple, and His mother says to Him: *Why hast Thou done so to us? Thy father and*

I have sought Thee sorrowing. And He: *Did you not know that I must be about my Father's business?*[44] This He said because the Son of God was in the temple of God.[45] The temple was not Joseph's, but God's.

"See," says someone, "He made no admission of being the Son of Joseph."

Give me a little more of your attention and patience, Brethren. Our time is short—we must make it suffice for the sermon. When Mary said, *Thy father and I have sought Thee sorrowing,* He answered, *Did you not know that I must be about my Father's business?* Obviously, He did not wish to be taken for their Son in such a sense as not to be understood to be also the Son of God. The Son of God is always the Son of God. He was even their Creator! But as the Son of man, which He was, having been born of a Virgin who conceived Him without her husband's seed, He still regarded them both as parents. And how do we prove this? Mary, as has already been shown, said: *Thy father and I have sought thee sorrowing.*

Women should imitate Mary's modesty and humility. Mary called Virgin and Mother. A symbol of faith.

18. But first, dear Brethren, we must not permit to remain unnoticed—especially because of the lesson there is in this for the women, our sisters—such holy modesty on the part of the Virgin Mary. She had given birth to Christ, an angel had come to her and said: *Behold, thou shalt conceive in thy womb, and shalt bring forth a Son; and thou shalt call His name Jesus. He shall be great, and*

*shall be called the Son of the Most High.*⁴⁶ She had merited to give birth to the Son of the Most High, yet was she most humble. She did not put herself before her husband, not even in the order of naming him, so as to say, "*I* and Thy father"; but she says, *Thy father and I*. She did not pay attention to the high distinction that came to her womb; but she did pay attention to her place as a married person. Indeed, the humble Christ would not have taught His mother to be proud!

Thy father and I have sought Thee sorrowing. Thy father and I, she says, *because the husband is the head of the wife.*⁴⁷ How much less ought other women be proud! In fact, even for Mary herself the term "woman" was used, not because she had lost her virginity, but because such use of the term is peculiar to her people.⁴⁸ The Apostle, too, for instance, said concerning the Lord Jesus Christ, *made of a woman;* ⁴⁹ but this does not mean that he thus destroyed the structure and texture of our faith by which we confess that He was born of the Holy Spirit and the Virgin Mary. For as a virgin she conceived, as a virgin she gave birth, a virgin she remained. But by a usage proper to the Hebrew tongue they called all females "women." Here is a most evident example of this. The first female made by God taking her from the side of the man, was termed a "woman" even before she lay with the man, which, so it is written, was after they went out of Paradise; for Scripture says, *He formed . . . her into a woman.*⁵⁰

Christ does not deny that Joseph is His father. The Child Jesus a model of obedience for children.

19. The fact, then, that the Lord Jesus Christ answers, *I must be about my Father's business,* does not emphasize that God is His Father in such wise as to deny that Joseph was His father also. How do we prove this? By following Scripture, which states as follows: *And He said to them: . . . Did you not know that I must be about my Father's business? And they understood not what He spoke unto them. And when He had gone down with them, He came to Nazareth, and was subject to them.*[51] It did not say, "He was subject to His mother," or "He was subject to her," but—*He was subject to them.* To whom was He subject? Was it not to His parents? They to whom He was subject were both His parents, by the same condescension by which He was the Son of man.

A moment ago the women were receiving their precepts: now let the children receive theirs—to be obedient to their parents and to be subject to them. The world was subject to Christ—Christ was subject to His parents!

Christ both the Son and the Lord of David.

20. You see, then, Brethren, that He did not say, *I must be about my Father's business,* as though we were to understand this as meaning, "You are not my parents." They were His parents in time; He, His Father in eternity. They were the parents of the Son of man; He, the Father of His Word and His Wisdom, the Father of His Power, through which He created all things. If all things were

created through It, which *reacheth from end to end mightily and ordereth all things sweetly*,[52] then were they also created through the Son of God, they to whom He Himself was later to be subject as the Son of man.

Again, the Apostle calls Him the Son of David, saying, *who was made to Him of the seed of David, according to the flesh*.[53] But yet the Lord Himself presents the Jews with a question which the Apostle solves in these very words; for when he said, *who was made to Him of the seed of David*, he added, *according to the flesh:* he wanted it understood that according to His divinity He was not the Son of David, but the Son of God, the Lord of David. For in another passage, too, the Apostle, setting forth the singular blessings of the Jewish people, speaks in the same vein: *Whose are the fathers*, he says, *of whom is Christ, according to the flesh, who is over all things, God blessed for ever*.[54] In that He is *according to the flesh*, He is the Son of David; but as being *over all things, God blessed for ever*, He is the Lord of David.

The Lord, then, says to the Jews, *Whose Son do you say Christ is?* They answered, *David's*.[55] This they obviously knew as something they readily gathered from the preaching of the Prophets; and He was, in fact, of the seed of David, but *according to the flesh* through the Virgin Mary, who was espoused to Joseph. When, therefore, they answered that Christ was David's Son, Jesus said to them: *How then doth David in spirit call Him Lord, saying: "The Lord said to my Lord: Sit Thou at my right hand, until I put Thy enemies under Thy feet"? If David then in spirit call Him Lord, how is He his Son?*[56] But the Jews could not answer Him. So we have it in the Gospel.

He did not deny that He was the Son of David, so that they were unaware that He was also the Lord of David. And, in fact, regarding Christ they grasped only what He became in time; they failed to understand in Him what He is in eternity. Wherefore, wishing to teach them His divinity, He asked them a question regarding His humanity; as though He were saying: "You know that Christ is David's Son. Tell me, then, how can He be also David's Lord?" And, to anticipate their saying, "He is not David's Lord," He introduced the testimony of David himself. And what is it that he says? The truth, of course, for you have God in the Psalms also saying the well-known words to David: *Of the fruit of thy womb I will set upon thy throne.*[57] Here you have the *Son of David!* And how is He also the Lord of David, He who is the Son of David? He says, *The Lord said to my Lord: Sit Thou at my right hand.*

Do you wonder that David should regard his Son as his Lord, when you see that Mary was the mother of her Lord? He is David's Lord because He is God; David's Lord because He is the Lord of all; and David's Son because He is the Son of man. He is both—Lord and Son: David's Lord, *who being in the form of God, thought it not robbery to be equal with God;* and David's Son because *He emptied Himself, taking the form of a servant.*[58]

Not carnal union, but conjugal love constitutes marriage. Abstinence in marriage by mutual consent.

21. And so it is not true that Joseph was not the Lord's father because he did not mingle with His mother in wedlock—as though lust and not conjugal love is what

makes a wife! Mark this, my dear Christians: After a while Christ's Apostle was to say in the Church: *It remaineth that they who have wives, be as if they had none.*[59] And we know many among the brethren bringing forth fruit in grace; we know that in the name of Christ and by mutual consent they mutually restrain the concupiscence of the flesh, without, however, restraining the conjugal love they have for each other. The more the former is restrained, so much the stronger and firmer does the latter become. Are they not husband and wife who live thus, people who do not seek from each other the enjoyment of the flesh, who do not exact from each other the debt of carnal concupiscence? And yet she is subject to her husband, because this is proper for her; and her subjection is the more complete, the greater her chastity is. Conversely, he truly loves his wife—as Scripture says—*in honor and sanctification,*[60] as a coheir of grace, *as Christ loved the Church.*[61]

If, then, this is a union, if this is a marriage; if the mere absence of an act which can also be consummated—but illicitly!—with other than a husband or wife does not mean that there is no marriage: then would that all could live thus! Many, however, lack the strength to do so. But they must not for that reason separate those who do have the strength, and deny that the man is a husband and the woman a wife, simply because they have no carnal relations, but only the union of their hearts.

*Carnal union for the sole purpose of procreation.
The marriage contract. Whence the word
"adultery"? When there is venial
sin in the marital act.*

22. Hence, my Brethren, understand the sentiments expressed by Scripture regarding those ancestors of ours who married for this reason only—because they wished to have children by their wives. For even those who, according to the time and custom of their nation, had a plurality of wives, lived with them so chastely as not to cohabit with them except for the purpose of procreation,[62] thus truly holding them *in honor*. But when a man desires his wife beyond the limit set in the rule, "for the purpose of procreating children," he acts contrary to the very contract by which he married her.

The contract is read, and read in the presence of all witnesses; and the words, "for the purpose of procreating children," are read; and this is called the marriage contract.[63] If it were not for this that wives are given, if this were not the reason for receiving them, what man could with unruffled mien give his daughter to the lust of another? But, that parents need not blush when they give away their daughters, the contract is read—making them parents-in-law, and not panderers. And what is read from the contract? The words, "for the purpose of procreating children." When he hears this provision of the contract, the father's countenance becomes bright and calm. Let us look at the countenance of the man taking a wife. If the father is ashamed to give her with any other stipulation, the husband, too, should be ashamed to take her under any other condition.

But should they prove unequal to this condition, then —to state again what we have said before—let them exact the debt. Let them not go to anyone but their debtors. Let both the woman and the man seek relief for their infirmity in themselves. Let him not go to another woman, and she must not go to another man. It is from this that "adultery" gets its name: it is, as it were, "a going to another." [64] And if they go beyond the bounds set for them by their marriage contract, let them at least not go beyond their own marriage bed.

It is not a sin, then, to exact the debt from one's companion in marriage more often than the procreation of children demands? It is indeed a sin, though only a venial one.[65] The Apostle says, *But I speak this by indulgence;*[66] he was referring to what he had been saying: *Defraud not one another, except by consent, for a time, that you may give yourselves to prayer; and return together again, lest Satan tempt you for your incontinency.*[67] What does this mean? That you should not impose upon yourselves anything that surpasses your strength, lest by your mutual continence you fall into adultery—*lest Satan tempt you for your incontinency.* And that he might not seem to enjoin what he was merely allowing (for it is one thing to make demands upon moral strength, and another to make allowances to weakness), he immediately added, *But I speak this by indulgence, not by commandment. For I would that all men were even as myself.*[68] This is as though he were saying, "I do not command you to do this; but I forgive you if you do."

The preservation of mankind rests upon two factors.

23. Now then, my Brethren, give me your attention. In the case of great men who live with wives for the purpose of procreating children, men such as we read the Patriarchs to have been, and we find this documented over and over again, with the holy pages attesting it without any equivocation whatsoever; if, as I was saying, there are those who are joined to wives for the sole purpose of bringing children into existence, if they could be given the opportunity of having children without marital intercourse, would they not embrace so great a privilege with the greatest enthusiasm? Would they not accept it with extraordinary joy?

There are two works of the flesh upon which the preservation of mankind depends. To these the wise and holy descend from a sense of duty, while the unwise rush into them because of passion. It is one thing, of course, to descend to something as a matter of obligation, and another to be precipitated into something through lust.

And what are these things by which humankind is preserved? The first concerns our own selves and has to do with taking nourishment, which obviously cannot be taken without some gratification of the flesh—with eating and drinking. If you do not do this, you will die. By this one support, then, of eating and drinking, and because this is so prescribed by its nature, does mankind subsist. But men subsist by this support only as far as they themselves are concerned; for they do not take measures for a succession by eating and drinking, but by marrying. This, then, is how the human race continues to exist: in the first place, by the fact that men live; but because whatever attention they may devote to the body they certainly cannot live forever, there is the logical provision that as people die, others are born to succeed them. For the race of man is, as Scripture says, like the leaves on a tree; that is to say, like the leaves on an olive, or a laurel, or some such tree which is never without foliage, yet does not always have the same leaves, because—in the words of Scripture—it puts forth some, and others it casts off,[69] for those that shoot forth replace the others as they fall down; and thus the tree is ever shedding leaves, yet always clothed with leaves. So, too, the human race does not sense the losses it sustains in those who die day by day, because of the replacements it receives in those who are born; and thus all humankind, true to the norms set for it, preserves its existence; and as leaves are ever seen on the trees, so is the earth found to be full of men. If, however, they were only to die and none were born, the earth would be stripped of all men, as certain trees are of all their leaves.

In providing for the indispensable things of life, some are guided by lust, others by reason.

24. Since, then, the human race subsists in such wise that two supports, about which enough has been said, are indispensable, the wise and prudent and faithful man descends to both from a sense of duty; he does not fall into them through lust. But how many are there who rush greedily to their eating and drinking, devoting their whole life to them, as if they were the final cause for living! For, whereas they eat to live, they think they live

to eat.[70] Such does every wise man, and Divine Scripture especially, censure as gluttons, drunkards, gormandizers, *whose God is their belly.*[71] Only the craving of the flesh, not the need of refreshment, brings them to the table; and so they fall upon their food and drink. Those, however, who descend to them because life obliges them to do so, do not live to eat, but eat to live. Accordingly, if these prudent and temperate people were offered the opportunity of living without food and drink, with what great joy would they welcome this benefaction, that they should not be compelled to descend to that into which they had not habituated themselves to fall, but could always lean upon the Lord, without having their aspirations diverted by the necessity of sustaining a body falling into ruin! How do you think the holy Elias received the cup of water and the cake of bread to serve him as nourishment for forty days?[72] With great joy, to be sure, for he ate and drank because he was obliged to do so in order to live, and not because he was in bondage to lust.

Try—if that be possible for you—to confer this same benefaction upon a man who places his whole well-being and happiness in the table, as cattle do in their cribs! He would hate your kind offer, he would thrust it away from him, he would regard it as a punishment. Thus, too, in that other necessary function, married life, men imbued with lust seek only its gratification when seeking for wives, and for this reason, once they have their wives, they are scarcely satisfied even with them.

And so, would that if they cannot or will not rid themselves of their lust, they would not suffer it to go beyond what is their due by their wives, and in this due I include what is conceded to weakness! For if you were to say to such a man, "Why do you marry?" he, perhaps blushing at the question, would answer you, "For the sake of children." But if someone in whose words he could place implicit trust were to say to him: "God is able to give you children, and He certainly will give them to you even without your performing that act with a wife"—he would certainly be cornered and confess that it was not for the sake of children that he was seeking for a wife. Let him, therefore, acknowledge his weakness; let him receive what he pretended to receive only because of his sense of duty.

The Patriarchs were permitted to have many wives for one reason only—that they might beget children.

25. As it was then, those holy men of antiquity—men of God they were—sought for children and wished to beget children. For this one purpose did they unite themselves to women, for this purpose did they have intercourse with women—the procreation of children. It is for this reason that they were permitted to have more than one wife. For if unbridled lust were pleasing to God, permission would have been given at that time for one woman to have more than one man, in the same way that one man had more than one woman.

And why was it that all chaste women did not have more than one man, whereas one man had more than one woman? Was it not because when one man has more than one woman this provides for a multiplication of offspring, while a woman cannot beget more children the more men she has? Wherefore, Brethren, if our forefathers entered marriage with women and had relations with them for no other purpose than the procreation of children, they would have been overjoyed, had they been able to have children without that carnal act. For the sake of having them, they did not rush into performing the act through lust, but descended to it because it was a matter of duty to them.

Was Joseph, therefore, not a father because he received a Son without concupiscence of the flesh? God forbid that Christian chastity should entertain such a thought which the Jews themselves did not entertain! Love your wives, but love them chastely. Ask their co-operation in the carnal act only to the extent that this is necessary for the procreation of children. And because you cannot otherwise have children, descend to it with sorrow. For here we have the punishment of that Adam from whom we are sprung. Let us not take pride in our punishment. It is the punishment of him who, because he made himself mortal by sin, brought it upon himself that he could beget only mortal offspring. This punishment God has not taken away, because man was to remember from what state he is called away and to what state he is called; and because he was to seek for that embrace in which there can be no corruption.

The dignity of virginity began with the Lord's Mother. Joseph is truly the father of Christ. The adoption of children. Natural children and children born in wedlock.

26. In that nation, then, it was necessary to provide for an abundant progeny up to the time of Christ, because

it required a great number of people to serve the prefigurement of all the lessons that were to be prefigured regarding the Church. Thus it was a duty to take wives: through the wives the nation was to grow, and in the nation the Church was to be prefigured.

But when the King of all nations Himself was born, then the glory of virginity took its beginning in the Mother of the Lord, who was privileged to have a Son and at the same time exempted from losing her virginity. Why, then, since their marriage was a true marriage and a marriage free from all defilement, should not the husband chastely receive what his wife had chastely brought forth? For as she was a chaste wife, so was he a chaste husband; and as she was a chaste mother, so was he a chaste father. Wherefore, anyone who says, "He should not have been called a father, because he did not receive his Son by begetting Him as fathers do," is motivated by lust in the procreation of children, and not by a sense of affection. A condition which another desires to fulfill in the flesh, he in a nobler manner fulfilled in the spirit. For assuredly, too, those who adopt children because they are unable to beget them by the flesh, beget them with the greater chastity by their hearts.

Consider, Brethren, the laws of adoption; consider how a man comes to be the son of a man of whose seed he was not born, and that to the extent that the will of the one who adopts him has more right over him than the one who begets him.[73] Not only, then, was it Joseph's right to be a father, but it was his very special right to be so. Indeed, men also beget children of women who are not their wives, and these are called natural children; but children born in wedlock are preferred to them.[74] As to the action of the flesh that begot them, they are born equal. Why is it that the latter are preferred, but because the love of a wife by whom children are procreated, is the more pure? Here the union of man and woman receives no attention, for this is the same in both women. In what, then, is the wife superior, if not in her desire to be faithful, her attitude toward married life, and her capacity for a sincerer and purer love? If, therefore, a man could beget children by his wife without intercourse, should he not do so with his joy all the greater as she whom he loves most, is a woman of greater chastity?

To reconcile Matthew and Luke we rightly postulate two fathers for Joseph.

27. Note now from what we have said that it is possible for a person to have not only two sons, but also two fathers. Since mention was made of the word "adoption," it should occur to you that this is possible. It is said, of course, that a man can have two sons, but two fathers he cannot have. On the contrary, the truth is that he can have two fathers also—if one has begotten him by seed, and another adopted him by love. Therefore, if one man can have two fathers, then it was possible for Joseph also to have two fathers—one who begot him, another who adopted him.

In the light of this possibility, what ground is there for the carping criticism of those who keep on talking about Matthew following one genealogy, and Luke another? As a matter of fact we do find that the one has followed one, the other another. For instance, Matthew has said that Jacob was the father of Joseph, and Luke, that it was Heli. And true it is—it could seem that one and the same man, whose son Joseph was, had two names. But inasmuch as they enumerate grandfathers and great-grandfathers and other more remote progenitors whose names are different, and the one mentions a greater number of names, and the other a lesser, it is clearly shown that Joseph did have two fathers.[75]

Thus this problem and the malice that proposes it is disposed of; for clear reasoning has demonstrated that the case is possible of one father begetting a child and another adopting him. Considering that here there were two fathers, it is not strange that in an ascending enumeration of grandfathers and great-grandfathers and other ancestors, these should appear different as coming from different fathers.

Adoption in Sacred Scripture. How the ancients could have intercourse with their maidservants without committing adultery.

28. And you must not think that the law of adoption is something foreign to our Scriptures, and that, as though it found a place in the practice of human legislation only, it is impossible to reconcile it with the record of the Divine Books. For it is a matter going back to antiquity and commonly referred to in the Church's canon of the Scriptures themselves,[76] that not only seminal birth but also a benevolent act of the will [77] may beget a child. For example, even women, if they themselves had remained childless, used to adopt children born of the seed of their husbands by their maidservants; indeed, they

would even bid their husbands to give them offspring in this way: thus did Sara, thus Rachel, thus Lia.[78] And by favoring them the husbands were not committing adultery, because they were only obeying their wives in that which has to do with the conjugal debt, according to the statement of the Apostle: *The wife hath not power of her own body, but the husband. In like manner the husband also hath not power of his own body, but the wife.*[79]

Moses, too, who was born of a Hebrew mother and was exposed, was adopted by Pharaoh's daughter.[80] True, there were not then the same legal instruments as now, but the free choice of the will was given the authority of law, as the Apostle again says in another passage: *For the Gentiles, who have not the law, do by nature those things that are of the law.*[81]

But if women were permitted to make those their children to whom they themselves had not given birth, why should not men have done the same with children whom they themselves had not begotten of the seed of the flesh, but of the love of adoption? Indeed, we read that even the Patriarch Jacob himself, the father of so many children, made his grandchildren, the sons of Joseph, his own children, speaking as follows: *These two . . . shall be mine, and they shall receive the land with their brethren; . . . but the others whom thou shalt have, shall be thine.*[82]

But perhaps someone will say that the word "adoption" actually is not found in Holy Scripture. As though it were of any importance what word is used for it, when the thing itself is there, that a woman may have a child to whom she has not given birth in the flesh, or a man one whom he has not begotten in the flesh! And let him, without any objection on my part, refuse to call Joseph adopted, as long as he concedes that he could also have been the son of a man of whose flesh he was not born.

Yet the Apostle Paul does continually mention also the word "adoption," and that in reference to a great mystery.[83] For example, though Scripture testifies that our Lord Jesus Christ is the only Son of God, he states that the brothers and coheirs whom He vouchsafed to have are made such by a kind of adoption through divine grace. He says: *But when the fullness of the time was come, God sent His Son, made of a woman, made under the law, that He might redeem them who were under the law, that we might receive the adoption of sons.*[84] And in another passage he says: *We groan within ourselves, waiting for the adoption . . . , the redemption of our body.*[85] Again, even when speaking of the Jews, he says: *I wished myself to be an anathema from Christ, for my brethren, my kinsmen according to the flesh; who are Israelites, to whom belongeth the adoption . . . , and the glory, and the Testament, and the giving of the Law; whose are the fathers, and of whom is Christ according to the flesh, who is over all things, God blessed forever.*[86] Here he shows that both the word "adoption" and the thing it stands for existed of old among the Jews, just as did the Testament and the giving of the Law, which he mentions together with it.

A kind of sonship peculiar to the Jews. The fact that the Lord's genealogies as given by the Evangelists do not harmonize, involves no falsification.

29. Furthermore, the Jews had another way of their own by which one might become the son of another of

whom he was not born according to the flesh. Kinsmen married the wives of their next of kin who died without children, that they might raise up seed to him who had died.[87] Thus he who was born was the son both of him of whom he was born and of him whom he was to succeed by his birth. All this has been said, so that no-one, thinking it impossible for two fathers to be mentioned properly for one man, should hold that one or the other of the Evangelists who have set forth the generations of the Lord ought to be charged with a lie, as it were. This would be a sacrilegious misrepresentation, especially when we see them warning us against this by the very words they use.

Matthew, in fact, who is understood to mention that father from whom Joseph was begotten, enumerates his generations thus: "So-and-so *begot* so-and-so," and thus he is able to come to what he says at the end, *Jacob begot Joseph*.[88] But Luke—because he cannot properly be said to be begotten who is made a son by adoption, or is born in the succession of a man deceased, of her who was his wife—did not say, "Heli begot Joseph," or "Joseph, whom Heli begot"; but he says, *who was the son of Heli*[89]— either by adoption, or by being begotten by a kinsman of the man deceased and born in the succession of the latter.[90]

*Why the genealogy is that of Joseph,
and not that of Mary.*

30. Now then, regarding the question why the generations are counted through Joseph and not through Mary, and that this should not perplex us, enough has been said; for as she was a mother without carnal concupiscence,

SERMONS: CHRISTMAS 63

so was he a father without carnal intercourse. Through him, then, let the generations descend, through him let them ascend. And let us not take exception to him merely because carnal concupiscence was excluded: let his greater purity rather confirm his paternity. Otherwise Holy Mary herself may censure us! For she would not mention herself before her husband; but she said, *Thy father and I have sought Thee sorrowing.*⁹¹ Wherefore, let not perverse faultfinders do what this chaste spouse did not do. And let us count through Joseph, because as he is in chastity a husband, so is he in chastity a father. Indeed, let us give the man precedence of the woman, according to the law of nature and the law of God. For if we should set him aside and put her in his place, he will say, and rightly, "Why have you cut me off? Why should not the generations ascend and descend through me?" Are we to say to him, "Because you are not a father by the operation of your flesh"? Obviously, he will answer, "And is she a mother by the operation of her flesh? What the Holy Spirit has wrought, He has wrought for both of us."

*Being a just man,*⁹² we read. Therefore, a just man, a just woman. The Holy Spirit, well-pleased with the justice of both, gave to both a Son. But in that sex for which it was proper to give birth, He disposed that a Son was born also to the husband. And therefore the angel bids both to give a name to the Child, and thus the authority of both parents is established. So, too, when Zacharias was still unable to speak, the mother wanted to give a name to the son who had been born. And when those who were present asked the father by signs what he would have him called, he took a writing-tablet and wrote what she had already said.⁹³ And to Mary it is said: *Behold thou shalt* *conceive . . . a Son; and thou shalt call His name Jesus.*[94] To Joseph, too, it is said: *Joseph, son of David, fear not to take unto thee Mary thy wife, for that which is conceived in her, is of the Holy Spirit. And she shall bring forth a Son; and thou shalt call His name Jesus. He shall save His people from their sins.*[95] It is also said, *And she brought forth a Son to him;*[96] and here we certainly have confirmation of his fatherhood, not in the flesh, but in love. Let him, therefore, be accepted as a father, as indeed he is.

The Evangelists, to be sure, with great circumspection and wisdom give their enumerations through him, whether Matthew in descending from Abraham down to Christ, or Luke in ascending from Christ through Abraham up to God. The one counts in a descending, the other in an ascending order—both through Joseph. Why? Because he was the father. Why was he the father? Because he was the more positively a father, the more chastely he was such. It is true, he was thought to be the father of our Lord Jesus Christ in another manner; that is to say, in the same way that men normally are fathers, by procreating children through the flesh, not by begetting them through love of the spirit alone. For Luke, too, said, *who was supposed to be the father of Jesus.*[97] Why "supposed"? Because men's thoughts and suppositions carried to what is usually the case with men. The Lord, then, was not of the seed of Joseph, though this was thought to be so; but yet to the piety and love of Joseph a Son was born of the Virgin Mary—He who was also the Son of God.

*Why Matthew counts downwards,
and Luke upwards.*

31. But why is it that in the one case we have a descending, in the other, an ascending enumeration? I beg you, do listen to this attentively, as the Lord sees fit to assist us; your minds are now at ease and do not have to contend with trumped-up charges. Matthew descends through his generations to signify our Lord Jesus Christ descending to bear our sins, that in the seed of Abraham all nations might be blessed. Hence he does not begin with Adam, for from him is the whole human race. Nor with Noe, because from his family, too, following the flood, the whole human race came into being. Nor could the man Christ Jesus, as descended from Adam, from whom all men are descended, serve the fulfillment of the prophecy given; [98] nor, as descended from Noe, from whom again all men are descended; but only as descended from Abraham, who at a time when the earth was already full of nations, was chosen that in his seed all nations should be blessed.

Luke, on the other hand, gives an ascending lineage. He does not begin to enumerate the generations from the very beginning, from the Lord's birth, but from that place where he relates His baptism by John. For as in His Incarnation the Lord takes upon Himself the sins of the human race that He may bear them, so does he take them in the consecration of His baptism to atone for them.

And so the one, signifying His descent to bear our sins, enumerates the generations in a descending order; whereas the other, signifying the atonement of sins—not His own, of course, but ours—follows an ascending enumeration. Now, the one descends through Solomon, by whose mother David sinned; the other ascends through Nathan, another son of the same David, through whom he was purged of his sin.[99] For we read that Nathan was sent to him to charge him with his guilt, and that he might redeem himself by doing penance.[100]

Both met in David—the one descending, the other ascending; and from there up to Abraham, or from Abraham to David, they differ in no generation. Thus Christ, both the Son of David and the Son of Abraham, ascends to God. For so, too, must we be made new in baptism and brought back to God by the remission of our sins.

The number forty in the generations of the Lord. What that number signifies.

32. In the generations which Matthew enumerates the number forty certainly stands out. Now, this is a common practice in the Divine Scriptures, that on occasion they do not count supernumerary items when presenting pre-established numbers. For example, thus it is also said to be four hundred years before the people of Israel went out of Egypt,[101] though actually it is four hundred and thirty.[102] Thus, too, the one generation which exceeds the number forty does not take away the primacy of this number.

Now, regarding this number, it signifies the life of toil which we spend here on earth, as long as *we are absent from the Lord* [103] and a provision for preaching the truth during this period is necessary. Moreover, the number ten, by which the sum total of happiness is signified,[104] when multiplied by four—because time is divided into four seasons and the world is divided into four parts—makes the number forty. This is why Moses [105] as well as Elias,[106] and the Mediator Himself, our Lord Jesus Christ,[107] fasted forty days; because in this temporal life it is necessary to restrain the temptations of the body. Forty years also did the people wander about in the desert.[108] Forty days the flood lasted.[109] For forty days after His Resurrection did the Lord abide with the disciples, convincing them of the reality of His risen body; [110] and here He signified that in this life in which *we are absent from the Lord—* and the number forty, as has been said, mystically intimates this—we must make commemoration of the Lord's Body, which we do in the Church *until He come.*[111]

Since, then, our Lord descended to this life, *and the Word was made flesh that He might be delivered up for our sins and rise again for our justification,*[112] Matthew followed the number forty. The one generation which there exceeds the number forty either does not prevent its perfection, just as those thirty years do not detract from the perfection of the number four hundred; or it even has this added meaning, that the Lord Himself, adding whom we have the number forty-one, descended to this life to bear our sins, but in such a way that He, because of His special and singular excellence, whereby He is man in such wise as also to be God, is found to be excepted from this life. For of Him alone it is said—and this never could be said in the past or can be said in the future of any holy man, however perfect his wisdom and righteousness—*the Word was made flesh.*[113]

Why Luke enumerates seventy-seven generations.

33. But Luke, who, taking his beginning from the baptism of the Lord, follows an ascending order in his generations, completes it with the number seventy-seven; he begins to ascend from our Lord Jesus Christ Himself through Joseph, and comes up to God through Adam. The reason for this is that the remission of all sins, which is accomplished in baptism, is signified by this number. Not that the Lord Himself had anything to be forgiven in baptism; but by humbly submitting to it Himself, He recommended its usefulness to us. And though that was only the baptism of John, yet there appeared in it, in a way perceptible to the senses, the Trinity of the Father and the Son and the Holy Spirit, and thus was consecrated the baptism of Christ Himself, in which the Christians were to be baptized: the Father, in the voice which came from heaven; the Son, in the Person of the Mediator Himself; the Holy Spirit, in the dove.[114]

The meaning of the number seventy-seven.

34. And now, why does the number seventy-seven stand for all sins which are forgiven in baptism? The following suggests itself as the probable explanation: The number ten expresses the perfection of righteousness and happiness, when the creature, signified by seven, cleaves to the Trinity of its Creator. Hence, too, the Decalogue of the Law expressed God's sanction in ten commandments; whereas transgression[115] of the number ten is signified by the number eleven; and sin is understood to be transgression in that a man, when seeking something

more, goes beyond the rule of justice. This is also why the Apostle calls avarice the root of all evils.[116] And to a soul separating itself from the Lord by the fornication of sin [117] it is said, in the person of the same Lord, "You were hoping that if you left me, you would have something more."

The sinner, then, because he wishes for some gratification all his own, causes his transgression, that is, his sin, to revert to himself alone; and for this reason, too, those who *seek the things that are their own, not the things that are Jesus Christ's,*[118] are censured, and charity which *seeketh not her own,*[119] is praised. Therefore, this number eleven by which trangression is signified, is multiplied, not by ten, but by seven, and the result is seventy-seven.[120] For transgression involves not the Trinity of the Creator, but the creature itself, that is, man himself, which creature the number seven designates—three, because of the soul, in which there is a certain image of the Trinity of the Creator, for in his soul man was made after the image of God; [121] four, because of the body, for everybody knows the four elements [122] of which the body is composed. And if anyone does not know them, he can easily see that the body of the world, on which our own bodies move about, also has, so to say, four principal parts, which even Divine Scripture mentions again and again—East and West, South and North.

And because sins are committed either by the soul, for example, in the will alone, or by works of the body also, and so visibly; therefore the Prophet Amos continually refers to God as threatening and saying, *For three and four impieties I will not turn away,*[123] that is, "I will not leave unnoticed." Three stands for the nature of the soul; four, for that of the body; it is of these two that man consists.

How to read the Scriptures.

35. Accordingly, then, seven times eleven, indicating, as has been said, the transgression of righteousness reverting to the sinner himself, makes the number seventy-seven. The signification is that it embraces all sins which are remitted in baptism. This is why Luke ascends through seventy-seven generations to God, showing that man is reconciled to God by the remission of all sins. Hence the Lord Himself says to Peter asking how many times he should forgive a brother: *I say to thee not seven times, but till seventy-seven times.*[124]

And so, whatever else there is to be said regarding these hidden treasures among God's mysteries, this is for others who are more diligent and more worthy than we, to bring out. At all events, we have spoken on this subject to the best of our ability, as the Lord assisted us and inspired us, and as the limitations of time permitted us. If there be anyone among you who has a profounder grasp of this, let him knock at the door of Him from whom we, too, receive what we are able to grasp, what we are able to say. But this do keep in mind before all else—you must not lose your composure over matters in Sacred Scripture which you do not yet understand; and when you do understand them, you must not feel conceit. What you do not understand, treat with reverence and be patient; and what you do understand, cherish and keep.

2

(Ben. no. 184 = pp. 74-76 Lambot) [1]

CHRISTMAS

THE BIRTHDAY OF OUR LORD JESUS CHRIST

The mystery of the Incarnation means nothing to the worldly-wise.

This is the birthday of our Lord and Savior Jesus Christ. It is the anniversary of the day on which *Truth sprang out of the earth,*[2] and the Day of Day [3] was born to bring light into our day. It is a day we ought to celebrate; *let us rejoice and take delight in it.*[4] Our Christian faith alone can convey to us what this sublime act of humility gave to us. It is something that utterly escapes the understanding of unbelievers; because God *has hidden these things from the wise and prudent, and has revealed them to little ones.*[5] Let the humble, therefore, make God's humility their own. With help such as this, with this to carry, as it were, the burden of their weakness,[6] they will arrive at the sublimity of God.

The "wise and prudent," referred to a moment ago, seek only the lofty things of God, and give no consideration to the lowly things; and because they ignore the latter, they will not compass the lofty things either. Foolish and fickle, proud and arrogant, they float, so to speak, in the air separating earth and sky. They are indeed wise and prudent, but of this world, and not of Him by whom the world was made. For if they had true wisdom, which is of God and is God, they would understand that it was possible for God to take on flesh, but that He could not be changed into flesh; they would understand that He took to Himself what He was not, and that He remained what He was; that He came to us as man without leaving the Father; that He remained with the Father [7] what He is, while appearing to us as what we are; that His power was placed in the body of an Infant, yet this power did not come from the earth. His work, inasmuch as He remains with the Father, is the whole universe; and, inasmuch as He comes to us, His work is the fruit of the Virgin's womb.

Verily, the Virgin Mother, as much a virgin after giving birth as before conceiving,[8] gave evidence of His majesty. Her husband discovered that she was pregnant; he had not made her so. She was with Man without the co-operation of a man.[9] Her fruitfulness was all the more wonderful as she was made fruitful without losing her virginity.

This great miracle those people prefer to regard as fiction rather than fact. So, because they cannot believe it, they disregard the humanity of Christ, the God-Man; because they cannot disregard His divinity, they do not believe it. But the more despicable to them, so much the more precious to us is the human body which God in His humility has assumed; and the more impossible to them, so much the more divine to us is the fruit of the Virgin's womb born man.

The birthday of Christ, a cause of joy for all.

2. Let us, then, celebrate the Lord's birthday with the full attendance and the enthusiasm that we should give it. Let men rejoice, let women rejoice. Christ was born Man; He was born of woman. Both sexes have been honored. Let him, therefore, who had been condemned before in the first man, now become a follower of the Second Man.[10] A woman had been the cause of our death; a woman, again, gave birth to life for us. *The likeness of sinful flesh* [11] was born to purify the sinful flesh. For that reason do not let the flesh be found with sin, but let sin die that nature may live; for He was born without sin, that he who was with sin might be reborn.

Young men, you who lead chaste lives,[12] who have chosen to follow Christ in a special manner, who do not seek marriage—rejoice! Not through marriage did He come to you, He in whom you have found your ideal: He wished to give you the strength to esteem lightly that through which you have come into being. You have come into being through carnal marriage, without which He came to join a spiritual marriage; and you to whom He has given a special vocation to marriage, He has enabled to spurn marriage.[13] Thus it is that you have no desire for that by which you have been born; because more than others have you loved Him who was not born in this manner.

Rejoice, chaste virgins. A virgin has brought forth for you Him to whom you may espouse yourselves without corruption. Neither in conceiving Him nor in giving birth to Him can you destroy what you love.[14]

Rejoice, you who are just. It is the birthday of Him who justifies.

Rejoice, you who are weak and sick. It is the birthday of Him who makes well.

Rejoice, you who are in captivity. It is the birthday of the Redeemer.

Rejoice, you who are slaves. It is the birthday of the Master.

Rejoice, you who are free. It is the birthday of Him who makes free.

Rejoice, you Christians all. It is Christ's birthday.

The nativity of Christ is twofold. The awesome miracle of the Divine Babe.

3. By His birth of an earthborn mother He hallowed this one day [15] who by His birth of the Father was the Creator of all ages. In the one birth a mother was impossible, while for the other no human father was required. In fact, Christ was born both of a father and of a mother, both without a father and without a mother; of a father as God, of a mother as man; without a mother as God, without a father as man. *Who, then, shall declare His generation?* [16] The one is without time, the other without seed; the one without beginning, the other without parallel; the one which has always been, the other which has never been before or since; the one which does not end, the other which begins where it ends.

Rightly, therefore, did the Prophets announce that He was to be born, and the heavens and the angels that He had been born.[17] He whose hands governed the world, lay in the manger; and Infant that He was, He was also the Word.[18] Him whom the heavens cannot contain, the womb of one woman bore. She ruled our Ruler; she carried Him in whom we are; she gave milk to our Bread.

O manifest infirmity, O wondrous humility, in which all the greatness of God lay hid! The mother to whom His infancy was subject, He ruled with His power; and to her at whose breasts He nursed, He gave the nourishment of truth.

May He who did not shrink from taking a beginning even like unto ours, perfect in us His gifts; and may He also make us children of God, He who for our sakes wished to become a child of man.

3
(Ben. no. 185) [1]

CHRISTMAS

*Truth sprang from the earth when
the Word was made flesh.*

When we speak of Christmas, we mean the day on which the Wisdom of God manifested Itself as a speechless babe [2] and the Word of God was heard in the voice of humankind when it cannot yet utter words. But that divinity, hidden though it was, was revealed to the Magi by a sign in the heavens and announced to the shepherds by the words of angels.

With due solemnity, therefore, do we celebrate the anniversary of the day on which were fulfilled the words of the prophecy: *Truth is sprung out of the earth, and justice hath looked down from heaven.*[3] The Truth which abides in the bosom of the Father, is sprung out of the earth to dwell also in the bosom of a mother. The Truth which contains the world, is sprung out of the earth to be borne in the hands of a woman. The Truth which is the food of incorruption for the angels, is sprung out of the earth to receive milk from the breasts of woman. The Truth which the heavens cannot contain, is sprung out of the earth to be placed in a manger!

For whose benefit was it that such Sublimity came in all this lowliness? Certainly, not for Its own; but, if we have faith, it was for our own great benefit. Wake up, O man—it was for you that God was made man! *Rise* *thou that sleepest, and arise from the dead; and Christ shall enlighten thee.*⁴ For you, I say, was God made man. Eternal death would have awaited you, had He not been born in time. Never would you be freed from your sinful flesh, had He not taken to Himself the likeness of sinful flesh. Everlasting would be your misery, had He not performed this act of mercy. You would not have come to life again, had He not come to die your death. You would have broken down, had He not come to help you. You would have perished, had He not come.

Justice was brought to us by Christ's Incarnation.

2. Let us joyfully celebrate the coming of our salvation and redemption. Let us celebrate the hallowed day on which the great Eternal Day came from the great Eternal Day ⁵ into this, our so short and temporal day. *Here He is made unto us . . . justice and sanctification and redemption: that, as it is written, "he that glorieth, may glory in the Lord."* ⁶ That is to say, we were not to be proud like the Jews, *who, not knowing the justice of God and wanting to establish their own, have not submitted themselves to the justice of God.*⁷ Therefore, when it was said, *Truth is sprung out of the earth,* there followed, *and justice hath looked down from heaven:* mortal man in his weakness was not to arrogate this justice to himself, he was not to say that these things were properly his own; and man was to be prevented from rejecting God's justice because he believed that he was justified by himself, that is, made just through his own power.

Truth, then, *is sprung out of the earth:* Christ who

said, *I am the truth,*[8] is born of a virgin. *And justice hath looked down from heaven:* man, believing in Him who has been born, has been justified not by himself, but by God.

Truth is sprung out of the earth, for *the Word was made flesh.*[9] *And justice hath looked down from heaven,* for *every best gift, and every perfect gift, is from above.*[10]

Truth is sprung out of the earth—flesh born of Mary. *And justice hath looked down from heaven,* for *a man cannot receive any thing, unless it be given him from heaven.*[11]

The glory of God in the gratuitous justification of men.

3. *Being justified therefore by faith, let us have peace with God through our Lord Jesus Christ; by whom we have also access into this grace, wherein we stand and glory in the hope of the glory of God.*[12] To this short passage from the Apostle, which you recognize with me, Brethren, it is interesting to join a passage from the Psalm quoted, and to note how they are in agreement: *Being justified by faith, let us have peace with God,* for *justice and peace have kissed each other;*[13] *through our Lord Jesus Christ,* for *Truth is sprung out of the earth; by whom we have also access into this grace, wherein we stand and glory in the hope of the glory of God.* He does not say, "of our glory," but "*of the glory of God*";[14] because *justice* does not proceed from us, but *hath looked down from heaven. He that glorieth,* therefore, *may glory,* not in himself, but *in the Lord.* Because of this, even when the Lord, whose birthday we celebrate to-day, was born

of the Virgin, the angels announced, *Glory to God in the highest; and on earth peace to men of good will.*[15]

Whence is peace on earth, if not from the fact that *Truth is sprung out of the earth,* that is, Christ is born of flesh? And *He is our peace, who hath made both one,*[16] that we might be men of good will, bound together by the sweet bonds of unity.

Let us, then, rejoice in this grace, that *our glory* may be *the testimony of our conscience,*[17] wherein we *may glory*, not in ourselves, but *in the Lord*. Obviously, it was because of this that it was said, *my glory, and the lifter up of my head.*[18] For what greater grace could have dawned upon us from God, than that He, who had only one Son, made Him the son of man, and so in turn made the son of man a son of God. Ask yourself whether this involved any merit, any motivation, any right on your part; and see whether you find anything but grace! [19]

4
(Ben. no. 186) [1]

CHRISTMAS

Christ born of a virgin. He did not cease to be God when He became man.

Brethren, let us be happy! Let the nations rejoice and exult! Not the visible sun, but the sun's invisible Creator gave us this holy day, when the Virgin Mother, from the fruitfulness of her womb and with her virginity preserved,[2] brought forth [3] Him who was made visible for us and by whom—invisible—she herself had been created.

A virgin who conceives, a virgin who gives birth; [4] a virgin with Child, a virgin delivered of Child—a virgin ever virgin! Why do you marvel at these things, O man? When God vouchsafed to become man, it was fitting that He should be born in this way. He who was made of her, had made her what she was.

Before He was made, He was; and His was the power, because He was all-powerful, to be made and to remain what He was. Abiding with His Father, He made for Himself a mother; and when He was made in the womb of His mother, He remained in the heart of His Father. How could He have ceased to be God when He began to be man, when He gave His mother the privilege of not losing her virginity when she gave birth? Precisely so, because the Word was made flesh, the Word did not become flesh by ceasing to be; on the contrary, the flesh, lest it should cease to be, was joined to the Word,[5] so that, just as man is body and soul, Christ might be God and man, not in a confusion of nature, but in the unity of a person.

In short, it was one and the same who from all time and forever is the Son of God begotten of the Father, who began to be the Son of man by His birth of the Virgin. And thus, too, was human nature added to the Son's divine nature. Yet the result was not a quaternity of persons, but the Trinity remains.

The Word remained unchanged, the Son of God and the Son of man became identically the same. Our Rule or Symbol of Faith in the matter.

2. Do not, therefore, let the opinions of certain people who pay too little attention to the Rule of Faith and the utterances of the divinely inspired Scriptures, steal in upon you. They say, for example: "The son of man has become the Son of God; but the Son of God did not become the son of man." To arrive at this formulation, they have studied the truth; but they have not proved competent to express the truth. For what have they considered? This only, that it was possible for human nature to be changed into something better, but that divine nature could not possibly be changed into something less good. This is true; but even so, that is, though the divinity has in no way been changed into something inferior, the Word *was* made flesh. The Gospel does not say, "The flesh was made the Word"; but it says, *The Word was made flesh—* [6] and the Word is God, because *the Word was God*.[7]

And what is "flesh" but "man"? For Christ's human

flesh was not without a soul; this is why He says, *My soul is sorrowful even unto death*.[8] If, then, the Word is God, and the flesh is man, what else does *The Word was made flesh* signify but that He who was God was made man? And thus He who was the Son of God, was made the son of man, by the assumption of a lesser thing, not by changing from something better; but by taking to Himself what He was not, not by losing what He was.

Indeed, how could we confess in the Rule of Faith that we believe in the Son of God born of the Virgin Mary, if He was born of the Virgin Mary not as the Son of God but as a son of man? Is any Christian going to deny that there was born of that woman a son of man—but, of course, as God made man, and so as man made God? For *God was the Word, and the Word was made flesh*. As I was saying, then, we must confess that the Son of God, in order to be born of the Virgin Mary, took to Himself the form of a servant and became the Son of man; that He, remaining what He was and taking to Himself what He was not, began to be that in which He is less than the Father, but remains at all times that in which He and the Father are one.

In the Incarnation the Son of God and the Son of man are the same.

3. Indeed, if He who is at all times the Son of God has not Himself become the Son of man, what does the Apostle mean when he says of Him: *Who being in the form of God, thought it not robbery to be equal with God, but emptied Himself, taking the form of a servant, being made*

in the likeness of men, and in habit found as a man? ⁹ Note that not someone else, but He Himself, who is certainly the only-begotten Son of God, in the form of God equal to the Father, *emptied Himself, being made in the likeness of men.* And not someone else, but *He* Himself, in the form of God equal to the Father, *humbled*—not someone else, but *Himself, becoming obedient unto death, even to the death of the Cross.*¹⁰ All of which the Son of God did only in the form in which He is the Son of man.

Likewise, if He who is at all times the Son of God, has not Himself been made the Son of man, what does the Apostle mean when he says to the Romans, . . . *separated unto the gospel of God, which He had promised before, by His prophets, in the Holy Scriptures, concerning His Son, who was made to Him of the seed of David according to the flesh?* ¹¹ Here you have it—the Son of God, which certainly He always was, was made what He was not, *of the seed of David according to the flesh.*

Again, if He who is the Son of God has not Himself been made the Son of man, how has *God sent His Son, made of a woman?* ¹² This noun in Hebrew ¹³ does not signify the lack of virginity, but indicates the female sex. And who was sent by the Father, if not the only-begotten Son of God? How, then, was He *made of a woman,* if not by the fact that the selfsame who was the Son of God with the Father, having been sent, was made the Son of man?

Born of the Father without day of time, born of a mother this day! He made the mother from whom He was made: so He also chose this day which He brought into existence, to be the day on which He was to be brought into existence. For even the day itself, beginning with which each succeeding day receives a longer period of light,[14] is symbolic of the work of Christ by which our inner man is made to gain in strength from day to day.[15] Certainly it was but right that the eternal Creator should have as His birthday in created time that day around which temporal creation was to move in harmony.

5
(Ben. no. 187) [1]

CHRISTMAS

Attributes which contradict each other are found in wondrous harmony in the Infant Christ.

My mouth will speak the praise of the Lord,[2] of the Lord through whom all things have been made and who has been made in the midst of all things; who is the Revealer of His Father, the Creator of His mother; who is the Son of God through His Father without a mother, the Son of man through His mother without a father. He is great as the Day [3] of the angels, small in the day of men; the Word God before all time, the Word made flesh at a suitable time. Maker of the sun, He is made under the sun. Disposer of all ages in the bosom of the Father, He consecrates this day in the womb of His mother; in Him He remains, from her He goes forth. Creator of heaven and earth, He was born on earth under heaven. Unspeakably wise, He is wisely speechless; filling the world, He lies in a manger; Ruler of the stars, He nurses at His mother's bosom. He is both great in the nature of God, and small in the form of a servant,[4] but so that His greatness is not diminished by His smallness, nor His smallness overwhelmed by His greatness. For He did not desert His divine works when He took to Himself human members. Nor did He cease *to reach from end to end mightily, and to order all things sweetly,*[5] when, having put on the infirmity of the flesh, He was received into the

Virgin's womb, not confined therein. Thus the food of wisdom was not taken away from the angels, and we were to taste how sweet is the Lord.

A comparison to show that the Word did not leave the Father when It was made flesh.

2. Why should we marvel at all this concerning the Word of God, when this sermon which we are giving enters the senses so freely that the hearer receives it without at the same time confining it? Obviously, if it were not received, it would instruct no-one; if it were confined, it would not reach anyone else.

It is clear, too, that the present sermon is made up of words and syllables. But you do not take out this and that as you do in the case of food for the stomach. No, all of you hear all of it; each one of you takes all of it. Nor need we fear as we talk to you, that someone listening will consume all that we say and nothing will remain for another to take. On the contrary, with no intention of depriving anyone's ear or mind, we want you all to be so attentive that each of you hears everything and leaves everything for the others to hear.

Nor is this done at one time for one person, and at another time for another person, so that when the sermon being spoken has entered you first, it goes out from you to enter another; but it comes to all of you at the same time, and all of it comes to each of you. And if it were possible to memorize all of it, you would each of you go home with all of it, just as you have all come to hear all of it.

How much more could the Word of God, through which all things have been made, and which, remaining in Itself, renews all things, which is not hemmed in by space, nor extended by time, nor varied by long and short pauses, nor composed by sounds, nor terminated by silence; how much more could this Word, this great Word, make fruitful the womb of Its mother with the body It took to Itself, and yet not leave the bosom of the Father! And go forth to reveal Itself to the eyes of men, and, on the other hand, illuminate the minds of the angels! And appear on earth, and, on the other hand, transcend [6] the heavens! And be made man, and, on the other hand, make men!

*The Word was not changed when
It was made flesh.*

3. Let no-one, therefore, believe that the Son of God was changed or transformed into the Son of man; but rather let us believe that He, remaining the Son of God, was made the Son of man, without loss of His divine substance and by a perfect assumption of the human substance.[7] Nor do the words, *The Word was God* and, *The Word was made flesh,*[8] signify that the Word was made flesh in such a way that It ceased to be God; for in the flesh itself, because the Word was made flesh, *Emmanuel, God with us,*[9] was born.

Take the word which we carry in our thoughts: it goes over into voice when we give expression to it by way of mouth; yet it is not transformed into voice, but, while the word is preserved entirely intact, the voice in which it finds expression is taken in addition to it. The result is that what is understood remains inwardly, and at the same time what is heard is sounded outwardly; but what is produced in sound is the same as had before been sounded in silence. Thus, when the word becomes voice, it is not changed into voice; but, remaining in the light of the mind, having assumed the voice bound to flesh, it goes forth to the one who hears it, and does not leave the one who thinks it. I am not referring to the voiced word itself as thought of in silence—be that in Greek, in Latin, or in any other language; but to the thing itself which is to be said, in its state anterior to any differentiation by language, when in the chamber of the heart it in a way shows itself naked to the one whose intellect grasps it; and when it proceeds to go forth, it is clothed in the voice of the speaker.

Both of these, however—what is given thought by the intellect and what is given sound in speech—are changeable and are unlike. The first will be no more when you have forgotten it; the second will be no more when you are silent. BUT THE WORD OF GOD REMAINS FOREVER, AND REMAINS UNCHANGEABLE!

The Word made flesh is God and man.

4. And when It took on flesh out of time that It might appear in our temporal life, Its eternity was not lost in the flesh; rather, It conferred immortality also on the flesh. So He Himself, *as a bridegroom coming out of his bride chamber, hath rejoiced as a giant to run the way.*[10] *Who being in the form of God, thought it not robbery to be equal with God; but, so that He might for our sakes be*

made what He was not, He *emptied Himself*, not destroying the form of God, but *taking the form of a servant,* and through this form *being made in the likeness of men,* not as in His proper substance, but *in habit found as a man.*[11]

All that we are, whether in body or in soul, is our nature; with Him it is His habit.[12] If we were not this, we would not be; if He were not this, He would at any rate be God. When He began to be this which He had not been, He, continuing to be God, was made man, so that He might most truly be said to be not one of these alone, but both; because He was made man—*for the Father is greater than I* [13]—and because He remained God—*I and the Father are one.*[14] For if the Word had been changed and converted into flesh, that is, God into man, only this would be true—*The Father is greater than I,* and for the simple reason that God is greater than man; and this— *I and the Father are one*—would be false, because God and man obviously are not one and the same.

But perhaps He could say, "I and the Father are not one, but we have been one." True, what He was and has ceased to be, He certainly is not, but has been. Actually, however, because of the true *form of a servant* which He had taken, He said truly, *The Father is greater than I;* and because of the true *form of God,* in which He remained, He said truly, *I and the Father are one.*

He emptied Himself, therefore, among men, not having become what He had not been in such a way that He was not what He had been, but hiding what He had been and showing what He had been made. Thus, because the Virgin conceived and gave birth to a Son—because of the manifest *form of a servant—A Child is born to us.*[15] And because the Word of God which remains forever was made flesh that It might *dwell among us*—because of the hidden but remaining *form of God*—we, as did Gabriel in the Annunciation,[16] call *His name Emmanuel.* For He, remaining God, was made man, so that even as the Son of man He is rightly called *God with us,* not "God in the one case, man in the other." [17]

Let the world, therefore, rejoice in those who believe. To save them, He came through whom the world was made—the Creator of Mary, born of Mary; the Son of David, Lord of David; the seed of Abraham, who was before Abraham; the Maker of the earth, made on the earth; He who brought the heavens into existence, brought into existence under the heavens. He Himself *is the day which the Lord hath made,*[18] and the day of our heart [19] is itself the Lord. Let us walk in His light, let us rejoice and take delight in it.

6
(Ben. no. 188) [1]

CHRISTMAS

The Word of God cannot be explained by man.

If we undertake to praise the Son of God as He is with the Father—equal to and coeternal with Him, in whom all things visible and invisible in heaven and on earth have been made, the Word of God and God, the Light and Life of men—it is not surprising that no human thought, no language can be equal to the task. Indeed, how can we worthily praise with our tongue Him whom we cannot yet see in our heart? There it is that He has placed the eye with which He can be seen;[2] but the condition is that the heart be cleansed of all iniquity and cured of weakness and that men make this apply to themselves: *Blessed are the clean of heart, for they shall see God.*[3] It is not surprising, I say, that we do not find words to give expression to that one Word, in which the command was spoken for us who would say something about that Word, to have existence.

Certainly, these words which are in our thoughts and which we deliver here, are formed by our mind, but it itself is formed by that Word. Man does not make words in the way in which he has been made through the Word; because the Father did not beget His only Word in the way in which He made all things through the Word. God indeed begot God; but the Begetter and the Begotten are at the same time one God. God, moreover, made the world; the world passes away, and God remains. And all things made certainly did not make themselves! So, too, He through whom it was possible for all things to be made, was made by no-one.

It is no wonder, then, that man, finding himself just one of all the things made, should not prove himself capable to explain in words the Word through which all things have been made.

For our sakes was the eternal Word born in time.

2. Now then, let us for a few moments turn our ears and minds to this and see if we can perhaps say something fit and worthy, not about the fact that *in the beginning was the Word, and the Word was with God, and the Word was God,*[4] but about *the Word made flesh;* to see if perhaps He may be spoken of by us because of the fact that He *dwelt among us;*[5] to see if perhaps there where He willed to be visible, it is possible to speak about Him. Indeed, it is for this reason also that we celebrate this day on which He deigned to be born of a virgin; in fact, He caused the story of His birth to be told by men as best they could.

But *who shall declare His generation*[6] in that eternity in which God of God was born? There there is no such day to celebrate solemnly. There day does not pass away to return with the year's rotation, but continues without sunset because it did not begin with sunrise. It is no other than the one and only Word of God, the Life, the Light of men—indeed, the eternal Day.

But that day on which He, united to man's flesh, was

made *as a bridegroom coming out of his bride chamber*,⁷ is now—to-day; tomorrow it will be yesterday. But yet this day extols the eternal Day born of the Virgin, for the eternal Day born of the Virgin has made this day holy.

And now, with what words shall we praise the love of God? What thanks shall we give? He so loved us that for our sakes He, through whom time was made, was made in time; and He, older by eternity than the world itself, was younger in age than many of His servants in the world; He, who made man, was made man; He was given existence by a mother whom He brought into existence; He was carried in hands which He formed; He nursed at breasts which He filled; He cried like a babe in the manger in speechless infancy—this Word without which human eloquence is speechless!

*The Word become a speechless infant,
a teacher of humility.*

3. See, O man, what God has become for you. Take to heart the lesson of this great humility, though the Teacher of it is still without speech. Once, in Paradise, you were so eloquent that you gave a name to every living being; ⁸ but your Creator, because of you, lay speechless, and did not call even his mother by her name. You, finding yourself in a boundless estate of fruitful groves, destroyed yourself by having no regard for obedience; He, obedient, came as a mortal man to a poor, tiny lodging that by dying He might seek the return of him who had died. You, though you were only man, wished to be God; and you were lost. He, though He was

God, wished to be man that He might find what had been lost. Human pride pressed you down so that divine humility alone could lift you up.

Mary gave birth to Christ without losing her virginity.

4. Let us, therefore, be happy and celebrate the day on which Mary gave birth to the Savior—she, given in marriage, to the Creator of marriage; she, a virgin, to the Prince of virgins; espoused to a husband, but a mother not by her husband; a virgin before marriage, a virgin in marriage—a virgin with Child, a virgin nursing her Child! For indeed, when her Omnipotent Son was born, He in no manner at all took away the virginity of His holy mother whom He had chosen when He was to be born.[9]

True it is, fertility in marriage is good; but virginity in a life of piety is better. For this reason Christ as man who as God—for He was both God and man—was able to give both, could never have given His mother the gift [10] which the married cherish, and thus deprive her of that better gift for the sake of which virgins pass over the opportunity of being mothers.

And so Holy Church, virgin that she is, celebrates this day the fruit of the Virgin's womb. It is to the Church that the Apostle says: *I have prepared you for one husband that I may present you as a chaste virgin to Christ.*[11] Why does he say *chaste virgin,* when there are so many peoples of both sexes, when there are so many of both groups—young men and women, and married fathers and mothers? Why, I say, does he say *chaste virgin,* if not because of the purity of her faith, her hope, and her charity? [12]

Accordingly, Christ, designing to establish virginity in the heart of the Church, first preserved virginity in the body of Mary. When men and women marry, the woman is given to her spouse and she will no longer be a virgin; but the Church could not be a virgin if she had not found the Spouse to whom she was given, to be the Son of a virgin.

7

(Ben. no. 189 = pp. 209-211 Morin) [1]

CHRISTMAS

The Day of Day—the Son of the Father.

The Day who has made all days has made this day holy for us. The Psalm sings about Him: *Sing ye to the Lord a new canticle, sing to the Lord, all the earth. Sing ye to the Lord and bless His name, bring the good tidings of the Day of Day, of His salvation.*[2] What is this Day of Day if not the Son of the Father, Light of Light? But that Day which begot this Day, who was born of the Virgin to-day—that Day has no sunrise, has no sunset. I am speaking of God the Father as Day. For Jesus would not be *Day of Day*, if the Father were not also Day.

What is Day but Light? Not light of eyes bound to flesh, not light common to man and beast, but the Light which shines upon the angels, the Light to see which our hearts are purified. Indeed, the night in which we are now living, in which the lamps of the Scriptures are lit for us, passes away; and there will come that which is foretold in another Psalm: *In the morning I will stand before Thee, and will contemplate Thee.*[3]

Mary, the earth from which Truth has sprung.

2. This Day, then, the Word of God, the Day whose light shines upon the angels, the Day whose light brightens that fatherland from which we have departed for foreign parts, put on flesh and was born of the Virgin Mary. The

birth took place in a wonderful manner. What is more wonderful than birth of a virgin? She conceived, and is a virgin. She gives birth, and is a virgin. In fact, He was brought into existence out of her whom He had brought into existence; and He made her fruitful without destroying her virginity.

Whence is Mary? From Adam. Whence is Adam? From the earth. If Adam is from the earth, and Mary from Adam, then Mary, too, is earth. If Mary is earth, let us realize what we are saying when we sing, *Truth is sprung out of the earth.*

And what favor was bestowed upon us? *Truth is sprung out of the earth, and justice hath looked down from heaven.*[4] For the Jews, as the Apostle says, *not knowing the justice of God, and wishing to establish their own, have not submitted themselves to the justice of God.*[5] How can a man be just? By his own power? What poor man gives himself bread? What naked person covers himself, unless someone has given him a garment? We were without justice, sin alone was present. Whence is justice? What justice is there without faith? For *the just man liveth by faith.*[6] He who is without faith and calls himself just, lies. And how could a man not lie if he had no faith? If he wishes to speak what is true, let him turn to the Truth.

But Truth was far away. *Truth is sprung out of the earth.* You were sleeping; It came to you. You were snoring; It aroused you. That It might not lose you, It made Itself a way for you to follow. Wherefore, because *Truth is sprung out of the earth*, our Lord Jesus Christ is born of a virgin; *justice hath looked down from heaven*, that men might have justice—not their own, but God's.

Man begins life with tears.

3. What signal dignity has been conferred on us! What indignation [7] had gone before! How did this His indignation show itself? We were mortal, we were bearing the load of our sins, we were burdened down by our punishments. Every human being at birth begins life with misery. Do not consult the Prophet about this [8]—ask the infant when it is born, look how it cries!

Such, then, was God's great indignation on earth. And what is this dignity conferred all of a sudden? *Truth is sprung out of the earth.* He who had brought all things into existence, was brought into existence in the midst of all things. He made the day—He came into the light of day. He who was before time, set His seal upon time.[9] Christ the Lord was forever without beginning with the Father; but look, what He is to-day! It is His birthday. Whose birthday? The Lord's. He has a birthday? Yes, He has. *In the beginning . . . the Word, God with God*— He has a birthday? Yes, He has. If He had not been begotten as a human being, we would not attain our divine rebirth; for He was born that we might be reborn.

Christ has been born; let no-one hesitate to be reborn. Christ has been begotten, but without need of being begotten anew. Indeed, for whom was a second begetting necessary, if not for him whose first begetting was condemned? May His mercy, therefore, be given to our hearts.

His mother carried Him in her womb; let us carry Him in our hearts. By the Incarnation of Christ was a virgin made fruitful; let our breasts be made fruitful by the faith of Christ. She gave birth to the Savior; let us give birth to good deeds. Let us not be sterile, let our souls be fruitful for God.

The wondrous fact of Christ's double birth.

4. Christ begotten of the Father without a mother, Christ begotten of a mother without a father—two wondrous facts! The first begetting, eternal; the second, temporal. And when was He born of the Father? What is that—"*when*"? Regarding the first case, you are asking *when*—a case in which you will not find time? No, here you must not ask "when." But regarding the second, you may ask "when." "When was He born of a mother?" is a legitimate question; not so, "When was He born of His Father?"

He was born, yet is not bound to time. He was born from eternity—eternal, coeternal. Why do you marvel? He is God. Consider His divinity, and the cause of your marvelling vanishes. And when we say, "He was born of a virgin," this is something extraordinary—you marvel. He is God! You must not marvel. Let our surprise yield to thanksgiving. Have faith; believe, for this really so happened. If you do not believe, then this happened and yet you remain an infidel. He deigned to become man: what more do you ask? Is it not enough that God has been humbled for you? He who was God was made man. His was a poor little hut; He was wrapped in swaddling clothes, placed in a manger—you heard it when the Gospel was being read.[10] Who would not be amazed?

He who filled the world, did not find a place at the

inn. Placed in a manger, He became our food.[11] In the two animals, let two peoples approach the manger: *The ox knoweth His owner, and the ass His master's crib.*[12] Look at the manger: do not be ashamed to be the Lord's beast of burden. You will be bearing Christ, you will not go astray as you go your way; the Way [13] is sitting upon you! Do you recall the ass's foal that was brought to the Lord? [14] Let no-one blush—we are that.[15] Let the Lord sit upon us, and let Him direct [16] us whither He will. Let us be His beast of burden—we are going to Jerusalem.[17] With Him sitting upon us, we shall not be burdened down, but raised up. With Him leading us on, we shall not go astray. We shall be going to Him, we shall be going through Him, we shall not perish.

8
(Ben. no. 190) [1]

CHRISTMAS

The mystical meaning of Christ's choice of the day on which He was born.

Our Lord Jesus, who was with His Father before He was born of His mother, chose not only the virgin from whom He was to be born, but also the day on which He was to be born. Misguided men very frequently go by certain dates. One man chooses a day for setting out new vines; another, a day for building; another, a day for starting on a journey; and sometimes, too, a man takes a special day for getting married.[2] When they do this, they have this in mind, that anything undertaken may for that reason thrive and prosper. But no-one is able to choose the day of his own birth; whereas the Lord, who was able to create both,[3] was also able to choose both.

Moreover, He did not make His choice of day after the manner of those silly people who think that the fates of men are bound up with the position of the stars.[4] Obviously, He was not made happy by the day on which He was born; but the day on which He deigned to be born was made a happy one by Him. For indeed, the day of His birth also shows the mystery of His light. The Apostle indicates this when he says: *The night is passed, and the day is at hand. Let us . . . cast off the works of darkness, and put on the armor of light. Let us walk honestly, as in the day.*[5] Let us recognize that it is day, let us be day ourselves. When we were living without faith, we were night. And, because this same lack of faith which covered the whole world like the night, had to be lessened by the growth of faith, so on the birthday of our Lord Jesus Christ the nights began to be shorter, while the days became longer.[6]

Let us, therefore, Brethren, keep this day with due solemnity; not, like those who are without faith,[7] on account of the sun, but because of Him who made the sun. For He who was *the Word, was made flesh*,[8] that for our sakes He might be under the sun. Under the sun, to be sure, in His flesh; but in His majesty, over the whole universe in which He made the sun. And now, too, He, incarnate, stands above that sun which is worshipped [9] as god by those who, intellectually blind, do not see the true Sun of Justice.[10]

The two births of Christ. Why He wished to be born of woman.

2. Let us, then, Christians, celebrate this day, not as that of His divine birth, but of His human birth, namely, the birth by which He spared us, so that through the Invisible made visible, we may pass from visible things to the invisible. With our Catholic faith we ought to hold fast that the Lord has two births, the one divine, the other human; the one timeless, the other in time. Both, moreover, are extraordinary: the one without a mother, the other without a father. If we fail to grasp the latter, when shall we explain the first? Who will grasp this prodigy of prodigies, so unique and unprecedented in the

world, this incredible thing made credible and, transcending belief, believed in the whole world: that a virgin conceived, a virgin gave birth, a virgin remained virgin when she gave birth?

What human reason cannot solve, faith comprehends; and where human reason fails, faith advances. Indeed, who would say that the Word of God through whom all things have been made, could not have made human flesh for Himself, even without a mother, just as He made the first man without a father and mother?

But because He Himself certainly had created both sexes, that is, male and female, even by His being born He wished to honor the sexes which He had come to free. You of course know the story of the fall of the first man—that the serpent did not venture to speak to the man, but used the woman to cause his downfall. Through the weaker one he got the stronger one; and so, by taking over the one, he triumphed over both. For this reason, that we might not, as with an impulse of just resentment, abominate woman as the cause of our death [11] and believe that she was condemned beyond the possibility of restoration, the Lord, coming to seek what had been lost,[12] wished to honor and distinguish both, because both had been lost. Regarding neither sex, therefore, ought we to affront the Creator; both have been favored by the Lord's Nativity with the hope of salvation.

The honor of the male sex comes from the body of Christ; the honor of the female sex is in the mother of Christ. The grace of Jesus Christ has won over the cunning of the serpent.

The Infant Christ in the manger for our sakes.

3. Let both sexes, therefore, be reborn in Him who was born to-day. Let both sexes celebrate this day, the day on which Christ the Lord did not begin to exist, but on which He, who had always been with His Father, brought into the light of this world the flesh which He received from His mother. Thus He gave fruitfulness to His mother, but He did not take away her virginity.

He is conceived, He is born, He is an Infant. Who is this "Infant"? For *infans,* as you know, means one incapable of *fari,* that is, unable to speak.[13] He, then, is both an Infant and the Word. Through the flesh He is silent, through the angels He teaches. The Prince and Shepherd of shepherds is announced to the shepherds, and He lies in the manger as the Food of the faithful beasts of burden. For it had been foretold through the Prophet, *The ox knoweth His owner, and the ass His master's crib.*[14] Hence, too, He sat upon an ass's foal when he entered Jerusalem to the cheering of the crowds that went before Him and followed Him.[15] Let us also recognize Him, let us go to the crib, let us eat our Food. Let us carry our Lord and Ruler, so that with Him as our guide we may come to the heavenly Jerusalem.

In His birth of a mother Christ became manifest in weakness; but, born of His Father, He shows His great majesty. Among time-bound days He has His day in time; but He Himself is the Eternal Day of the Eternal Day.[16]

The birth of Christ to be celebrated.

4. Rightly are we carried away by the language of the Psalm, by the sound of a heavenly trumpet, as it were, when we hear: *Sing ye to the Lord a new canticle. Sing to the Lord, all the earth. Sing ye to the Lord and bless His name.*[17] Let us acknowledge, then, let us herald the Day of Day, who on this day was born in flesh. The Day, Son of Day, the Father—God of God, Light of Light! This indeed is the salvation that is spoken of elsewhere: *May God have mercy on us, and bless us. May He cause the light of His countenance to shine upon us, that we may know Thy way upon earth, Thy salvation in all nations.*[18] Here the phrase, *upon earth,* is repeated in the words, *in all nations.* The phrase, *Thy way,* is repeated in *Thy salvation.* We recall that the Lord Himself said, *I am the way.*[19]

And just now when the Gospel was read,[20] we heard that Simeon, a most saintly old man, received a divine revelation that he would not taste *death before he had seen the Christ of the Lord.*[21] And when he had taken the infant Christ in his hands and recognized the Child for His greatness, he said: *Now Thou dost dismiss Thy servant, O Lord, according to Thy word in peace; because my eyes have seen Thy salvation.*[22] Let us, then, with eloquent tongue proclaim *the Day of Day, His salvation.*[23] Let us announce *His glory among the Gentiles, His wonders among all people.*[24]

He lies in a manger, but He holds the world. He nurses at His mother's breasts, but He feeds the angels. He is wrapped in swaddling clothes, but He gives us the garment of immortality. He is given milk, but at the same time is adored. He finds no room at the inn, but He builds a temple for Himself in the hearts of those who believe.

That infirmity might be made strong, strength has been made weak. Let us, therefore, admire the more also His human birth instead of looking down upon it; and let us in His presence try to realize the abasement that He in all His majesty accepted for our sakes. And then let us be kindled with love, that we may come to His eternity.

9
(Ben. no. 191) [1]

CHRISTMAS

The Word was made flesh that It might submit to what It did not deserve for the sake of the undeserving.

When the Maker of time, the Word of the Father, was made flesh, He gave us His birthday in time; and He without whose divine bidding no day runs its course, in His Incarnation reserved one day for Himself. He Himself with the Father precedes all spans of time; but on this day, issuing from His mother, He stepped into the tide of the years.

Man's Maker was made man, that He, Ruler of the stars, might nurse at His mother's breasts; that the Bread might be hungry, the Fountain thirst, the Light sleep, the Way be tired from the journey; that the Truth might be accused by false witnesses, the Judge of the living and the dead be judged by a mortal judge, Justice be sentenced by the unjust, the Teacher be beaten with whips, the Vine [2] be crowned with thorns, the Foundation be suspended on wood; that Strength might be made weak, that He who makes well might be wounded, that Life might die. He was made man to suffer these and similar undeserved things for us, that He might free us who were undeserving; and He who on account of us endured such great evils, merited no evil, while we who through Him were so bountifully blessed, had no merits to show for such blessings. Therefore, because of all this, He who before all ages and without a beginning determined by days was the Son of God, saw fit in these latter days to be the Son of man; and He, who was born of the Father but not made by the Father, was made in the mother whom He had made, that He might sometime be born here on earth of her who could never have been anywhere except through Him.

Christ's birth did not impair His mother's virginity.

2. Thus there was fulfilled what had been foretold in the Psalm, *Truth is sprung out of the earth*.[3] Mary was a virgin before she conceived, a virgin after she gave birth. God forbid that in this earth, that is, in this flesh from which Truth is sprung, virginity should have been lost! Indeed, after His Resurrection, when He was thought to be a spirit, and not a body, He said: *Handle and see: for a spirit hath not flesh and bones, as you see me to have*.[4] And, despite the mass of His body, a body in the flower of manhood, He entered in where His disciples were behind locked doors.[5] Why, then, if in adult age He was able to enter through closed doors, should He not have been able as an infant to issue from His mother and leave her members unimpaired?[6] But the unbelieving will not believe the one thing or the other. For where there is faith, all the more readily are both believed; but where there is no faith, neither is believed. This is precisely what constitutes unbelief, that Christ is held to be without any divinity whatsoever. But when faith believes that God was born in the flesh, it does not doubt that both things were possible for God: His manifestation

of His mature body to persons in a house with doors barred, as well as His appearance, as an Infant Spouse, from His bridal chamber,[7] that is, from the womb of a virgin, without having impaired His mother's virginity.

Abstractly, the Church is both virgin and mother.

3. For truly in this manner the only-begotten Son of God saw fit to join to Himself human nature, designing to unite the immaculate Church to Himself as her immaculate Head. It is her that the Apostle Paul calls a virgin. He does not have in mind such only as are actually virgins in body; but he is referring to all, expecting them to have pure hearts. He says: *For I have espoused you to one husband that I may present you as a chaste virgin to Christ.*[8] The Church, therefore, imitating the mother of her Master, though she could not be such in body, yet spiritually is both a mother and a virgin.[9] And so, too, Christ, who established His Church as a virgin by redeeming her from the fornication of demons, in no wise deprived His mother of her virginity when He was born.

And you whom the Church out of her unsullied virginity has begotten as holy virgins,[10] you who, disdaining earthly marriage, have chosen to be virgins also in the flesh: joyfully and solemnly celebrate this day the Virgin Birth. He indeed was born of a woman, He who was not conceived of the union of man and woman. He who brought you what you should cherish, did not take what you do cherish from His mother. Heaven forbid that He who heals in you what you have inherited from Eve, should injure what you have loved in Mary.

We should imitate the virginity of Mary.

4. She, then, whose footsteps you follow, not only did not cohabit with a man that she might conceive, but in giving birth remained a virgin. Imitate her to the best of your ability—not in her fecundity, for this you cannot do and still preserve your virginity. She alone was privileged to have both, and of these it is your wish to have only one; because if you wished to have both, you would lose the one. She alone could have both, for she gave birth to the Omnipotent, through whom this was made possible for her. It was but right that only the only Son of God should become a son of man in this unique way.

And yet the fact that He is the offspring of only one virgin is no reason that Christ should not mean something special to you. As a matter of fact, Him whom you were not privileged to beget as a son in the flesh, Him have you found as your Spouse in your hearts; a Spouse, too, your Redeemer, to whom you should cling and feel happy, without fear of defilement in your virginity. For He did not deprive her of her virginity even when He was born of her body; all the more does He preserve it for you in His spiritual embrace.

And you must not think of yourselves as sterile merely because you remain virgins. For it is precisely this holy purity of the flesh that also leads to fruitfulness of the spirit. Do what the Apostle says. Since you are not considering *the things of the world, how you may please your husbands,* consider *the things that belong to God, how you may please Him* in all things.[11] And do this so that you may have, not a womb fruitful with offspring, but a spirit fruitful with virtues.

Finally, I address myself to you all, I speak to you all. I have this appeal to make to the universal chaste Virgin whom the Apostle has espoused to Christ: What you admire in the flesh of Mary, do in the inner chamber of your soul. He who believes with the heart unto justice conceives Christ. He who *confesses by mouth unto salvation* [12] gives birth to Christ. In this manner may your spirits be blessed with both bounteous fecundity and persevering virginity.

10
(Ben. no. 192) [1]

CHRISTMAS

The admiration we should show for the Incarnation of the Son of God for man.

To-day *Truth is sprung out of the earth.*[2] Christ is born of flesh. Rejoice on this solemn occasion. On this day be reminded also of the Eternal Day and think upon It, and with a profound hope desire the eternal gifts. Since you have received the power *to be made the sons of God,*[3] presume that you are such. For your sakes has the Maker of time been made in time. For your sakes has the Maker of the world appeared in flesh. For your sakes has the Creator been born.

Why do you mortal beings continue to take delight in mortal things, and why do you try, if it were possible, to hold on to your fleeting life? A far brighter hope has beamed forth upon the earth—life in heaven promised to the dwellers on earth. To make us believe this, we were first asked to accept a thing still more unbelievable. Designing to make gods of those who were men, He, who was God, was made man.[4] Without losing what He was, He determined to be Himself made what He had made. It was He Himself who made what He would be; for He only added human nature to His divine nature and did not lose His divine nature in becoming man.

We marvel at the birth of the Child by the Virgin and we try to make the incredulous accept this extraordinary way of being born: a Child was conceived in her womb which no seed had entered, and her body which had never submitted to a carnal embrace, brought forth the Son of man for whom there was no human father; and her perfect virginity remained inviolate when she conceived, and unimpaired when she gave birth.

This is a manifestation of power that is astonishing indeed; but deserving of greater admiration is the act of mercy, that He who was able to be born in such a way, determined to be born. Begotten the only Child of His mother, He already was the Only-begotten of His Father; and He, Maker of His own mother, was made in His mother. Existing from eternity with His Father, He is to-day born of His mother! Made from His mother after His mother, but from the Father before all things—without having been made! Without Him the Father never was, and without Him His mother would never have been!

The birth of Christ a cause for joy to virgins, widows, and the married. The Church a mother and virgin.

2. Rejoice, you virgins of Christ! The mother of Christ is one of you. You have not been privileged to give birth to Christ; but because of Christ you have not wished to bear children. He was not born of you, but He was born for you. And yet, if you bear His word in mind as you should, then, because you are doing the will of His Father, you are also His mothers. For He Himself has said, *Whosoever does the will of my Father . . . , he is my brother, my sister, and my mother.*[5]

Rejoice, you widows [6] of Christ! To Him who has made virginity fruitful, you have vowed holy continence.

Rejoice also, all you who live in nuptial chastity, living faithfully with your spouses! What you have lost in your bodies, preserve in your hearts. Where the flesh can no more be inviolate because of the use of marriage, let your good conscience in matters of the faith be a virgin, in the same sense that the universal Church is a virgin.[7]

In Mary holy virginity gave birth to Christ. In Anna the widowhood of advanced years recognized the Child. In Elizabeth conjugal chastity and fertility of old age were put in the service of Christ. His faithful members in all stations of life brought to their Head [8] what they were by His grace able to bring. In the same manner, because Christ is Truth, Peace, and Justice, conceive Him by faith, give birth to Him through your works, so that your heart may be doing in the law of Christ what the womb of Mary did in the flesh of Christ.

Moreover, why should you not be concerned in the Virgin's childbearing, seeing that you are the members of Christ? Mary gave birth to your Head; the Church gave birth to you.[9] For the Church herself is also both mother and virgin: a mother through loving charity, a virgin through the soundness of her faith and sanctity. She gives birth to peoples, but her members belong to the One only of whom she herself is the body and the spouse. In this, too, she bears the likeness of that other Virgin, the fact that she is also the mother of unity [10] among many.

Truth from the earth, justice from heaven. Why Christ was born on the shortest day of the year.

3. Let us, therefore, all of us, one heart and soul, with chaste hearts and holy desires, celebrate the birthday of the Lord, the day on which *Truth,* as we stated at the beginning of this sermon, *is sprung out of the earth.* What follows in the same Psalm has indeed also come to pass. For, while it is He who *is sprung out of the earth,* that is, born of flesh, because He came from heaven and *is above all,*[11] so, without a doubt, when He ascended to the Father, He was likewise that *justice which hath looked down from heaven.* He Himself with His own words speaks in praise of this justice when He promises the Holy Spirit. He says: *He will convince the world of sin, and of justice, and of judgment. Of sin: because they believed not in me; of justice: because I go to the Father; and you shall see me no longer.*[12] This is the justice which has looked down from heaven. For *His going out is from the end of heaven. And His circuit even to the end of heaven.*[13]

But no-one was to despise Truth because it is *sprung out of the earth,* when like a bridegroom It came out of Its bride chamber, that is, out of the Virgin's womb where the Word of God was united to human creation by a marriage which it is impossible to define; no-one was to despise this Word and, though It was born in a wonderful manner and is wonderful both for Its words and for Its deeds, yet, because of Its likeness to sinful flesh, refuse to believe that Christ is anything more than man; therefore, when it was said, *He as a bridegroom coming out of His bride chamber, hath rejoiced as a giant to run the way,* there was immediately added, *His going out is from the end of heaven.*[14] Wherefore, when you hear *Truth is sprung out of the earth,* you hear of a distinction conferred, not of something that had to be; this is a story of mercy, not of misery.

Truth, that it might spring out of the earth, came down from heaven; regarding the Bridegroom, that He might come out of His bride chamber, *His going out is from the end of heaven.* Here you have the reason that He was born *to-day*—than which there is no shorter day on earth; though after it the days grow longer. He—to repeat—who bent down and raised us up, chose the day which was shortest, but beginning with which the daylight grows longer. By His very coming under such circumstances He, without uttering a sound, exhorts us, as though by a stentorian voice, that in Him who was made poor for our sakes, we may learn to be rich; that in Him who took the form of a servant for our sakes, we may accept freedom; that in Him who *is sprung out of the earth* for our sakes, we may possess heaven.

11
(Ben. no. 193) [1]

CHRISTMAS

The words of the angels were addressed to all mankind.

When the Gospel was read, we heard the words with which the angels announced to the shepherds that the Lord Jesus Christ was born of the Virgin: *Glory to God in the highest; and on earth peace to men of good will.*[2] Festive words these are, words of felicitation addressed not alone to the woman whose womb gave birth to the Child, but to the human race for whom the Virgin gave birth to the Savior. To be sure, it was but right and entirely becoming, that this new mother, who had begotten the Lord of heaven and earth and who had remained a virgin after her Child was born, should have her childbearing proclaimed not by mere women with human solemnities, but by angels singing the praises of God.[3] And now let us, too, say and let us say it with all the rejoicing of which we are capable—we who cannot bring the news of His birth to the shepherds of the flocks, but who, with His sheep, celebrate the feast of His birth; let us, I repeat, say with faithful hearts and devout voice: *Glory to God in the highest; and on earth peace to men of good will!*

And let us with our best effort study and examine these divine words, these praises of God, this joy of the angels, and meditate on them with faith and hope and charity.

For as we believe and hope and desire, so shall we also be *glory to God in the highest,* when in the resurrection of our spiritual bodies we are taken up in the clouds before Christ, provided only that we pursue peace with good will while we are on earth. For, to be sure, our life will be *in the highest,* because there is the place of the living; and there, where the same Lord Himself is, the good days are, and there life knows no end of years. And *he that desireth life and loveth to see good days, let him refrain his tongue from evil, and let not his lips speak guile; let him turn away from evil and do good;* and so let him be a *man of good will. Let him seek after peace and pursue it,*[4] because *on earth peace to men of good will.*

Man in his weakness should ask God for help.

2. Now, should you, O man, say: "Look, *to will is present with me, but to accomplish that which is good, I find not";*[5] and *you are delighted with the law of God, according to the inward man, but you see another law in your members, fighting against the law of your mind, and leading you captive in the law of sin, that is, in your members,*[6] then persist in good will, and cry aloud what follows: *"Unhappy man that I am, who shall deliver me from the body of this death? The grace of God, by Jesus Christ our Lord."*[7] For He is *peace on earth to men of good will* after the war in which *the flesh lusteth against the spirit and the spirit against the flesh . . . , so that you do not the things that you would;*[8] because *He is our peace, who hath made both one.*[9]

Let good will, therefore, persist against bad desires,

and persisting let it implore the help of the grace of God through Jesus Christ our Lord. The law of the carnal members fights against it, and see, even now it is being made captive. Let it beg for help, let it not rely on its own strength. When it is exhausted, let it be humble enough to admit it. For He will be there to help, He who said to those whom He saw were already believing in Him: *If you continue in my word, you shall be my disciples indeed. And you shall know the truth, and the truth shall make you free.*[10] Truth will be there to help and to deliver you *from the body of this death.* Certainly, therefore, *Truth,* whose birthday we are celebrating, *is sprung out of the earth,*[11] that *peace* may be *to men of good will.* Indeed, who is qualified to will and to be able, unless He who by calling us has caused us to will, by inspiring us helps us to be able? Because His mercy has everywhere anticipated us, so that we who did not will, were called, and so that we receive the strength to be able to do what we do will. Let us, therefore, say to Him: "*I have sworn and am determined to keep the judgments of Thy justice.*[12] Yes, I am determined, and because Thou hast commanded it, I have promised obedience; but because *I see another law in my members fighting against the law of my mind and leading me captive in the law of sin that is in my members,*[13] *I have been humbled, O Lord, exceedingly: quicken Thou me according to Thy word.*[14] Behold, *to will is present with me:*[15] wherefore, *the free offerings of my mouth approve, O Lord,*[16] that there may be *peace on earth to men of good will.*"

Let us voice these sentiments and whatever else comes to us through our piety taught by holy reading, so that we may not celebrate without profit the feast of the Lord born of a virgin. We have received good will to start with, and we are to be perfected with the richest measure of charity; and this, too, *is poured forth in our hearts,* not by us ourselves, *but by the Holy Spirit who is given to us.*[17]

12
(Ben. no. 194) ¹

CHRISTMAS

The twofold birth of Christ. The birth of Christ and John.

Hear, children of light, you who have been adopted into the kingdom of God! Hear, my dearest brethren, hear and *rejoice in the Lord, O ye just,* that this may apply to you—*praise becometh the upright!* ² Hear what you already know, think of what you have heard; love what you believe, proclaim what you love.

To-day we are celebrating an anniversary, so you should expect a sermon proper for the occasion.

Christ has been born: as God of the Father, as man of His mother; of the immortality of His Father, of the virginity of His mother; of His Father without a mother, of His mother without a father; of His Father without time, of His mother without seed; of His Father as the beginning of life, of His mother as the end of death; of His Father as the Ruler of all days, of His mother as the Sanctifier of this day.

He sent before Him a man, John, to be born at the time when days begin to grow shorter,³ while He Himself was born when they begin to grow longer. This was to be a prefigurement of what the same John says: *He must increase, but I must decrease.*⁴ That is to say, human life should mean less and less to itself, but make progress in Christ, *that they who live, may not now live to themselves,* *but unto Him who died for all, and rose again;* [5] and that each one of us may say what the Apostle says: *And I live, now not I, but Christ liveth in me.* [6] Indeed, *He must increase, but I must decrease.*

The Word is the food of the angels in heaven, and the food of men in the manger.

2. Most worthily do all His angels praise Him who is their eternal food, who quickens their life with incorruptible sustenance; for He is the Word of God by whose life they live, by whose eternity they live forever, by whose goodness they live forever happy. Most worthily do they praise Him—God with God—and give *glory to God in the highest.*

But we are His people and the sheep of His hands: [7] may we by our showing good will be reconciled with Him and, to the extent this is possible for our weakness, merit peace. For certainly these same words which the angels themselves uttered in their joy when the Savior was born for us, have their application to-day: *Glory to God in the highest; and on earth peace to men of good will.* [8] They praise Him as they ought; let us, too, praise Him in obedience. They are His heralds; let us, on our part, be His flocks. He has filled their table in heaven; He has filled our manger on earth. For them the fullness of their table consists in this: that *in the beginning was the Word, and the Word was with God, and the Word was God.* [9] For us the fullness of our manger is the fact that *the Word was made flesh, and dwelt among us.* [10] In order that man might eat the bread of angels, the Creator of the angels was made man. They give praise by living, we by believing; they by enjoying, we by asking; they by taking, we by seeking; they by entering in, we by knocking.

*After this life we shall be refreshed
by the sight of the Lord.*

3. Who among men knows all the treasures of wisdom and knowledge hidden in Christ and concealed in the poverty of His flesh? Because *being rich He became poor for our sakes, that through His poverty we might be rich.*[11] When He took on mortality and destroyed death, He appeared in poverty; but He promised riches which had only been deferred—He did not lose riches that had been taken from Him.

How great is the multitude of His sweetness which He has hidden for them that fear Him, and which He has wrought for them that hope in Him! [12] *For we know in part . . .* until *that which is perfect is come.*[13] That we might show ourselves fit to receive this perfection, He, *equal to the Father in the form of God,* made like to us *in the form of a servant,*[14] reforms us to the likeness of God; [15] and the only Son of God, having been made a son of man, makes many sons of man sons of God; and the servants that have been nourished by the visible form of the servant, are made freemen by Him so that they may see the form of God. For *we are the sons of God; and it hath not yet appeared what we shall be. And we know that when He shall appear, we shall be like to Him: because we shall see Him as He is.*[16] Indeed, what kind of treasures of wisdom and knowledge are they, what kind of divine riches are they, if they are not such that are sufficient for us? And what is that multitude of sweetness, if not one that will satisfy us? *Show us, therefore, the Father, and it is enough for us.*[17] And in one of the Psalms someone of us, either among us or for us, says to Him, *I shall be satisfied when Thy glory shall be made manifest.*[18] But He Himself and the Father are one;[19] who sees Him sees also the Father.[20] Therefore, *the Lord of Hosts, He is the King of glory.*[21] Turning us around, He will show us His face, *and we shall be saved*,[22] and we shall be satisfied, and He will be sufficient for us.

Conclusion.

4. Therefore, let our hearts say to Him: *I have sought Thy face; Thy face, O Lord, will I seek. Turn not away Thy face from me.*[23] And let Him reply to our hearts: *Who loveth me, keepeth my commandments. And he that loveth me, shall be loved of my Father: and I will love him and will show myself to him.*[24] They to whom He said this certainly saw Him with their eyes and heard the sound of His voice with their ears, and thought of Him as a man with a human heart; but He promised *what eye hath not seen, nor ear heard, neither hath it entered into the heart of man*—He promised to show Himself *to those who love Him.*[25] Until this is done, until He shows us what is sufficient for us, until we drink Him as the fountain of life and are filled, let us while we, walking on through faith,[26] are absent from Him,[27] while we thirst and hunger for justice,[28] while we crave with an ineffable passion for the beauty of the form of God—let us in the

meanwhile with humble devotion celebrate His Nativity in *the form of a servant*.

We are not yet able to contemplate the fact that He was *begotten* by the Father *before the daystar;* [29] but let us keep in our thoughts the fact that He was born of a virgin during the hours of night. We do not yet grasp the fact that *His name continueth before the sun;* [30] let us recognize *His tabernacle set in the sun*. We do not yet perceive the only Son remaining in His Father; let us remember *the Bridegroom coming out of His bride chamber*.[31] We are not yet prepared for our Father's banquet; let us recognize the manger of our Lord Jesus Christ.

13

(Ben. no. 195) [1]

CHRISTMAS

Christ has two births; both are beyond description.

Our Lord Jesus Christ, the Son of man as well as the Son of God, born of the Father without a mother, created all days. By His birth from a mother, but without a father, He consecrated this day. In His divine birth He was invisible; in His human birth, visible; in both births, awe-inspiring. Hence, it is difficult to determine which birth the Prophet was speaking about in particular, when he prophesied concerning Him: *Who shall declare His generation?* [2] Was he speaking of the birth in which He, regarding whom it was never true that He was not yet born, has a coeternal Father? Or of the birth in which He, born in time, had already made the mother in whom He was made? Or of the birth in which He, who always was, was always born? And who will tell how Light was born of Light, and both Lights are one? How God was born of God, and there was no increase in God's number? How one may speak of His being born as of an accomplished fact, when in that birth there was no passage of time resulting in time past, nor time preceding so that it should be impending, nor present time so that it should be in progress and not yet brought to conclusion? Wherefore, again, *who shall declare this generation,* seeing that what is to be declared remains above the realms of time, whereas the words of the one who would declare it, pass away in time?

And regarding the fact of this generation by a virgin—who shall declare this, noting that His conception as a man did not come about in the manner of men, that His birth in the flesh brought fruitfulness to her who nourished Him, but did not deprive her of her virginity when she bore Him?

Indeed, *who shall declare His generation*—the one or the other—or even both?

Christ, the Son of a virgin, the Spouse of a virgin.

2. This is the Lord our God, this is the Mediator of God and man: a Man, our Savior; who, born of the Father, created even His mother; who, born of His mother, glorified even the Father. Without birth by woman, He is the only Son of the Father; without embrace of man, His mother bore Him as her only Son. This is He who is *beautiful above the sons of men*,[3] Son of holy Mary, Bridegroom of Holy Church whom He has made like His own mother; for He has given her to us to be our mother and keeps her a virgin for Himself. It is to her that the Apostle says: *I have prepared you for one husband that I may present you as a chaste virgin to Christ.*[4] And concerning her he says again that our mother is not a bondwoman, but a freewoman, and *many are the children of the desolate, more than of her that hath a husband.*[5] The Church, too, then, like Mary, has perpetual virginity and inviolate fecundity. For what Mary has merited in the flesh, the Church has preserved in the soul.[6] But whereas the one gave birth to only One, the

other gives birth to many, who through the One are to be gathered into one.

Why Christ came in the flesh.

3. So this is the day on which the Maker of the world came into the world, the day on which He who had never been absent in His power, became present in flesh; because He was in this world, and *He came into His own. He was in the world, but the world knew Him not,* because *the light shone in darkness, and the darkness did not comprehend it.*[7] He came, therefore, in the flesh to cleanse the vices of the flesh. He came born of the earth, a Physician to heal our inner eyes which this our outer world had made blind;[8] thus, when He has healed them, we who were *heretofore darkness* are made *light in the Lord,*[9] and the light will no longer shine in darkness as a light present for such as are absent, but will become visible to seers of the truth. This is why *the Bridegroom has come out of His bride chamber* and *rejoiced as a giant to run the way.*[10]

Fair as a bridegroom, strong as a giant, lovable and terrible, severe and serene, beautiful to the good, harsh to the wicked, He, remaining in the bosom of His Father, has filled the womb of His mother. In that bridal chamber, that is, in the Virgin's womb, His divine nature united itself to the human; and thus *the Word was made flesh* for us, that, proceeding from a mother, It might *dwell among us;*[11] that, going before to the Father, It might prepare a place for us in which to dwell. Let us, therefore, joyfully and solemnly celebrate this day; and through the Eternal One who was born for us in time, let us faithfully long for the day eternal.

14

(Ben. no. 196) [1]

CHRISTMAS

Christ has two births. The Son was always and without beginning begotten by the Father.

To-day, a festive day for us, has dawned as the birthday of our Lord Jesus Christ. It is His birthday, the day on which He was born. And this is to-day, because beginning with to-day the day begins to grow.[2]

Our Lord Jesus Christ had two births, the one divine, the other human. Both were miraculous. The first was without woman for a mother, the other, without man for a father. What the holy Prophet Isaias says, *Who shall declare His generation?*[3] can be referred to both begettings. Who could find the proper words to explain God's act of begetting? Who could properly explain the childbearing of the Virgin? The former was without day; the latter, on a definite day. Both transcend human estimation, both strike us with great awe.

Consider that first begetting: *In the beginning was the Word, and the Word was with God, and the Word was God.*[4] Whose Word was it? God's own. What Word? The Son Himself. The Father never was without the Son; yet He who was never without the Son, begot the Son. He begot Him, but He did not give Him a beginning. He who was begotten without a beginning, has no beginning. Yet He is the Son, yet He was begotten.

Man would say: "How was He begotten when He has

no beginning? If He was begotten, He has a beginning. If He has no beginning, how was He begotten?"

How, I do not know. You are asking a *man* how *God* was begotten? Your question embarrasses me. But I appeal to the Prophet: *Who shall declare His generation?*

Come with me to that other begetting, the human one; come with me to that begetting in which *He emptied Himself, taking the form of a servant.* See whether we can perhaps comprehend it, or whether perhaps we can say something about it. After all, who could grasp—*Who being in the form of God, thought it not robbery to be equal with God?*[5] Who could grasp this? Who could give this the thought it deserves? Whose mind could presume to investigate this? Whose tongue could be emboldened to proclaim this? Whose reasoning could comprehend this? For the time being, let us drop this. It is too much for us.

That, however, this might not be too much for us, He *emptied Himself, taking the form of a servant, being made in the likeness of men.*[6] Where? In the Virgin Mary. Well, let us say something about this, if that should be possible. The angel announces; the virgin hears, believes, and conceives. She has faith in her soul, and Christ dwells in her womb. A virgin conceived—we marvel. A virgin gave birth—we marvel the more. After she had given birth, she remained a virgin.[7] Verily, *who shall declare this generation?*

*Three lives—wedlock, widowhood, and virginity—
bear witness to Christ.*

2. My dearest friends, I have something to say that will interest you. In the Church there are three ways of life for the members of Christ: wedlock, widowhood, and virginity.[8] Because it was precisely these ways of life, of life spent in chaste virtue, that were to inform Christ's holy members, all three bore witness to Christ.

First, there is wedlock. When the Virgin Mary conceived, Elizabeth herself, the wife of Zachary, had also conceived. She was bearing the Herald of this Judge in her womb. Holy Mary came to see her, to greet her cousin. The infant leaped in the womb of Elizabeth. He rejoiced, she prophesied.[9] This is chaste virtue bearing witness in the married state.

And widowhood? It is exemplified in Anna. Just now when the Gospel was read,[10] you heard that she was a holy prophetess, a widow of eighty-four years, who had lived for seven years with her husband. She made many visits to the temple of the Lord, serving Him in prayer night and day. And the widow, too, recognized Christ. Though when she saw Him, He was small, she recognized Him for His greatness. And she, too, testified. She exemplifies for you life in widowhood.

In Mary you have the life of virginity.[11]

Let each make his own choice of these three lives as he will. One who does not wish to follow one of these ways of life, fails to take his place among the members of Christ.

Let not married women say, "We do not belong to

Christ." There are holy women who have had husbands. Let not virgins sing their own praises. *The greater they are, the more let them humble themselves in all things.*[12]

Examples of all the ways to be saved have been set before us to see. Let no one go beyond his due limits. Let no one have to do with woman except his wife; and it is better to be without wife.

If you look for conjugal chastity, you have Susanna. If you look for chaste widowhood, you have Anna. If you look for chastity in virginity, you have Mary.

God an infant for our sakes.

3. The Lord Jesus willed to be man for our sakes. Do not disdain His mercy. Wisdom came to dwell upon earth. *In the beginning was the Word, and the Word was with God, and the Word was God.*

O Food and Bread of the angels! From Thee do the angels have their fill, by Thee are they satisfied, and they are not surfeited. From Thee they have life; from Thee they have wisdom; from Thee they have happiness. Where is it that Thou art for my sake? In a little hovel, in swaddling clothes in a manger. And on account of whom?

The Ruler of the stars nurses at a mother's breasts, He who feeds the angels! He who speaks in the bosom of His Father, is silent in the bosom of His mother. But He is going to speak when He is of the age to do so. He is going to do for us all the things mentioned in the Gospel. On account of us is He going to suffer, because of us is He going to die; He is going to rise again as a token of our reward, ascend into heaven before the eyes of His disciples, and come down from heaven for the Judgment.

SERMONS: CHRISTMAS 133

There you see Him who was lying in the manger—He was made small, but He did not destroy Himself. He took to Himself what He was not, but remained what He was. Here we have the Infant Christ—let us grow with Him.

The superstitious festival of the first of January.

4. Let this suffice for you, my beloved.[13] Because I see so many present here on account of this solemn feast, I must make a remark.

The first of January is coming. You are all Christians. By the favor of God, the city is a Christian one.[14] There are two kinds of people here, Christians and Jews.[15] Let nothing happen that is odious to God—iniquitous games, shameless amusements.[16] Let not men make judges for themselves,[17] lest they come into the hands of the true Judge. Listen: you are Christians, you are the members of Christ—think of what you are, consider at what great price you have been purchased!

Finally, if you wish to know what you are doing—I speak here to those who are doing it; do not feel hurt, if such things do not appeal to you. I am speaking only to those who are doing it and who find pleasure in doing it. Do you wish to know what you are doing and what sorrow you are causing us? Are the Jews doing it? Well, then, be so ashamed that you will not do it. On the Nativity of John,[18] that is, six months ago—for there are that many months between the Herald and the Judge—Christians, copying a superstitious pagan rite, went to the sea and there bathed themselves.[19] I was absent at the time, but, as I learned, the presbyters, thoroughly aroused by the matter of Christian conduct involved, disciplined certain parties as the Church's norms require. There was grumbling and some said: "What was so extraordinary about this that we should be taken to task for it? Had we been warned ahead of time, we would not have done it. Had these same presbyters warned us before, we would not have done it."

Your bishop is forewarning you. I warn you, I state this publicly, I make this an official declaration. Hear your bishop commanding you! Hear your bishop admonishing you! Hear your bishop pleading with you! Hear your bishop adjuring you! I adjure you in the name of Him who was born this day. I adjure you, I make this your responsibility—let no-one do it!

This is all I have to say in the matter. It is better that you should give heed to my words of warning than that you should feel my severity.

15

(Ben. no. 140) [1]

CHRISTMAS (?)

THE WORDS IN THE GOSPEL OF JOHN, 12.44-50: *HE THAT BELIEVETH IN ME, DOTH NOT BELIEVE IN ME, BUT IN HIM THAT SENT ME,* AGAINST A STATEMENT BY THE ARIAN BISHOP MAXIMINUS WHO BLASPHEMED WHEN HE WAS STATIONED IN AFRICA WITH THE COUNT SIGISVULT.[2]

Faith in Christ

What is it, Brethren, we have heard the Lord saying: *He that believeth in me, doth not believe in me, but in Him that sent me?* [3] It is good for us to believe in Christ, especially because He Himself has also stated expressly what you have now heard, that is, that He *had come a light into the world, and that one who believes in Him, shall not walk in darkness, but shall have the light of life.*[4] It is good, therefore, to believe in Christ. It is a great good to believe in Christ, and it is a great evil not to believe in Christ. But because Christ the Son is, whatever He is, from the Father, while the Father is not from the Son, but is the Father of the Son: He indeed recommends faith in Himself, but refers the honor to His Author.

The two births of Christ.

2. For hold to this as a definitely established truth, if you wish to continue as Catholics, that God the Father begot the Son without time, and made Him of a virgin in

time. The first birth transcends time; the second throws a bright lustre upon time. Both births are wonderful: the one without a mother, the other without a father. When God begot the Son, He begot Him of Himself, not of a mother. When the mother begot the Son, she begot Him as a virgin, not by a man. He was born of the Father without a beginning. Of His mother He was born to-day with a definite beginning. Born of the Father, He made us; born of His mother, He remade us. He was born of the Father that we might be; He was born of His mother that we might not be lost. But the Father begot Him equal to Himself, and whatsoever the Son is, He has all from the Father. But what God the Father is, He does not have from the Son. And so we say that God the Father is from no-one, that God the Son is from God. Therefore, all the wonderful things that the Son does, all the truth that He speaks, He attributes them to Him of whom He is. Yet He cannot possibly be aught else than He of whom He is. Adam was made man; he was able to be other than he was made. For example, he was made just, and was able to be unjust. But the only-begotten Son of God, what He is, cannot be changed: He cannot undergo a change into something else, He cannot be diminished; what He was He cannot but be, He cannot but be equal to the Father. But obviously He who gave all things to the Son at His birth, did not give them to Him because He lacked them. Without a doubt this very equality, too, with the Father was given by the Father to the Son. How did the Father give it? Did He beget Him less and add to His character so as to make Him an equal? If He had done this, He would have been bestowing something that was wanting. But I have told you already what you ought to hold as your most firm conviction: namely, that the Father gave the Son all that He is, but gave it to Him in His birth, not as to one who was lacking it. If He gave it to Him in His birth and not as to one lacking it, then doubtless He both gave Him equality and, in giving Him equality, begot Him an equal. And though the one be one Person, and the other another, it does not follow that the one is one thing, and the other another. But what the one is, that the other is also. He who is the one, is not the other; but what the one is, that the other is also.

Why Christ is called the true Son of God.

3. He *who sent me*, you have heard Him say. *He who sent me*, He says, *He gave me commandment what I should say and what I should speak. And I know that His commandment is life everlasting.*[5] It is John's Gospel—cling to it!

He who sent me, He gave me commandment what I should say and what I should speak. And I know that His commandment is life everlasting. O that He would give me strength to say what I wish to say! My want in the presence of His abundance distresses me.

He, says He, *gave me commandment what I should say and what I should speak. And I know that His commandment is life everlasting.* Look in the Epistle of this John the Evangelist for what he has said concerning Christ. *Let us believe,* he says, *in His true Son, Jesus Christ. This is the true God and life everlasting.*[6] What is *true God and life everlasting?* The true Son of God is *true God and life everlasting.* Why did he say, *in His true Son?* Because

God has many sons, therefore a distinction had to be made by adding that He was the "true" Son. Not by simply saying that He is "the Son," but, as I said, by adding that He is "the true Son"—for this reason had He to be distinguished, because of the many sons which God has. We are sons by grace, He by nature. We have been made by the Father through Him. As for Him, what the Father is, that He is also. Are we, too, what God is?

No-one except Christ has dared to say that he is one with the Father.

4. Contrary to expectation, however, some man not knowing what he is talking about, says, "For this reason was it said, *I and the Father are one*,[7] because They have between Themselves an agreement of will, and not because the Son's nature is the same as the Father's. For the Apostles, too"—and this is what he said, not I—"for the Apostles, too, are one with the Father and the Son." Horrible blasphemy! "And the Apostles," he says, "are one with the Father and the Son, because they obey the will of the Father and the Son."

He has dared to say this? Then let Paul say, "I and God are one." Let Peter say, let the Prophets, any and all of them, say, "I and God are one." They do not say it; God forbid they should! They know that they have a different nature, a nature that needs to be healed. They know that they have a different nature, a nature that needs to be enlightened.

No-one says, "I and God are one." No matter what progress he may make, no matter how he may distinguish himself by his sanctity, no matter by what eminence of virtue he may excel: he never says, "I and God are one." Because if he is virtuous and therefore says as much, by saying it he has already lost what he had.

The Son's equality with the Father.

5. Believe, therefore, that the Son is equal to the Father; but yet that the Son is of the Father, and the Father is not of the Son. The source is with the Father, equality with the Son. For if He is not equal, He is not a true Son. Indeed, what are we saying, Brethren? If He is not equal, He is less.[8] If He is less, I put this question to the man who needs to be restored to health, who believes what is wrong—how was He born less? Answer me: being less, does He grow or not? If He grows, then the Father also grows old. But if He will remain what He was born, then, if He was born less, He will also remain less. He will be complete with His something less, having been born complete with something less than the nature of the Father; and He will never attain the nature of the Father. Thus do you commit sacrilege and deliver over the Son! Thus do you heretics blaspheme the Son!

What, then, does the Catholic faith say? The Son is God of God the Father; God the Father is God, but not of the Son. At the same time God the Son is equal with the Father—born equal, not born less; not made equal, but born equal. What the one is, the other who was born is also.

Has the Father ever been without the Son? Heaven forbid! Take away the word "ever" where there is no time.

The Father has always been, the Son has always been. The Father is without beginning of time, the Son is without beginning of time. Never was the Father before the Son, never was the Father without the Son. But yet—because the Son is God of God the Father, and the Father is God, but not of God the Son: let us not therefore fret over honoring the Son in the Father. In fact, when we honor the Son, we give honor to the Father; we do not detract from His divinity.

The Word of God, the Commandment of the Father.

6. Because, therefore, I was speaking of what I had quoted Him as saying, *And I know that His commandment is life everlasting,* do pay attention, Brethren, to these words—*I know that His commandment is life everlasting.* And we read in the same John concerning Christ, *This is the true God and life everlasting.* If the commandment of the Father is life everlasting, and Christ the Son Himself is life everlasting, then the Son is Himself the commandment of the Father. For how is not that the Father's commandment which is the Word of the Father? Or if you take the commandment given to the Son by the Father in the manner of men, as if the Father said to the Son, "This I command you; I want you to do that"—what words did He use in speaking to the only Word? Did He look for words, when He gave the commandment to the Word? That, then, the commandment of the Father is life everlasting, and the Son Himself life everlasting, this do believe and accept, believe and understand, because the Prophet says, *Unless you believe, you shall not under-*

*stand.*⁹ You do not grasp this? Open your hearts! Hear the Apostle: *Open your hearts! Do not be bearers of the yoke with unbelievers.*¹⁰ Those who do not wish to believe this before they grasp it, are unbelievers. And because they are determined to be unbelievers, they will remain ignorant. Let them believe, therefore, that they may understand.¹¹

To sum up: The commandment of the Father is life everlasting. Therefore, the commandment of the Father is the Son Himself who was born this day—a commandment not given by time, but a commandment born. The Gospel of John exercises our minds, sharpens and spiritualizes them, so that our comprehension of God is not sensual, but spiritual.

Let this, then, suffice for you, Brethren; we must not permit the length of our discussion to cause the sleep of forgetfulness to steal over you.

16
(Ben. no. 197)[1]

NEW YEAR'S DAY
A SERMON AGAINST THE PAGANS

God's anger is revealed against all impiety and wrongdoing.

For the wrath of God is revealed from heaven against all ungodliness.[2] Whose ungodliness is meant? Is it not that of both the Jews and the Gentiles? But to anticipate an objection: "Why against the ungodliness of the Gentiles? The Gentiles never received the Law, did they? How could they transgress it? As for the Jews, rightly is the wrath of God made manifest against them. The Law was given to them, and they refused to observe it; but it was not given to the Gentiles." Observe, Brethren, and see how it is shown that all stand accused, and that all are in need of God's salvation and mercy: *For the wrath of God is revealed from heaven against all ungodliness and injustice of those men that detain the truth of God in injustice.*[3] Mark that it is not said, "do not have the truth," but, *detain the truth in injustice*. And as though in answer to your objection, "How can they have the truth when they did not receive the Law?" there follows, *Because that which is known of God is manifest in them.*[4] And how could that *which is known of God* have been manifest in such as did not receive the Law? The text continues: *For the invisible things of Him, from the creation of the world, are clearly seen, being understood by the things that are* *made; His eternal power also, and divinity.*⁵ Here we obviously supply *are clearly seen, being understood.* For why should a man notice the works, but not inquire about their Maker? You notice the earth producing fruits, you see the sea with its teeming animal life, you notice the air full of birds, you notice the sky radiant with stars, and so on; and you do not look for the Author of this great work?

But you say to me, "I see these things, but I do not see Him."

That we might see these things, He gave our body eyes; that we might see Him, He gave us our mind. You do not see man's soul either! ⁶ Therefore, in the same way that you recognize the presence of the soul which you do not see, from the activity and government of the body, so, too, from the government of the whole universe and from the directing of the souls themselves, recognize that there is a Creator.⁷

But to recognize Him is not enough; for those people recognized Him, and see what the Apostle says: *Because that, knowing God, they have not glorified Him as God, or given thanks; but became vain in their thoughts, and their foolish heart was darkened.*⁸ Why had they deserved this, if not because of their pride? Indeed, note what follows: *Professing themselves to be wise, they became fools.*⁹ They should not have prided themselves on what He had given them, nor boasted about what they did not have from themselves, but from Him. They should have given Him credit for what they had; then retention of what they were able to see would have been made possible for them by being restored to health by Him to whom they owed it that they could see at all. Had they done this, they would have preserved humility; and they could have been cleansed, and would have participated in that most blessed contemplation.

But because they were given to pride, the proud Liar and Deceiver intervened, promising them that their souls would be cleansed in some extraordinary manner by pride, and he made demon-worshippers of them. This is the source of all the rites celebrated by the pagans, which, so they say, have the power to cleanse their souls.[10] Note therefore, the logical conclusion of the Apostle and his statement, that these things were visited upon them to punish them for their pride in not honoring God as He should be honored.

And they changed the glory of the incorruptible God into the likeness of the image of a corruptible man.[11] Now he is speaking of images; and here he refers to all the Greeks and the other nations who have them in the likeness of men. But the greatest and most superstitious idolatry is that of the Egyptians, for Egypt has filled the world with images such as the Apostle now lists. He followed up his words, *into the likeness of the image of a corruptible man,* with, *and of birds, and of four-footed beasts, and of creeping things.* Have you, Brethren, perhaps seen in other temples a statue with the head of a dog or a bull and images of the other irrational animals? These, as you know, are the idols of the Egyptians. The Apostle, then, combining both classes, says: . . . *into the likeness of the image of a corruptible man, and of birds, and of four-footed beasts, and of creeping things. Wherefore God gave them up to the desires of their heart, unto uncleanness, to dishonor their own bodies among themselves.*[12] Those evils of theirs exist because of the ungodliness of their pride. But these their sins, because they derive from their pride, are not only sins, but also punishments. For the words, *God gave them up,* already indicate a punishment for some sin, as a result of which they do such things.

Who changed the truth of God into a lie.[13] What is the meaning of *changed the truth of God into a lie?* Obviously, they changed it *into the likeness of the image of a corruptible man, and of birds, and of four-footed beasts, and of creeping things.* And so that none of them could say, "It is not the image that I worship, but that which the images stand for," there was immediately added, *and worshipped and served the creature rather than the Creator.*[14] Understand this clearly. They worship either the image or the creature. If it is the image a man worships, he is perverting God's truth into a lie. The sea, for instance, is a true thing; but Neptune [15] stands for a lie fabricated by man, for here the truth of God is twisted into a lie. To be sure, God made the sea, whereas man made the image of Neptune. Similarly, God made the sun; man, however, by making an image of the sun, perverts God's truth into a lie. But, lest they say, "I do not worship the image, but it is the sun I worship," for this reason it was stated that they *worshipped the creature rather than the Creator.*

Christ chose humble men for His disciples.

2. But perhaps someone will say, "Even though He was born humbly, He wished to glory in the nobility of His disciples." He did not choose these from among kings, or senators, or philosophers, or orators; no, indeed, He chose men of the people—paupers, men unlearned, fishermen. Peter was a fisherman, Cyprian an orator.[16] Had not the

fisherman gone before in faith, the orator would not have followed in humility.[17] Let no-one be despondent and lose hope for himself. Let him cling to Christ, and his hope will not be deceived; and so on.

Simon was proud, Paul humble.

3. What did Simon want, but to be praised in miracles, to be extolled because of his pride? Pride it was that drove him to think that the gift of the Holy Spirit could be bought with money.[18] In contrast to this pride, the Apostle, remaining humble, not relaxing his zeal in the heat of day, and a shining example of prudence, says: *Neither he that planteth is anything, nor he that watereth; but God that giveth the increase;* [19] and this he says because he had stated, *I have planted, Apollo watered, but God gave the increase.*[20] He says again: *Was Paul then crucified for you? or were you baptized in the name of Paul?* [21] See how he rejects the idea of being worshipped in the place of Christ, and how he refuses to present himself in the place of the Spouse to a soul committing fornication. Does it not seem to be a great thing to plant and to water? But *neither he that planteth is anything, nor he that watereth.* How has he expressed his "fear"? [22] He does not call himself anything toward the salvation of those whom he desired to build in Christ.

Paul did not want us to place our hope in him.

4. Nor did the same Apostle want hope to be placed in himself, but in the truth which he was proclaiming. What

was being said through him was better than his person through whom it was being proclaimed. *Though we,* he starts to say. But this is not enough for him—hear what follows: *or an angel from heaven,* he says, *announce to you anything besides that which you have received, let him be anathema.*[23] He saw that a false mediator could transfigure himself into an angel of light and announce something false. Therefore, just as proud men want themselves to be adored in the place of God, to be credited with whatever they can, to hear their names mentioned, and, if that were possible, to outstrip Christ Himself in glory, the devil and his angels do the same. The Donatists[24] hold to Donatus in place of Christ. Should they hear some pagan disparaging Christ, the chances are that they would tolerate it and bear it rather than if they heard him disparaging Donatus.

Christ to be loved in His saints.

5. Christ Himself speaks in His saints, as the Apostle says, *Do you seek a proof of Christ that speaketh in me?*[25] And though he says, *Neither he that planteth is anything, nor he that watereth, but God that giveth the increase,* and not because he wanted himself to be loved, but God, he bears testimony to a certain group, saying: *You received me as an angel of God, even as Christ Jesus.*[26] In all His saints, therefore, He is to be loved who says, *I was hungry, and you gave me to eat.*[27] For He does not say, "you gave those people," but *you gave me.* Such is the love of the Head for Its body!

We must beware of those who would deceive us.

6. What is Juno? Juno, they say, is the air.²⁸ A while ago we heard the suggestion that we worship the sea in an image of earth; now we are being asked to worship the air. These are the elements of which this world consists. Hence the Apostle Paul, setting this forth in his Epistle, says: *Beware, lest any man cheat you by philosophy and vain deceit . . . according to the elements of this world.*²⁹ He was referring to those who would give learned interpretations of the meaning of idols. This is why when he had mentioned *philosophy,* he said in the same passage, *according to the elements of this world:* he was admonishing them, not so much that they should beware of image-worshippers in general, but of the would-be-learned interpreters of what the images represent.

17

(Ben. no. 198)[1]

NEW YEAR'S DAY

The festival of the first of January.

We see, beloved Brethren, that you have come together to-day as for a feast and that for this day you have gathered here in greater numbers than usual. We urge you to remember what you sang a moment ago; otherwise it will only mean that your tongue made some noise while your heart remained still. The sounds you have produced in each other's ears, these it is for your love to reproduce with loud voice in the ears of God. Now, this is what you were singing: *Save us, O Lord, our God; gather us from among the Gentiles that we may give thanks to Thy holy name.*[2] On this day the Gentiles celebrate their festival with worldly joy of the flesh, with the sound of most vain and filthy songs, with banquets and shameless dances. If what the Gentiles do in celebrating this false feast does not please you, then you will be *gathered from among the Gentiles.*

Our separation from the Gentiles by Christian faith, hope, and charity.

2. Indeed, this is what you have sung, and the sound of the divine strains is still fresh in your ears—*Save us, O Lord, our God; and gather us from among the Gentiles.*

Who can be *gathered from among the Gentiles* except when he is saved? Consequently, those who associate with the Gentiles are not saved; whereas such as are *gathered from among the Gentiles* are saved by the salvation of faith, the salvation of hope, the salvation of most sincere charity, by salvation of the spirit, by the salvation of God's promises.

The simple fact, therefore, that a man believes, hopes, and loves does not mean that he is saved forthwith. For it makes a difference what he believes, what he hopes, and what he loves. It is quite obvious that no-one in any walk of life spends his days without his soul experiencing these three things—believing, hoping, loving. If you do not believe what the Gentiles believe, do not hope what the Gentiles hope, do not love what the Gentiles love, you are *gathered from among the Gentiles,* you are segregated, that is, you are separated from the Gentiles. And in the face of all that separates you in soul, you must not let the physical contacts you make frighten you. For what, for instance, could be accounted a greater separation than the fact that those people believe in demon gods, while you believe in Him who is the one and true God? That they hope in the foolish things of the world, while you place your hope in eternal life with Christ? That they love the world, but you love the Artisan of the world? Let him, then, whose faith, whose hope, whose love is different from theirs, prove it by his life, show it by his deeds.

You are going to observe the practice of giving New Year's presents [3] like a pagan, you are going to play at dice, and you are going to make yourself drunk? How can this be a different faith, a different hope, a different love? How can you have the effrontery to sing, *Save us, O Lord, our God; and gather us from among the Gentiles?* For you segregation from the Gentiles consists in leading a life different from theirs despite your contacts with them. And what such segregation means, you will realize if you will but put it into effect, if you will but give proof of it.

Do not forget—our Lord Jesus Christ, the Son of God, who became man for our sakes, has paid a price for us. It was His price, His own, that He paid. His reason for paying it was that He wished to redeem us, *to gather us from among the Gentiles.* But if you associate with the Gentiles, you do not want to follow Him who has redeemed you. You associate with the Gentiles by the life you live, by your deeds, your heart; by believing as they do, by hoping as they do, by loving as they do. You prove yourself ungrateful to your Redeemer, you do not acknowledge the price paid for you—the Blood of the Immaculate Lamb.[4] That you may, therefore, follow your Redeemer who has redeemed you with His Blood, you must not be associated with the Gentiles by behaving and acting like them.

They give New Year's presents: you give alms! They entertain themselves with debauched singing: find your entertainment in the words of the Scriptures! They run to the theater: you go to church! They get drunk: you practice fasting! If you cannot fast to-day, at least eat with moderation. If you do this, you have sung rightly, *Save us, O Lord, our God; and gather us from among the Gentiles.*

Christians separate themselves from the pagans by pious works. False gods are pleased with the evil behavior of their worshippers.

3. And so, many will struggle to-day in their hearts with the words they have heard. For we said, "Do not give New Year's presents; give to the poor." It is not enough that you give only so much; give even more. You do not want to give more? Well, give at least that much.

But you say to me, "When I give New Year's presents, I receive them in return." What? When you give to a poor person, do you receive nothing in return? Surely, you do not believe what the Gentiles believe; surely, you do not hope what the Gentiles hope. But if you say that you receive nothing when you give to a poor person, then you belong to the Gentiles; you have had no reason to sing, *Save us, O Lord, our God; and gather us from among the Gentiles.* Do not forget that rule which says, *He that giveth to the poor shall never want.*[5] Have you already forgotten what the Lord is going to say to those who have given to the poor—*Come, ye blessed of my Father, take possession of the kingdom?*[6] And what He will say to those who have not given—*send them into everlasting fire?*[7]

Now, there certainly are among you those who liked to hear His words, standing [8] with others who did not like to hear them. I am now speaking to true Christians: if your faith is different from that of others, if your hope is different, if your love is different, then lead different lives and show by your different conduct that your faith, hope, and charity are really different. Hear the forceful reminder of the Apostle: *Bear not,* he says, *the yoke with unbelievers. For what participation hath justice with injustice? Or what fellowship hath light with darkness? . . . Or what part hath the faithful with the unbeliever? And what agreement hath the temple of the Lord with idols?*[9] And in another place he says: *For the things which the heathens sacrifice, they sacrifice to devils, and not to God. I would not that you should be made partakers with devils.*[10] Their gods, therefore, are pleased by their behavior. But he who said, *I would not that you should be made partakers with devils,* wanted his addressees to separate themselves, by their life and by their behavior, from people who serve demons. For the devils referred to are truly delighted by a worthless show and all the foul things that happen in the theaters, by the folly of the circus, the cruelty of the amphitheater, the spirited rivalries of men who take up strifes and contentions by championing people bent only on mischief—a mimic, an actor, a pantomime, a charioteer, a fighter in the arena. Those who do these things are, as it were, taking incense from their hearts and placing it before devils. For the seducers of the spirit rejoice over those seduced, and they feed upon the evil behavior and the filthy and infamous lives of those whom they have seduced and deceived.

But you, as the Apostle says, *have not so learned Christ, if so be that you have heard Him and have been taught in Him.*[11] *Be not therefore partakers with them. For you were heretofore darkness, but now light in the Lord. Walk then as children of the light,*[12] so that we, too, who preach the Lord's word to you, may be able to rejoice with you and because of you in that light eternal.

18

(Ben. no. 199)[1]

EPIPHANY

Christ soon joins in Himself Jews and Gentiles.

A few days ago we celebrated the day on which the Lord was born of the Jews; to-day we are celebrating the day on which He was adored by the Gentiles. *For salvation is of the Jews;*[2] but this *salvation is even to the ends of the earth.*[3] Thus, too, on the first day the shepherds adored; to-day, the Magi.[4] Angels announced Him to the former; a star, to the latter. When they saw the King of heaven on earth, both learned from heaven that *there was glory to God in the highest, and on earth peace to men of good will.*[5] *For He is our peace who hath made both one.*[6] Thus already as an infant when He was born and announced, did He manifest Himself as that celebrated Cornerstone,[7] already in the very beginning of His Nativity did He appear as such. Already was He beginning to join together in Himself two walls coming from different directions: He was leading the shepherds from Judea and the Magi from the East, *that He might make the two in Himself into one new man, making peace; . . . peace to those that were afar off, and peace to those that were nigh.*[8] And so, too, those approaching on the day itself from close by, and these coming to-day from afar off, signified two days to be celebrated by posterity, though they both saw the one Light of the world.

*The faith of the Magi and the
faithlessness of the Jews.*

2. But to-day we should speak of the men whom faith brought to Christ from remote parts of the earth. They came and sought Him, saying: *Where is He that is born King of the Jews? For we have seen His star in the east, and are come to adore Him.*[9] They announce Him and ask about Him, they believe in Him and seek Him, signifying, as it were, those who *walk through faith* and desire to see clearly.[10]

Had there not been ever so many other kings of the Jews born in Judea in the past? Why is it that this one is recognized in the heavens by men coming from foreign lands and is sought by them on earth? Why does He shine on high, but lie hidden in lowliness?

The Magi see a star in the East and know that a King is born in Judea. Who is this King, so small and so great, who is not yet speaking on earth, but who even now is giving commands in heaven? Though He had given the Magi so clear a sign in the sky and though He had revealed to their hearts that He had been born in Judea, still He wanted them to believe His Prophets concerning Himself; and this for our sakes, because He wanted us to become acquainted with His Holy Scriptures. Thus while seeking the city in which He had been born whom they were anxious to see and to adore, they were obliged to make inquiries of the Jewish rulers. In this manner by the grace of faith these unbelievers—themselves liars but truthful in spite of themselves—were to give information to believers, drawing upon Sacred Scriptures which they carried on their lips, not in their hearts.

What a magnificent thing it would have been, had they joined those seekers of Christ, when they heard from them that they had seen His star and had come to adore Him! If they personally had led them to Bethlehem of Juda, which they had pointed out from the divine books; if they had also seen Him, also understood Him, also adored Him! But actually, after they had shown the Fountain of life to others, they themselves perished of thirst. They served them as milestones—they gave some information to travellers on the road, but they themselves remained stock-still.

The Magi were seeking for the purpose of finding; Herod's search was for the purpose of destruction. The Jews read of the city of His birth, but they did not understand the time of His coming. In the interval between the edifying expression of the love of the Magi and the cruel manifestation of Herod's fear, these same men who pointed out Bethlehem disappeared from the scene; later, however, they were to deny Christ who was born there, whom they did not look for at that time, but whom they saw later; and they were to kill Him, not then when He was still speechless, but later when He was grown and spoke.[11] Happy the ignorance of the infants whom Herod persecuted when he was terrified—happier than the knowledge of the men whom He consulted in his confusion! The first were able to suffer for Christ whom they had not yet been able to confess; the latter did not follow the truth of the Teacher, the city of whose birth they were able to know.

The error of astrology.

3. To be sure, the star led the Magi to the exact place where God the speechless Word was. Here is the place for sacrilegious stupidity to blush for shame—a certain, to put it that way, unlearned learning which holds, merely because it was written in the Gospel that when He was born the Magi saw His star in the East, that Christ's birth was decreed by the stars. That would not be true, not even if human beings were born under a decree of this sort; because men are not born of their own free will, like the Son of God was born, but as dictated by their mortal nature.

Actually, the proposition that Christ was born by a star-determined fate is so inconsistent with truth, that whosoever really believes in Christ believes that no man is born in this way. But let these empty-minded men speak their foolish opinions about the natal stars of men. Let them deny the will by which they sin, let them invent the necessity by which they defend their sins. Let them even try to blame the heavens for their wretched morals which make men despise them on earth, and let them trump up the lie that their morality comes from the stars. But let each one of them see how and by what power he thinks that, not his life, but his household should be ruled. Obviously this his viewpoint does not permit him to flog his own slaves when they do wrong in his house. He would first have to blaspheme his gods glittering in the sky! Even so, not even according to their own most insipid conjectures, nor according to their books—which of course do not speak prophetically, but speak altogether falsely—can they believe that Christ was born under a decree of the stars merely because the Magi saw a star in the East when He was born. For it follows from this that Christ appeared, not under its rule, but rather as its Ruler; because that star did not keep to the ways of the stars in the sky, but showed the men who were seeking Christ the way to the place in which He had been born. Hence it was not a case of the star causing Christ to live in a wonderful manner, but of Christ causing it to appear in a wonderful manner. Nor did the star itself decree the miracles of Christ; on the contrary, Christ produced it among His own miracles.

He Himself, when born of His mother, made a new star [12] appear in heaven and showed it to the earth, He who, born of the Father, had created heaven and the earth. At His birth a new light was revealed in the star, and at His death the sun's ancient light was veiled. When He was born, the heaven-dwellers above became radiant with new glory; when He died, the inhabitants of the infernal regions trembled with new fear. When He rose again, the disciples burned with new love, and when He made His ascent, the heavens opened up with new loyalty.

Let us, then, devoutly and solemnly celebrate this day, too, on which the Magi of the Gentiles recognized and adored Christ,[13] just as we celebrated the day on which the shepherds of Judea saw the born Christ.[14] For our Lord God Himself chose the Apostles of Judea as the shepherds through whom He was to gather together and save sinners among the Gentiles as well.

19
(Ben. no. 200)[1]

EPIPHANY

The feast of Christ's Manifestation.

The Magi came from the East to adore the newborn Child of the Virgin. We celebrate this day to-day with all due solemnity and a sermon. That first day dawned upon them; it has returned to us on its yearly feast. They were the first fruits of the Gentiles; we are the people of the Gentiles. The mouth of the Apostles announced this to us; the star, as the mouth of the heavens, announced it to them. And the same Apostles, like the heavens, expounded to us the glory of God.[2] Why, indeed, may we not acknowledge them as heavens, seeing that they became the seat of God—as it was written, *the soul of the just is the seat of wisdom?*[3]

The Maker and Dweller of the heavens thundered through these heavens; the world trembled violently with this thunder, and, behold, it now believes. Here we have a great mystery. He was at that time lying in a manger, and yet was leading the Magi from the East. He lay hidden in a stable, yet He was acknowledged in the heavens, so that He, acknowledged in the heavens, might be made manifest in the stable, and this day might be called "Epiphany," which may be expressed in Latin as "Manifestatio." This day extols His loftiness and at the same time His humility: He who was shown by a star appearing as a sign in the open sky, was found in a tiny resting place when he was sought; He, weak in His infant limbs, wrapped in infant's swaddling clothes, was adored by the Magi, feared by the wicked.

Herod's fright.

2. Yes, King Herod feared Him when the same Magi, still seeking the Child who they knew from the evidence in the sky had already been born, brought the news to him. What will the tribunal of His judgment be when the cradle of His infancy terrified proud kings? How much more reasonable are kings to-day who are not, as was Herod, bent upon slaughter! But rather, like the Magi, they find delight in adoring Him—Him above all who even for His enemies endured at the hands of His enemies that same death which His enemy desired then to inflict, and who, when He was slain in His own body, slew death itself. Let our kings to-day stand in pious fear of Him who is even now sitting at the right hand of His Father, Him whom that wicked king feared when He was still nursing at His mother's breasts. Let them heed what Scripture says: *And now, O ye kings, understand: receive instruction, you that judge the earth. Serve ye the Lord with fear, and rejoice unto Him with trembling.*[4]

That King, the Chastiser of wicked kings, the Ruler of pious kings, was not born in the same way that worldly kings are born; because He was also born that one *whose kingdom is not of this world.*[5] The nobility of the Child appeared in the virginity of His mother; and the nobility of the mother was made manifest in the divinity of her Child. Never, in fact, though so many kings of the Jews had already been born and had died, were there Magi who sought for any of them to adore them; because no voice of heaven had told them about any one of them.

The blindness of the Jews expressed in the enlightenment of the Magi. The Scriptures neglected among the Jews brought faith to the Gentiles.

3. But now, and this must not be left unmentioned, in this enlightening of the Magi there is eloquent testimony of the blindness of the Jews. The former were seeking in the land of the latter for Him whom the latter did not acknowledge in their own land. Among the Jews the Magi found the Infant whom the Jews were to deny when He was teaching among them. Here, in the same land in which these strangers coming from afar adored the Christ Child when He was not yet uttering words, His own countrymen crucified Him when He was a young man working miracles. The first recognized God in His tiny body; the others, when He was performing great deeds, did not spare Him even as a human being. Apparently, it was a greater prodigy to see a new star shining at His Nativity than to see the sun in mourning at His death!

Further, there is the fact that the star which guided the Magi to the place where the Divine Infant was with the Virgin Mother and which obviously could have led them straight to the city where He was born, disappeared. It was not seen again until they had made inquiry of these selfsame Jews regarding the city in which Christ was to be born: the Jews themselves were to name it to them on the authority of the Divine Scriptures, saying: *In Bethle-*

hem of Juda. For so it is written: "And thou Bethlehem the land of Juda art not the least among the princes of Juda: for out of thee shall come forth the captain that shall rule my people Israel."⁶ What else has Divine Providence signified here than that the Divine Scriptures alone would remain with the Jews—for the instruction of the Gentiles, but for their own blinding? These Scriptures they were to carry with them, not to help them toward their own salvation, but to give witness to our salvation. To-day, for instance, when we cite the early prophecies concerning Christ which have been made clear in the light of things fulfilled, and pagans whom we wish to win over say that these prophecies were not made so long in advance, but only devised by us after the event in order to create the belief that what has happened had been prophesied, then we quote the volumes of the Jews to remove the doubts of the pagans. These latter were already foretokened by the Magi whom the Jews, quoting the Divine Scriptures, provided with information regarding the city in which Christ was born, without, however, making any inquiry about Him themselves or acknowledging Him.

Gentiles as well as Jews are united with Christ through love.

4. Now then, my beloved, children and heirs of grace, see your calling, and with a most enduring love cleave to Christ—to the Cornerstone, as it were, made manifest to the Jews and the Gentiles.

He was made manifest in the very cradle of His infancy to those close by and to those far away; to the Jews, in the shepherds near-by, to the Gentiles, in the Magi coming from afar. The former are believed to have come to Him on the very day He was born, the others, on this day. He was made manifest, then—and not to learned people in the first instance, nor to just [7] people in the second. For certainly ignorance is characteristic of shepherds in the field as irreligion marks the unholy practices of Magi.

That Cornerstone has fitted both to Himself; He, to be sure, came *to choose the foolish things of the world that He might confound the wise,*[8] and *to call not the just, but sinners,*[9] so that no man might pride himself on his greatness and no man despair because of his lowliness. And for this reason the Scribes and Pharisees, preening themselves on their superior learning and justice, in their building rejected Him the city of whose birth they had pointed out by quoting from the sayings of the Prophets. But because He *is become the head of the corner,*[10] and what he showed at His birth He fulfilled in His Passion, let us cling to Him with the other wall containing *the remnant* of Israel *saved according to the election of grace.*[11]

The shepherds prefigured those to be joined to Him from close by, so that we, too, whose call from afar was signified by the coming of the Magi, may now be not strangers and tenants, but fellow citizens of the saints and with them members of the family of God, built side by side on the foundation of the Apostles and the Prophets, with the cornerstone itself Christ Jesus, *who has made both one.*[12] He has made us one that we may love unity and to inspire us with an untiring love for the task of gathering up the branches that were grafted on from even the wild olive, but were broken off because of pride and became heretics; *for God is able to graft them in again.*[13]

20

(Ben. no. 201)[1]

EPIPHANY

Christ made manifest to the Gentiles.
The star, a tongue of heaven.

Only a few days ago we celebrated the Lord's birthday. To-day we are celebrating with equal solemnity, as is proper, His Manifestation, in which He began to manifest Himself to the Gentiles. On the one day the Jewish shepherds saw Him when He was born; on this day the Magi coming from the East adored Him.

Now, He had been born that Cornerstone, the Peace of the two walls coming from very different directions, from circumcision and uncircumcision. Thus they could be united in Him who has been made our peace, and *who has made both one.*[2] This was foretokened in the Jewish shepherds and the Gentile Magi. From this began what was to grow and to bear fruit throughout the world. Let us, therefore, with joy of the spirit hold dear these two days, the Nativity and the Manifestation of our Lord. The Jewish shepherds were led to Him by an angel bringing the news; the Gentile Magi, by a star showing the way.

This star threw into confusion the idle calculations and divinations of the astrologers when it showed them who adored the stars, the Creator of heaven and earth who should rather be adored. For He when He was born showed forth the new star, He who when He was slain obscured the ancient sun. In the light of the one the faith of the Gentiles took its beginning; the perfidy of the Jews stood accused by the darkness of the other.

What was that star which had never before appeared among the stars, and which afterwards did not remain to be pointed out? What was it but an eloquent tongue of heaven to tell of the glory of God, to proclaim with its wondrous lustre the wondrous fruit of the Virgin's womb, to be succeeded later when it disappeared by the Gospel preached throughout the world? And what did the Magi say when they came? *Where is He that is born King of the Jews?* What does this mean? Had not a great many kings of the Jews been born before? Why were they so intent upon knowing and adoring a king of a foreign nation? *For, they said, we have seen His star in the east, and we have come to adore Him.*[3] Would they have pressed their search with such great devotion, would they have shown such tender affection for the object of their desire, if they had not recognized Him as the King of the Jews, who is also King of the ages?

Pilate and the Magi were types of the Gentiles to be brought into the Church from the East and from the West.

2. Hence, even Pilate was inspired by at least a trace of truth when at the time of His Passion he composed the title, *King of the Jews.*[4] The false Jews tried to change this title. He answered them, *What I have written, I have written;*[5] because it had been foretold in the Psalm, *Do not falsify the inscription of the title.*[6]

Let us, then, turn our attention to this great and wonderful mystery. The Magi were of the Gentiles; and Pilate himself also came from the Gentiles. They saw the star in the sky; he wrote the title on the Wood; yet in both instances it was not a king of the Gentiles, but the King of the Jews that was sought or acknowleged. But as for the Jews themselves, they neither followed the star nor agreed with the title. Even then was there foretokened what the Lord Himself was to state later: *Many shall come from the East and the West, and they shall sit down with Abraham, and Isaac, and Jacob in the kingdom of heaven; but the children of the kingdom shall go into the exterior darkness.*[7]

For the Magi had come from the East, Pilate from the West. This is wherein they both bore witness to the King of the Jews—they to Him in the East, that is, at His birth; he to Him in the West, that is, at His death.[8] Thus could they sit down in the kingdom of heaven with Abraham, Isaac, and Jacob, from whom the Jews traced their origin. They were not descended from these people by the flesh, but were grafted into them by faith. Thus they were already foreshowing the wild olive of which the Apostle says that it is to be grafted on to the true olive.[9] It was obviously for this reason that not the King of the Gentiles, but the King of the Jews was sought or acknowledged by these same Gentiles; because the wild olive was coming to the true olive, not the true olive to the wild olive.

The branches, though, which were to be broken off, that is, the unbelieving Jews, answered the Magi inquiring where Christ was to be born, *In Bethlehem of Juda;*[10] and when Pilate was reproaching them for wanting their King to be crucified, they remained obdurate and became raving mad. And so, while the Jews pointed out the place of Christ's birth, the Magi adored. The lesson? It is in the Scriptures, accepted by the Jews, that we become acquainted with Christ. Pilate, a Gentile, washed his hands when the Jews were demanding the death of Christ; [11] it is in the Blood shed by the Jews that we wash away our sins.—But we must reserve for another occasion, Passiontide, a discussion of the testimony given by Pilate in the title on which he wrote of Christ as the King of the Jews.

The Jews are the custodians of the Scriptures for the salvation of the Gentiles.

3. But now let us state briefly what remains to be said about the Manifestation of the born Christ. This "Manifestation" is called *Epiphania* in Greek. It is the day on which He began to "manifest" Himself to the Gentiles in the adoration of the Magi. It is interesting indeed to reflect again and again how the Jews answered the Magi who were asking where Christ was born—*In Bethlehem of Juda;* whereas they themselves did not go to Him. But, while they remained aloof, the Magi were led to the place where the Infant was, by the star they had seen before. Thus it became evident that it could have guided them to the city directly; but it disappeared for a while to permit them to make inquiry of the Jews. And the reason that inquiry was made of the Jews was this: it was to be shown that they are the carriers of God's testimonies not for their own instruction and salvation, but for that of the Gentiles. Indeed, here we have the reason that this nation was driven from its kingdom and dispersed throughout the earth: they were to bear witness every-

where to the faith whose enemies they are. Though, to be sure, they have lost their temple, their sacrifice, their priesthood, and their kingdom itself, they preserve their name and nationality in a few ancient rites to keep them from intermingling with the Gentiles and, thus losing their own identity, disappearing entirely and losing the testimony of truth. They are like Cain in receiving a special mark: no-one was to kill him who, because he was envious and proud, had killed his just brother.[12]

Doubtless, it is not inadmissible either to take it that this is what is meant in the fifty-eighth Psalm also where Christ is found speaking in His mystical body, saying: *My God has shown to me in my enemies. Slay them not, lest they at any time forget Thy law.*[13] For it is in these enemies of the Christian faith that the Gentiles are shown how Christ was prophesied. Otherwise, seeing the prophecies so strikingly fulfilled, when passages are read to them containing predictions about Christ which obviously have come to pass, they might think that the Scriptures containing them are only forgeries made by the Christians. In such case the Jews enter the picture with their codices, and thus God manifests Himself to us in our enemies. These He has not slain, that is, He has not destroyed them entirely from the face of the earth,[14] for the reason that they were to preserve their law from oblivion. By reading in it and by observing, though only externally, certain of its precepts, they have preserved its memory—to bring judgment upon themselves and to bear witness for us.

21
(Ben. no. 202) [1]

EPIPHANY

Epiphany, Christ's Manifestation.

To-day's feast is known throughout the whole world. What joy it brings us, or what lesson the feast has for us on its annual return—the season suggests that we also make this the topic of the sermon which we give at this time each year.

The Greek *Epiphania,* it is clear, can be rendered in Latin by the word *Manifestatio.* It is on this day that the Magi are said to have adored the Lord. They were prevailed upon to do this by a star which appeared to them and were led on by the star going before them. On the day He was born they saw the star in the East; and they knew whose birth was signified by the star. From that day, then, to this did they hasten to find Him. They frightened King Herod with the news. When in answer to their inquiry the Jews had quoted to them the prophecies contained in the Scriptures, they found the city of Bethlehem where the Lord had been born. Then, with the same star as their guide, they came to the place where the Lord was. When they recognized Him, they adored Him. They offered Him gold, incense, and myrrh. They returned by another way.[2]

The Lord was also made manifest, and that on the day

of His birth, to the shepherds who were informed by an angel. And on that day news of Him was given by a star also to those men still far off in the East; and this is the day on which they adored Him. Therefore, the universal Church of the Gentiles adopted this day as a day to be celebrated in a most devout manner; for even these Magi, what were they but the first fruits of the Gentiles?

The shepherds were Israelites, the Magi, Gentiles. The first lived near-by, the latter, far away; yet both met at the Cornerstone. *Coming*, to be sure, as the Apostle says, *He preached peace to us that were afar off, and peace to these that were nigh. For He is our peace who has made both one, and has made the two in Himself into one new man, making peace, and has changed both to God in one body, killing the enmities in Himself.*[3]

*In the Magi were the first fruits
of the Gentiles harvested.*

2. With good reason have the heretical Donatists [4] never wished to celebrate this day with us: they neither love unity, nor are they in communion with the Eastern Church where that star appeared. Let us, however, celebrate the Manifestation of our Lord and Savior Jesus Christ on which He harvested the first fruits of the Gentiles, in the unity of the Gentiles.

For at that time when He was a Child, before He knew how to call His father or mother, as had been prophesied of Him, He accepted *the strength of Damascus and the spoils of Samaria;*[5] that is, before He uttered human words through His human flesh, He accepted the strength of Damascus, namely, that on which Damascus prided itself. Indeed, by the standards of the world it was a flourishing city and because of its riches had once given itself airs. But among riches the first place is given to gold, and this the Magi humbly offered to Christ. As for the spoils of Samaria, these were quite the same as the people who were living there: "Samaria" was taken as synonymous with "idolatry"; for there the people of Israel turned away from the Lord and gave themselves to the worship of idols. Christ, who was of course going to vanquish the kingdom of the devil throughout the world with a spiritual sword, as a Child took these first spoils away from the domination of idolatry. Thus He was to convert the Magi from the curse of their superstition to the adoration of Himself; and because He was not yet speaking on this earth through His tongue, He was to speak from heaven through a star. He was to show, not by a voice of flesh, but by the power of the Word made flesh, who He was, whither He had come, and for whose sake He had come.

This Word, which in the beginning was God with God, now also made flesh that He might dwell among us, had come to us—but He was also remaining with the Father. Without deserting the angels on high, He was employing the angels to gather men to Himself below. Because He was the Word, He shone with the light of unchangeable truth upon the dwellers in heaven; and at the same time, because His lodging was so small, He was lying in a manger.

It was He who showed the star in the sky, and it was He who showed Himself to be adored on earth. And yet this Infant, so powerful, so great, fled into Egypt, a Child borne there by His parents—because of the hostility of

Herod. Thus He says to His members, though not yet in words but as implied by His actions: *If you are persecuted in one city, flee into another.*[6]

He was, to be sure, wearing the garment of mortal flesh, that therein He might serve us as a model; and in it He was also to die for us at the opportune time. This is why He had received from the Magi not only the gold of honor and the incense of adoration, but also the myrrh of burial. In the little ones whom Herod had slain, He also showed what kind of people were going to die for His name, how innocent, how humble they would be. For indeed their age of two years also signified the number of precepts on which the whole law and the Prophets depend.[7]

The Jews show Christ by their own ceremonies and Scriptures.

3. But whose thoughts are not already directed to the significance of the fact that the Jews quoted Scripture when replying to the question of the Magi concerning the place where Christ was born, but themselves refrained from adoring Him? Do we not see this even now, when the very practices of religion to which their obduracy is exposed, point to nothing else but the Christ in whom they do not want to believe? Even when they kill their sheep and eat the passover,[8] do they not point out to the Gentiles the Christ whom they themselves do not adore with them? Indeed, what of the fact that in the case of prophetic testimonies by which Christ was announced beforehand and regarding which doubting individuals think that Christians may have composed them— not when they were still in the future, but when they

were accomplished facts—we often cite the writings of the Jews to settle the doubts they have in their minds? Do not the Jews even then show the Gentiles the Christ whom they do not wish to adore with the Gentiles?

After repentance we should not return to our former way of life.

4. We, therefore, Beloved, of whom the Magi were the first fruits, we are the inheritance of Christ even to the ends of the earth. For our sake a part of Israel was overtaken by blindness that the fullness of the Gentiles might come in.[9] We have learned to know our Lord and Savior Jesus Christ, who that He might console us, did then lie in a tiny lodging, who that He may raise us up, now sits in heaven. Let us so proclaim Him on this earth, in this our mortal life, that we may not return the way we have come, nor retrace the footsteps of our former way of life. This is why, too, the Magi did not return the way by which they had come. A change of way meant a change of life.

To us also did *the heavens show forth the glory of God;* [10] we, too, have been led to the adoration of Christ by the truth shining forth from the Gospel, like a star from the sky; we, too, have listened faithfully and have understood the prophecy honored in the Jewish race—a testimony, as it were, of the Jews refusing to go on with us; we, too, by acknowledging and praising the King, the Priest, the Christ who died for us, have honored Him, so to speak, in gold and incense and myrrh. It only remains for us to be heralds of His Gospel and go a new way, and not return the way we have come.

22

(Ben. no. 203)[1]

EPIPHANY

Rightly has the feast of Epiphany been established.

For the Greek word *Epiphania* we say *Manifestatio* in Latin. On this day, then, the "manifested" Redeemer of all nations has made a solemn feast for all nations. And so we are celebrating to-day the Manifestation of Him whose Nativity we celebrated only a few days ago.

Now, tradition has it that our Lord Jesus Christ, born twelve days ago,[2] was adored by the Magi on this day. That they adored Him is a truth spoken by the Gospel; on what day they did so, is proclaimed by the fact that this glorious feast is observed everywhere. For, inasmuch as the Magi were the first among the Gentiles to learn of Christ the Lord; and because they, not yet benefiting from His speech, followed the star which appeared to them and which, in place of the Infant Word, spoke to their sight—like a tongue of heaven:[3] it is but right, and right it truly is, that the Gentiles should gratefully acknowledge the day of the first fruits of their salvation, and with thanksgiving and solemn homage dedicate it to Christ the Lord.

Obviously, the first fruits of the faith and revelation of Christ among the Jews were the shepherds who, coming from the immediate vicinity, saw Him on the very day He was born. The news was given to them by the angels, to the others by the star. *Glory to God in the highest*[4] was said to them; in the others there was fulfilled, *The heavens tell of the glory of God.*⁵ Indeed, like the beginnings of two walls coming from different directions—the circumcised and the uncircumcised—both have met at the Cornerstone, so that He might be their Peace, making both one.⁶

The Jews received grace first, but the Gentiles had greater humility.

2. But, as I was saying, the first-mentioned praised God because they had seen Christ; ⁷ the others, however, also adored the Christ whom they had seen.⁸ The former had grace before the latter; the latter had greater humility. Now, perhaps the shepherds, being less sin-laden, rejoiced more spontaneously over their salvation, whereas these Magi, being burdened with many sins, more humbly felt the need of forgiveness.

This is that humility which Divine Scripture extols more in those who were of the Gentiles than in the Jews. For instance, the centurion was a Gentile, who, though he had welcomed the Lord with all his heart, nevertheless said that he was unworthy to receive Him into his house. He did not even want his sick one to be seen by Him, but merely wanted him to be made well by command.⁹ Thus within himself he was holding present in his heart Him whose presence he was in a respectful manner trying to keep from his house. Therefore, the Lord said: *I have not found so great faith in Israel.*

The Canaanite woman also was of the Gentiles: when she heard the Lord refer to her as a dog and one unworthy to have the bread of the children cast to her, she asked for the crumbs as though she were a dog. And hence she merited not to be one—because she did not deny what she had been; for she, too, heard the Lord say to her: *O woman, great is thy faith.*[10] Her humility had made her faith great because she had made herself small.

The salvation of all nations symbolized.

3. The shepherds, then, come from near-by to see, and the Magi come from afar to adore. This is the humility which made the wild olive worthy of being grafted onto the true olive[11] and of—contrary to its nature—bearing olives; because grace made it worthy of changing its nature. For, although the whole world was growing wild and bitter with this wild olive, it was made fertile through the grace of the grafting and became resplendent with fruit.

According to Jeremias, they come from the end of the earth, saying: *Surely, our fathers have cultivated lies.*[12] And they come, not from one part of the globe, but, as the Gospel according to Luke says, *from the East and the West, from the North and the South,* to sit down with Abraham, Isaac, and Jacob in the kingdom of heaven.[13] Thus the whole world is, by the grace of the Trinity,[14] called from the four points of the compass to the Faith. And according to this reckoning, when four is taken three times, we have the sacred number of the twelve Apostles,[15] prefiguring, as it were, the salvation of the whole globe from the four parts of the world into the grace of the Trinity.

This number was signified also by the disc which was shown to Peter full of all the animals [16]—full of all the nations, as it were. For here, too, suspended from heaven, as it were, by four lines, it was lowered and taken up three times; so that three times four made twelve. So, too, it was perhaps for this reason that twelve days after the Lord's birthday the Magi, the first fruits of the Gentiles, came to see and adore Christ, and merited not only to receive their own salvation, but also to signify the salvation of all nations.

Wherefore, let us in a most devout manner celebrate this day also; and let us adore the Lord Jesus residing in heaven whom those first fruits of ours adored when He was lying in His lodging place. They, to be sure, venerated in Him as something to come that which we venerate as a thing fulfilled. The first fruits of the Gentiles adored Him, nursing at the bosom of His mother; the Nations adore Him sitting at the right hand of God the Father.

23

(Ben. no. 204)[1]

EPIPHANY

Epiphany, Christ's Manifestation.

A few days ago we celebrated the Lord's Nativity; to-day we are celebrating Epiphany—a Greek word meaning "manifestation," and referring to what the Apostle says: *Without doubt, great is the mystery of godliness which was manifested in the flesh.*[2] Accordingly, both days pertain to Christ's manifestation. In fact, on the first He was born a human being of His human mother, He who without beginning was God with the Father. But He was manifested in the flesh to the flesh; because the flesh was not able to see Him as He was in the spirit. And it was also on that day, which is called His birthday, that the Jewish shepherds saw Him; whereas on this day, which is properly called "Epiphany," that is, "Manifestation," the Gentile Magi adored Him. Angels announced Him to the former, but a star to the latter. The heavens are inhabited by the angels and are adorned by the stars; to both, then, did *the heavens show forth the glory of God.*[3]

Christ, the Cornerstone for the union of Jews and Gentiles.

2. Indeed, to both was He born as a Cornerstone, *that, as the Apostle says, He might make the two in Himself*

*into one new man, making peace, and might change both to God in the one body by the Cross.*⁴

What is a corner but the joining of two walls coming from different directions, which then, as it were, exchange the kiss of peace? The circumcised and the uncircumcised, that is, the Jews and the Gentiles, obviously were mutual enemies; and that because two radically different things separated them—the worship of the one true God by the former, the worship of many and false gods by the latter. Since, therefore, the one group was close by, but the other, far off, He led both to Himself, He who *changed both to God in the one body, by*—as the same Apostle adds appropriately—*the Cross killing enmities in Himself.* And coming, he says, *He preached peace to you that were afar off, and peace to those that were nigh, because by Him we have access both in one spirit to the Father.*⁵ See if this is not a description of the two walls coming from different directions of enmity, as also of the Cornerstone, Jesus the Lord, to whom they have both approached from different directions, in whom they have both agreed, that is, both those of the Jews and those of the Gentiles who have believed in Him. It was as if it had been said to them: Both you from near-by and you from afar, *come ye to Him and be enlightened, and your faces shall not grow red with shame.*⁶ For it is written: *Behold, I lay in Sion a cornerstone, elect, precious. And he that shall believe in Him shall not be confounded.*⁷

They heard and obeyed; they came both from near-by and from afar; they kept peace, they put an end to their hatreds. The first fruits of both were the shepherds and the Magi. In them did the ox begin *to know his Owner, and the ass his Master's crib.*⁸ The horned animal stands for the Jews—among whom the horns of the Cross were being prepared for Christ. The long-eared animal stands for the Gentiles—hence it had been foretold: *A people which I knew not, hath served me: in the hearing of the ear they have obeyed me.*[9] Clearly, the Owner of the ox and the Master of the ass in His own person was lying in the crib and offering to both a common food.

Because, therefore, peace had come to those who were afar off, and peace to those who were nigh, the Israelite shepherds, representing those nigh, on the day Christ was born came to Him, saw Him, and rejoiced; and the Gentile Magi, representing those afar off, after many days had elapsed from the day He was born, arrived to-day, found Him, and adored. It was therefore proper for us, that is, the Church gathered from the Gentiles, to add the celebration of this day, the day on which Christ was made manifest to the first fruits of the Gentiles, to the celebration of that day on which Christ was born of the Jews, and to preserve the memory of so great a mystery in a twin festival.[10]

Some of the Jews were rejected, some chosen. Jacob blessed in his lameness.

3. When we reflect upon those two walls, the one consisting of the Jews, the other of the Gentiles, which by cleaving to the Cornerstone *preserve unity of spirit in the bond of peace,*[11] our minds should not be shocked by the great number of Jews rejected, among them the builders,[12] that is, those who wished to be teachers of the Law, but whom the Apostle describes as *understanding*

neither the things they say, nor whereof they affirm.[13] It was because of this their mental blindness that *they rejected the stone which is become the head of the corner.*[14] But it would not have become the head of the corner, if it did not offer the two peoples coming from different directions a joining effected by grace and making for peace.

Therefore, do not regard as being part of the Israelite wall the persecutors and killers of Christ who were, so to speak, building the Law and destroying the faith, rejecting the Cornerstone and preparing the downfall of an unfortunate city. And do not consider as part of that wall the many, many Jews scattered throughout the world bearing witness to the divine writings which they carry with them without understanding them. For Jacob is limping in these, he whose breadth of the thigh was stricken and paralyzed,[15] thus signifying the great number of his descendants limping from their paths.

On the other hand, consider as being within the holy wall which came away from them to the peace of the Cornerstone, those in whom Jacob was blessed; for, in fact, the same man was both blessed and lame: blessed in those made holy, lame in those rejected. Regard as within that wall the multitude of those who went before and followed the Savior on the ass's colt, crying with loud voice, *Blessed is He that cometh in the name of the Lord.*[16] Think of those among them who had been chosen disciples and who became Apostles. Think of Stephen, called in Greek by the name "Crown," and the first to be crowned by martyrdom after the Lord's Resurrection.[17] Think also of the many thousands who were of the number of persecutors, but who believed when the Holy Spirit came. Think of the churches of whom the Apostle says:

And I was unknown by face to the churches of Judea which were in Christ. But they had heard only that he who persecuted us in times past, doth now preach the faith which once he ravaged; and they glorified God in me.[18]

Thus should we think of the wall of Israel. Let it be joined to the wall coming from the Gentiles, a wall which is now strikingly in evidence. And so the Cornerstone, first placed in a crib, then raised to the summit of heaven, is found—Christ the Lord, who was not foretold in vain.

NOTES

LIST OF ABBREVIATIONS

AC	F. J. Dölger, Antike und Christentum
ACW	Ancient Christian Writers
CE	Catholic Encyclopedia
CIL	Corpus inscriptionum latinarum
CSEL	Corpus scriptorum ecclesiasticorum latinorum
DACL	Dictionnaire d'archéologie chrétienne et de liturgie
DTC	Dictionnaire de théologie catholique
LTK	Lexikon für Theologie und Kirche
ML	P. J. Migne, Patrologia latina
OCD	Oxford Classical Dictionary
PS	Patristic Studies
RAC	Reallexikon für Antike und Christentum
RE	Realenzylopädie der classischen Altertumswissenschaft
SCA	Studies in Christian Antiquity
SPCK	Society for Promoting Christian Knowledge
TLL	Thesaurus linguae latinae
TWNT	Theologisches Wörterbuch zum Neuen Testament

INTRODUCTION

[1] *Vita S. Augustini* 31. Possidius, the contemporary biographer of St. Augustine, had been his intimate friend for nearly forty years and a fellow bishop (of Calama) for more than thirty years. His life of Augustine was edited by H. T. Weiskotten, *Sancti Augustini vita scripta a Possidio episcopo* (diss. Princeton 1919); also by A. C. Vega, in *Opuscula Sancti Possidii, episcopi Calamensis* (El Escorial 1934).

[2] Cf. in the present collection *Serm.* 1(51).6.

[3] See M. M. Getty, *The Life of the North Africans as Revealed in the Sermons of Saint Augustine* (PS 28, Washington 1931); also A. Degert, *Quid ad mores ingeniaque Afrorum cognoscenda conferant S. Augustini sermones* (diss. Paris 1894); H. Pope, *Saint*

Augustine of Hippo (London 1937 [repr. Westminster, Md. 1949]) 26-77, 139-94.

⁴ This fact makes it possible to date many of Augustine's sermons; cf. A. Kunzelmann, 'Die Chronologie der Sermones des hl. Augustinus,' *Miscellanea Agostiniana* 2 (Rome 1931) 417-520.

⁵ *Conf.* 1. 26 f.

⁶ *Ibid.* 3. 6.

⁷ It is interesting to note how Augustine's interest in rhetoric helped lead him to the Church, how Augustine the orator was influenced by another orator, St. Ambrose, bishop of Milan. Augustine turned to the *facundia* of the celebrated Ambrose because of his professional interest in rhetoric (*Conf.* 5. 23). To his surprise he found that Ambrose could explain the Scriptures to his satisfaction (*ibid.* 5. 24, 6. 6). It was divine grace working through the public sermons of St. Ambrose that changed Augustine's attitude toward the Scriptures and led him on to a favorable view of Christianity.

⁸ See M. I. Barry, *St. Augustine, the Orator. A Study of the Rhetorical Qualities of St. Augustine's Sermones ad Populum* (PS 6, Washington 1924); M. Comeau, *La rhétorique de saint Augustin d'après les Tractatus in Ioannem* (Paris 1930); J. Finaert, *Saint Augustin rhéteur* (Paris 1939).

⁹ Valerius, a Greek, was unable to speak Punic and was not very fluent in Latin. One day early in 391 when Augustine happened to be in the church at Hippo, Valerius told the people he needed a priest to help him. The people laid hands on Augustine and brought him, protesting and weeping, to the bishop, who promptly ordained him. See Possidius, *op. cit.* 4; also Augustine's *Ep.* 21. 2 and *Serm.* 355. 2. Four or five years later the primate of Numidia, Megalius, consecrated Augustine coadjutor bishop of Hippo (Possidius, *op. cit.* 8). After the death of Valerius, in 395 or 396, Augustine was in complete charge of the diocese of Hippo.

¹⁰ Cf. Possidius, *op. cit.* 5; also Augustine, *Ep.* 41. 1.

¹¹ See the evidence gathered by Pope, *op. cit.* 140-42.

¹² An early Roman tribute to Augustine's eminence as an orator and preacher may be seen in the inscription, discovered in 1900 by a French architect, P. Lauer, beneath a fresco appearing on a wall below the Sancta Sanctorum Chapel opposite the Lateran Palace. The fresco, dating from the sixth or even the fifth century, portrays an elderly man with the features and dress of a scholar,

seated (the position used by the preacher in antiquity) and interpreting—with his right hand raised in a gesture—from a folio lying open on a low lectern before him. The name of St. Augustine does not occur in the inscription; but the authorities agree that he is represented. The inscription, a distich, reads:

> Diversi diversa Patres s[ed hic] omnia dixit
> Romano eloqu[io] mystica sensa tonans—

'The Fathers have spoken on a variety of subjects, the one on this, the other on that; but this Father has spoken with Roman eloquence on all subjects, uttering memorable words on the mysteries he fathomed.' For the picture and text, cf. P. Lauer in *Mélanges d'archéologie et histoire* (1900) 274, pl. 9 and 10; J. Wilpert, *Römische Mosaiken und Wandmalereien der kirchlichen Bauten* (Freiburg i. Br. 1916) 1. 149 ff.; 2 pl. 140; M. Grabmann-J. Mausbach, *Aurelius Augustinus, Die Festschrift der Görres-Gesellschaft zum 1500. Todestage des heiligen Augustinus* (Cologne 1930), frontispiece and the description—ix and x—by J. Sauer.

[13] D. C. Lambot in the preface to his *Sancti Aurelii Augustini sermones selecti duodeviginti* (Stromata patr. et med. 1, Utrecht-Brussels 1950) appears to deny this point; but note the remark of the Maurists in their preface (5. ii = ML 38. 11 f.): 'Certum est praeterea conciones plurimas ab eodem Doctore, aut nondum pronuntiatas, aut etiam postquam eas iam pronuntiasset, dictatas esse, sive ut ipsas iuberet in ecclesia sua recitari, sive ut iisdem alii quoque uti libere possent.' Cf. Pope, *op. cit.* 165.

[14] For a good summary of how these sermons have been preserved to this day, see Lambot, *op. cit.* 5-10; also C. Mohrmann, *Sint Augustinus, preken voor het volk* (Monumenta christiana, 1 reeks 1, Utrecht-Brussels 1948) xiii-xxvii.

[15] Cf. Possidius, *op. cit.* 7; Augustine, *Enarr. in Ps.* 51. 1; Mohrmann, *op. cit.* xv-xvi.

[16] *Sancti Aurelii Augustini Hipponensis episcopi opera* 5: *Sermones ad populum* (Paris 1683) = ML 38 and 39.

[17] Two years ago Lambot made a most welcome contribution when he published 18 sermons in a new critical edition (cf. above, n. 13).

[18] Cf. A. Wilmart, 'La collection tripartite des sermons de S. Augustin,' *Miscellanea Augustiniana* (Nijmegen 1930) 419; also Mohrmann, *op. cit.* xxii.

[19] The sifting of this mass of sermons is the major accomplishment of another Benedictine—Dom G. Morin, *Sancti Augustini sermones post Maurinos reperti* = vol. 1 of *Miscellanea Agostiniana* (Rome 1930); cf. his *praefatio*, vii-xi.

[20] E.g. *De patientia* (CSEL 41. 663-91); *De cantico novo* (ML 40. 677-86); etc.

[21] Cf. Mohrmann, *op. cit.* xiv.

[22] Lambot, *op. cit.* 9 (cf. the list of his articles on p. 11 f.), claims to have discovered 20 since Morin published his *sermones post Maurinos reperti* in 1930.

[23] See below, n. 1 to *Serm.* 1 (51).

[24] See below, n. 1 to *Serm.* 15 (140).

[25] Below, *Serm.* 20 (201). 1.

[26] *De Trin.* 4. 5. 9: 'Natus autem traditur octavo Kalendas Ianuarias.'

[27] Below, *Serm.* 22 (203). 1.

[28] *De div. quaest.* 1. 56, where Augustine, following the ancient usage of counting both initial and terminal days, says that from conception to birth there are 276 days—'novem menses (here *mensis* = period of 30 days) et sex dies'; cf. also *Quaest. in Hept.* 2. 90. See L. Duchesne, *Christian Worship* (tr. from the 5th French ed. by M. L. McClure, London 1919 [repr. 1949]) 257-65.

[29] Cf. A. C. Rush, *Death and Burial in Christian Antiquity* (SCA 1, Washington 1941) 72-87.

[30] Cf. H. Frank, 'Weihnachten,' LTK 10 (1938) 776; Duchesne, *op. cit.* 258.

[31] Cf. G. Wissowa, *Religion und Kultus der Römer* (2nd ed. Munich 1912) 364-68; H. J. Rose, 'Sol,' OCD 847.

[32] The sun as a deity, Sol of the pagan Roman religion, was equivalent to Helios of the Greeks. Augustine frequently denounces the Manichaeans for identifying Christ with Sol; cf. *In Ioan. Ev. tract.* 34. 2; *C. Faust. Man.* 20. 6-8; etc. Regarding Christ as the *Sol Iustitiae*, 'Sun of Justice' (Mal. 4. 2), see F. J. Dölger, *Die Sonne der Gerechtigkeit und der Schwarze* (Liturgiegesch. Forsch. 2, Münster i. W. 1918) 100-110.

[33] Below, *Serm.* 4 (186). 1.

[34] Below, *Serm.* 8 (190). 1. Cf. F. J. Dölger, 'Natalis Solis Invicti und das christliche Weihnachtsfest. Der Sonnengeburtstag und der Geburtstag Christi am 25. Dezember nach Weihnachtspredigten des vierten und fünften Jahrhunderts,' AC 6 (1940) 23-30.

35 The chronicler (Dionysius Philocalus?) in the so-called *Philocalian Calendar* (cf. below, n. 1 to *Serm.* 1 [51]), drawn up in the year 354, states in the table called *Depositio martyrum*: 'viii kal. ian. (= Dec. 25th), natus Christus in Betleem Iudae'; in his *Depositio episcoporum* he presupposes the same date for the year 336. Cf. Frank, *loc. cit.;* H. Leclercq, 'Nativité de Jésus,' DACL 12. 1 (1935) 910-15.

36 Below, *Serm.* 21 (202). 2. On Donatism, cf. n. 4 to the same.

36a Cf. H. Rahner, *Griechische Mythen in christlicher Deutung* (Zurich 1945) 190 ff.; literature: 191 n. 2.

37 Cf. A. Wilmart, 'Un sermon de saint Optat pour la fête de Noël,' *Revue des sciences religieuses* 2 (1922) 279 f.

38 Cf. C. Martindale, 'Epiphany,' CE 5 (1909) 504-506; L. Eisenhofer, *Grundriss der Liturgik des römischen Ritus* (5th ed. Freiburg i. Br. 1950) 145-149; B. Botte, *Les origines de la Noël et de l'Epiphanie* (Louvain 1932); G. Dix, *The Shape of the Liturgy* (Westminster 1945) 357 f.

39 Below, *Serm.* 1 (51). 1.

40 Augustine's spirited arguments for the paternity of St. Joseph as presented in this Sermon 51, are noticed and extensively quoted in the work by J. Müller, *The Fatherhood of St. Joseph* (tr. from the German by A. Dengler, St. Louis 1952)—cf. esp. ch. 2.

41 Cf. Ps. 84. 12, quoted often by Augustine.

42 See also below, n. 1 to *Serm.* 15 (140).

43 See below, n. 16 to *Serm.* 14 (196).

44 Cf. Augustine, *De civ. Dei* 5. 1 ff., and the excellent article by W. Gundel, 'Astrologie,' RAC 1 (1950) 817-31.

45 This treatise was addressed to Deogratias, a deacon of the Church of Carthage. For a recent translation of this work, with commentary, cf. J. P. Christopher, 'The First Catechetical Instruction,' ACW 2 (1946). The theory of homiletics is developed further in the fourth book of *De doctrina christiana*, published in the year 426.

46 Cf. the interesting examples gathered by Pope, *op. cit.* 142-48, 162.

47 O. Bardenhewer, *Geschichte der altkirchlichen Literatur* (Freiburg i. Br. 1924) 3. 353 f., 4. 495.

48 *Ibid.* 4. 495.

49 *Serm.* 19 (200). 3. The passage is also noted by Bardenhewer, *ibid.* 4. 447. On the function of parallelism and antithesis in

Augustine's sermons, see Mohrmann, *op. cit.* xliii-xlv; also Comeau, *op. cit.* ch. 3.

⁵⁰ Cf. Mohrmann, *op. cit.* xlv.

⁵¹ Cf. Mohrmann, 'Das Wortspiel in den Augustinischen Sermones,' *Mnemosyne* 3 (1936) 33-61.

⁵² Pope, *op. cit.* 154. Cf. also Mohrmann, *op. cit.* xlvii-xlix.

⁵³ *Serm.* 150. 1. Cf. Pope, *op. cit.* 155.

⁵⁴ In 394 or 395 Augustine wrote a letter (*Ep.* 28) to Jerome concerning the translation Jerome was making of the Old Testament. Augustine very frankly urges that such translation be made from the Septuagint rather than from the Hebrew. He further suggests that Jerome revise his interpretation of the controversy between Peter and Paul at Antioch (Gal. 2. 11-14). When the letter failed to reach the addressee, Augustine wrote another (*Ep.* 40), in which he expressed further criticism of Jerome's exegesis of the celebrated passage in the Epistle to the Galatians. When this letter also miscarried and Jerome five years later received a garbled account of it from others, he became very angry, as appears from his reply (*Ep.* 102) to Augustine. These and subsequent letters of the celebrated exchange have been published, with introduction and notes, by J. Schmid, *SS. Eusebii Hieronymi et Aurelii Augustini epistulae mutuae* (Florilegium Patristicum 22, Bonn 1930).

⁵⁵ See the initial notes to the individual sermons.

⁵⁶ Regarding Augustine and the Bible, see D. De Bruyne, 'Saint Augustin reviseur de la Bible,' *Miscellanea Agostiniana* 2 (Rome 1931) 521-606; C. H. Milne, *A Reconstruction of the Old Latin Text or Texts of the Gospels Used by Saint Augustine* (Cambridge 1926); M. Pontet, *L'exégèse de S. Augustin prédicateur* (Paris 1946).

⁵⁷ The greater part of *Serm.* 19 (200) appears in the second nocturn of the Roman Breviary for the second and third days within the octave of Epiphany, and was rendered into English by J. Marquess of Bute, *The Roman Breviary* (new ed. Edinburgh-London 1908) 192 f.

SERMON 1 (51)

¹ This sermon is also listed by the Maurists as *De diversis* 63. Possidius takes note of it in his record of Augustine's writings—*Indiculus* 8. In a sermon probably delivered on Pentecost, 417 (cf. A. Kunzelmann, 'Die Chronologie der Sermones des hl. Augustinus,'

Misc. Agost. 2 [Rome 1931] 471), Augustine expresses the hope that God will give him the opportunity to give a sermon such as the present: cf. *Serm.* Mai 158.2 (382 Morin); therefore, probably this sermon cannot antedate that year. Kunzelmann, *ibid.* 427, notices that Augustine says early in the present sermon that his audience will remember: 'On Christmas morning (*matutina Natalis Domini*) we postponed the question which we had proposed to solve . . . .' Kunzelmann concludes that our present discourse was delivered 'soon after Christmas.' He points out further (*ibid.* 427 n. 2) that very early in the sermon we learn that the gladiatorial shows—the *Munera*—were still on. But this confronts us with a serious chronological difficulty: the season for these shows was fixed, for December 2-24, with interruptions, as we know from the celebrated calendar of Philocalus: cf. *Fasti Philocali,* in T. Mommsen, CIL 1. 1. 278, 336. Kunzelmann himself (507) is aware of these dates, yet he thinks the present sermon delivered 'soon after Christmas,' which feast was celebrated on December 25 even in Augustine's time (see above, the Intro.). In two other sermons, 19 (title) and Caillau 2. 19. 7 (270 Morin), the *Munera* are mentioned, and Kunzelmann (507, 495) therefore dates them as of December (that is, Dec. 2-24). In the case of the present sermon (51) should we perhaps say that since it was given on one of the days of the *Munera,* it should rather be dated as given *shortly before Christmas?* In that case the reference to the *matutina Natalis Domini* would be actually to the last previous Christmas, probably of the year 416; and the present sermon on the genealogy of Christ could be regarded as peculiarly suited in preparation for, or anticipation of, Christmas, 417, then only a very short time away.—Regarding the history of the *Munera* or gladiatorial shows, cf. K. Schneider, 'Gladiatores,' RE Suppl. 3 (1918) 760-84; L. Friedländer, *Roman Life and Manners under the Early Empire* 2 (tr. from the 7th German ed. by J. H. Freese and L. A. Magnus, London 1908 [?]) 41-62.

[2] *Caritatis vestrae*: regarding this form of address, occurring especially in letters, and used also in speaking or writing to inferiors, cf. M. B. O'Brien, *Titles of Address in Christian Latin Epistolography to 543 A.D.* (PS 21, Washington 1930) 52-54.

[3] 2 Cor. 4. 7.

[4] The complaint that there are those who stay away from the sermon to attend the gladiatorial shows—'sunt qui propterea hodie

non venerunt, quia *munus* est'—is also found in an *enarratio* delivered at Carthage probably late in the year 412: cf. *Enarr. in Ps.* 147. 7, and S. M. Zarb, *Chronologia Enarrationum S. Augustini in Psalmos* (Valetta-Malta 1948) 140-45, 175, 254.

[5] Matt. 10. 22.
[6] Ps. 21. 17.
[7] *Ibid.* 21. 18.
[8] 1 Cor. 4. 9.
[9] Augustine is referring of course to the fact that his hearers by deciding to be present at his sermon have sacrificed their opportunity to witness the shows in the arena. In this section it is quite impossible to give an adequate account in English of all his wordplays with *spectare, spectator, spectaculum,* etc.
[10] John 16. 33. Augustine has *gaudete*, while the Vulgate reads, *sed confidete,* 'but have confidence.'
[11] Christ is called *Imperator,* a term used earlier by Tertullian, Cyprian, and others in descriptions of the life of a Christian as a life of combat. The title (*Dux* is also used) is discussed by E. L. Hummel, *The Concept of Martyrdom according to St. Cyprian of Carthage* (SCA 9, Washington 1946) 56-58.
[12] Gen. 22. 18.
[13] 1 Cor. 1. 27 f.
[14] It is quite impossible to convey in English the full, double connotation of the Latin—'quia *fideles* estis': 'because you are the faithful,' that is, 'believers,' and 'because you are faithful,' that is, to the faith.
[15] Col. 2. 6 f.
[16] *Ibid.* 2. 3.
[17] Cf. 2 Cor. 3. 16.
[18] This section, referring to Augustine's first memorable experience with the Scriptures, has its celebrated counterpart in his *Confessions.* In 3. 4. 7 f. he recounts how at the age of nineteen he read Cicero's *Hortensius,* which made such a profound impression on him. But failing to find Christ's name in that work—*quod nomen Christi non erat ibi*—he decided to see what the Sacred Scriptures were like (9). And here, too, he states that he undertook a task that needed to be approached in humility, not with pride: 'et ecce video rem non compertam superbis neque nudatam pueris, sed incessu humilem, successu excelsam et velatam mysteriis, et non eram ego talis . . . .' The simple language of the Scriptures

could not measure up to the majestic rhetoric of Cicero, and Augustine turned elsewhere—to the Manichaeans. A dozen years later, at Milan, St. Ambrose in his Sunday sermons was to introduce him again to the Scriptures—and God placed him back in the nest from which he had fallen (6. 3. 3 ff.).

[19] Matt. 1. 1.
[20] *Ibid.* 1. 2-5.
[21] *Ibid.* 1. 6-16.
[22] *Ibid.* 1. 17.
[23] *Ibid.* 1. 18.
[24] *Ibid.* 1. 18 f.
[25] *divulgare* for *traducere*: so Augustine in *Serm.* 82. 10. For evidence of this variant in the African manuscripts of the New Testament, cf. H. v. Soden, *Das lateinische Neue Testament in Afrika zur Zeit Cyprians* (Texte u. Untersuchungen 33, Leipzig 1909) 367 f.
[26] Matt. 1. 20 f.
[27] 'in our language' = *latine*.
[28] *Sanctitas vestra.*
[29] *sacramenta.*
[30] The figure of the 'little ones,' *parvuli*, who have only a *simplicior fides* and when beset by the criticism of heretics turn to their mother, the Church, for the milk of further enlightenment in the faith, undoubtedly contains a reminiscence of St. Paul's First Epistle to the Corinthians (3. 2): 'Tamquam *parvulis* in Christo *lac vobis potum dedi* . . . . Cf. also Heb. 5. 12-15.
[31] 1 Cor. 11. 19.
[32] *magnum sacramentum;* so also in the following paragraph.
[32a] *mysterium futurorum.*
[33] Jechonias had been king of Juda only three months and ten days when in the year 597 B.C. he was deposed and carried away to Babylon (as foretold by Jeremias, 22. 25 f.) with 10,000 Jewish leaders and craftsmen. There he was kept in prison for more than thirty-five years. In 561 B.C. he was set free by Evilmerodach, successor to Nabuchodonosor. He was restored to his royal rank, though not permitted to return to Jerusalem.
[34] For this and the following, cf. Jer. chs. 27 and 29; also 38.2 f., 17 ff.
[35] Rom. 11. 1.
[36] Cf. 1. Cor. 15. 6.

[37] Cf. Acts 1. 15 and 2. 1-4.
[38] Acts 13. 46, freely quoted.
[39] Jer. 29. 7, freely quoted.
[40] 1 Tim. 2. 1 f.; for 'intercessions' the Vulgate has *postulationes,* Augustine, *interpellationes.*
[41] Cf. Ps. 117. 22; Isa. 28. 16; Matt. 21. 42; Mark 12. 10; Luke 20. 17; Acts 4. 11; Eph. 2. 20; 1 Peter 2. 6.
[42] Ps. 117. 22, etc.—cf. the previous note.
[43] Matt. 1. 20.
[44] Luke 2. 48 f.
[45] The Douai-Rheims translation reads 'about my Father's business' for *in his quae Patris mei sunt.* Msgr. Knox renders 'in the place which belongs to my Father'—a version which is in excellent accord with the way Augustine interprets the passage.
[46] Luke 1. 31.
[47] Eph. 5. 23.
[48] Augustine here distinguishes between *femina* and *mulier*: the first designates 'woman' in general and sexually as the opposite of 'man'—'female' as against 'male' (*mas*); whereas *mulier*, originally designating 'woman' (the grown 'female') as the carrier of all the characteristics that set her off from 'man,' more particularly and most commonly—and this is the meaning Augustine is concerned with here—denotes a 'married woman' as distinguished from a 'virgin' (*virgo*). Sometimes it is also used for 'wife' (*uxor*). Cf. A. Walde-J. B. Hofmann, *Lateinisches etymologisches Wörterbuch* (3rd ed. Heidelberg 1938 ff.) *s. vv.*

The Hebrew word referred to is *ishshah*, which is used in a most general sense: the 'female human being,' 'woman' without distinction of age or sexual status. Cf. L. Koehler-W. Baumgartner, *Lexicon in Veteris Testamenti libros* (Leiden 1948) *s. v.* See below, *Serm.* 4 (186). 3 and n. 13.

[49] Gal. 4. 4. Regarding this passage and the concluding part of this paragraph, see below, § 3 of *Serm.* 4 (186) and n. 13 to the same.

[50] Gen. 2. 22. Augustine has simply *formavit eam in mulierem,* while the Vulgate reads, *Et aedificavit Dominus Deus costam, quam tulerat de Adam, in mulierem.*

[51] Luke 2. 49-51.
[52] Wisd. 8. 1. The words referred by Augustine to God's power (*virtus*), are here spoken of wisdom.

53 Rom. 1. 3.
54 *Ibid.* 9. 5.
55 Matt. 22. 42, condensed.
56 *Ibid.* 22. 43-45, with quotation of Ps. 109. 1. Compared with the Vulgate, Augustine's text lacks '*scabellum*' after '*inimicos tuos*,' but adds '*in spiritu*' before '*vocat eum Dominum.*' There is excellent MS-authority for both divergences.
57 Ps. 131. 11.
58 Phil. 2. 6 f.
59 1 Cor. 7. 29.
60 1 Thess. 4. 4. The Vulgate has 'in sanctification and honor.'
61 Eph. 5. 25.
62 Cf. also Augustine, *De doct. christ.* 3. 26 f.; *De bono coni.* 15.
63 *tabulae matrimoniales* (also *t. nuptiales, nuptiale instrumentum,* etc.). These 'tables' or 'tablets' were a form of contract read and witnessed as a part of the betrothal or marriage ceremonies. The practice of drawing up such contracts dates from early Imperial times. While no examples of these marriage documents survive, it appears that the formula, 'for the purpose of procreating children,' was used in the contract from the beginning. Cf. B. Kübler, 'Tabulae nuptiales,' RE 2. R. 4 (1932) 1949-55.

Though the *tabulae* were not essential for the validity of a marriage, the practice of drawing up such contracts in writing appears to have become quite general (Kübler 1952). This is also verified for the Christians in Africa by Augustine's frequent mention of the *tabulae* (cf., besides the present passage, *C. Faust. Man.* 15. 7; *De grat. Christi et de pecc. orig.* 2. 43; *De Gen. ad litt.* 11. 56; *Conf.* 9. 19; *De civ. Dei* 14. 18; *C. Iul. Pel.* 3. 43; *Enarr. in Ps.* 80.21; *Serm.* 9. 18; 37. 7; 278. 9; 332. 4; etc.). The fact that Augustine so often reverts to the *tabulae* and the obligations they place upon marriage; also the fact mentioned by Augustine (*Serm.* 332. 4) that the officiating bishop affixed his signature to the contract, may well indicate that the reading of the contract was considered one of the most important ceremonies in the celebration of a Christian marriage, at least in St. Augustine's time; cf. B. A. Pereira, *La doctrine du mariage selon saint Augustin* (Etudes de théol. hist., 2nd ed. Paris 1930) 153. For an interesting, though mutilated, representation of the ceremony of a Christian marriage, in which the bridegroom is shown holding the *tabulae* in his left hand, cf. DACL 10. 2 (1932) figure 7647; also the interpretation, col. 1905 f.

⁶⁴ This etymology of *adulter* (*adulterium*) is also given by Festus (epitomized by Paulus Diaconus), *De verborum significatu* p. 22 (Müller): '*adulter et adultera* dicuntur, quia et ille *ad alteram* et haec *ad alterum* se conferunt.' The derivation is questioned by modern authors—cf. Walde-Hofmann, *op. cit. s. v.*

⁶⁵ This severe limitation of the purpose and liceity of connubial intercourse is clearly expressed in many other passages in St. Augustine's writings. As J. Mausbach puts it — *Die Ethik des heiligen Augustinus* (2nd ed. Freiburg i. Br. 1929) 1. 250 f.: According to Augustine, 'where this rational purpose [procreation] is wanting, the exacting of the matrimonial debt constitutes venial sin. This is a view which Augustine consistently maintained throughout his writings. In the austerity which characterizes it, he went beyond not only the directions of Paul (1 Cor. 7. 5), but the teaching of other Fathers and later Catholic moral theology as well.'

Regarding the *sedatio concupiscentiae*, the quieting of the passions, which the theologians regard as also belonging to the essential end of marriage, Augustine makes the following clear distinctions (*De bono coni.* 6): 'Intercourse sought in marriage for the purpose of begetting children does not involve sin; but when it is sought for the purpose of satisfying concupiscence, and this is sought from one's spouse, then, because marital fidelity is preserved, (only) venial sin is present (*venialem habet culpam*); adultery, however, and fornication constitute mortal sin.' Cf. also *Enchir.* 78; *De bono vid.* 5; *De nupt. et conc.* 1. 16 f.; *C. Iul. Pel.* 3. 43; etc.

As Mausbach points out (*loc. cit.* n. 2), for corroboration of his severe attitude in this matter St. Augustine often appeals to the formula found even in the civil marriage contract, the *tabulae matrimoniales* (see above, n. 63), that marriage is contracted *liberorum procreandorum causa.* The following passage, in which he wishes to illustrate which lesser sins—*quotidiana peccata*—can be wiped away by almsgiving, is also taken from a sermon (9. 18) and illustrates further the appeal made to this argument in the present sermon:

Cum ipsa uxore si exceditur concumbendi modus procreandis liberis debitus, iam peccatum est. Ad hoc etenim ducitur uxor: nam id etiam tabulae indicant, ubi scribitur, LIBERORUM PROCREANDORUM CAUSA. Quando tu uti uxore amplius quam necessitas procreandorum liberorum cogit, volueris, iam peccatum est; et ipsa talia peccata quotidianae eleemosynae mundant.

Cf. also *C. Faust. Man.* 15. 7; *De grat. Christi et de pecc. orig.* 2.43; *C. Iul. Pel.* 3. 43; *Serm.* 278. 9; etc.

A second argument is based by Augustine on his reading of the celebrated text in St. Paul's First Epistle to the Corinthians (7. 5 f.): 'Defraud not one another, except, perhaps, by consent, for a time . . . ; and return together again, lest Satan tempt you for your incontinency. But I speak this *by indulgence,* not by commandment.' For the phrase 'by indulgence'—κατὰ συγγνώμην, Vulgate *secundum indulgentiam* — Augustine regularly reads *secundum veniam,* which likewise means 'by way of indulgence, permission, concession,' etc.; but which also shades over into signifying 'by way of remission, forgiveness, pardon,' etc., and is so interpreted by Augustine; note, for instance, the following in *De nuptiis et concupiscentia* (1. 16): quoting 1 Cor. 7. 3-6, he comments on the last sentence cited, 'Hoc autem dico *secundum veniam,* non secundum imperium'—

> Ubi ergo venia danda est, aliquid esse culpae nulla ratione negabitur. Cum igitur culpabilis non sit generandi intentione concubitus, qui proprie nuptiis inputandus est, quid secundum veniam concedit Apostolus, nisi quod coniuges, dum se non continent, debitum ab alterutro carnis exposcunt non voluntate propaginis, sed libidinis voluptate? *Quae tamen voluptas non propter nuptias 'cadit in culpam, sed propter nuptias accipit veniam.* Quocirca etiam hinc laudabiles *nuptiae,* quia et *illud,* quod non pertinet ad se, *ignosci faciunt propter se.* Neque enim etiam iste concubitus, quo servitur concupiscentiae, sic agitur, ut inpediatur fetus, quem postulant nuptiae.

Cf. also *C. Faust. Man.* 30. 5; *De bono coni.* 11; *De grat. Christi et de pecc. orig.* 2. 43; etc. In *Serm.* 351. 5 Augustine states regarding the Apostle's injunction, 'Defraud not one another . . . , and return together again':

> Quod ut *peccatum esse* demonstraret, sed infirmitati concessum, subiecit statim: 'Hoc autem dico secundum veniam, non secundum imperium.' *Sola enim generandi causa est inculpabilis sexus utriusque commixtio.*

While in the next-to-last passage quoted, Augustine states clearly that marital intercourse sought for the purpose of *sedatio concupiscentiae* involves guilt (*culpa*), he adds later that such guilt *propter nuptias accipit veniam;* that the marriage effects forgiveness of the guilt—*ignosci faciunt propter se.* Elsewhere (*De bono vid.* 5), too, he states the evil (*malum*) which is present 'quod ultra liberorum procreandorum necessitatem modum concumbendi aliquatenus concupiscentia carnalis excedit,' is *veniale propter nuptiarum bonum;* also 'it is forgiven by the nuptial good coming between'—*interventu boni nuptialis ignoscitur.* (Cf. also *De cont.* 27.) Here it is said that the marriage act in question is not merely 'venial' in the sense that it is 'forgivable,' but that it is actually 'forgiven' by the mediation of the *bonum nuptiale.* Therefore, no state of sin should persist after the act has been consummated. But elsewhere—see above the text quoted from *Serm.* 9. 18—Augustine cites intercourse sought in marriage 'amplius quam necessitas procreandorum liberorum cogit,' as an example of the *quotidiana peccata* which the practice of giving alms takes away! Cf. also *Serm.* 278. 9 f.

It is quite evident that Augustine's high regard for the state of virginity, his constant insistence on its primacy over the married state, led him to an enthusiastic and ceaseless advocacy of chastity and continence within marriage itself. At the same time he never controverts St. Paul's counsel to the married — 'Nolite invicem fraudare . . . et iterum ad ipsum estote, ne vos tentet satanas . . . .' For the realization and preservation of the second great blessing and purpose of marriage—*fides,* conjugal fidelity—he allows those 'concubitus coniugum qui non fiunt causa generandi, sed victrici concupiscentiae serviunt' (*De nupt. et conc.* 1. 16); he allows a minor evil, a *veniale peccatum,* to prevent the deadly crime—*mortiferum, letale, damnabile crimen, scelus, flagitium*—of marital infidelity, adultery. For the safeguarding of this *fides,* he not only allows the *sedatio,* but, as we have seen in the present sermon, commands it: 'Sed si non possunt . . . , exigant debitum.' Further, if the unmarried are unable to remain continent, let them follow the Apostle's counsel (1 Cor. 7. 9) and marry; by marrying for this reason—*per incontinentiam*—they will be committing a *minus peccatum,* but avoiding the grievous sin of fornication (*De bono coni.* 10 f.).

Thus the conclusion seems inescapable that Augustine puts his hearers and readers into a moral dilemma: for the sake of safeguarding the second *bonum matrimonii* against the grievous sin of adultery, he allows the *sedatio concupiscentiae;* the difficulty is not quite solved by Augustine—he appears to permit, and even recommend, sin, however *veniale* and *quotidianum,* in order to avoid sin.

By way of explanation, the following considerations among others may be briefly alluded to. In very large part St. Augustine's doctrine on marriage was developed under the stress of heresy. The Manichaeans, for instance, taught that man's existence is an evil, his birth an imprisonment; hence their abomination of the

SERMONS: CHRISTMAS 199

primary object of marriage — *proles,* procreation. Hence, too, Augustine's insistence on this same primacy, his persistent endeavor to protect marriage against becoming a mere instrument and outlet for lust (cf. *C. Faust. Man.* 15. 7). Again, according to the Pelagians as represented by Julian of Eclanum, marriage could be defined only as a *corporum commixtio*—carnal knowledge (cf. *C. Iul. Pelag.* 5. 62). Augustine objects vehemently: it is not *voluptas,* but *voluntas* that creates the bonds of marriage; *fides* and *sacramentum* (indissolubility), the second and third purposes of marriage, are not conditioned by marital intercourse; as Augustine has stated in the present sermon, 'Quasi uxorem libido faciat et non caritas coniugalis!' Because of the naturalistic interpretation of marriage by the Pelagians, Augustine constantly strives to elevate its spiritual character. He would have all married people practice continence—'utinam possent omnes, sed multi non possunt!' Cf. Mausbach, *op. cit.* 1. 321 f.

Lastly, St. Augustine's severe opinion regarding 'remedial' intercourse in marriage does not stand alone in Christian antiquity. With the notable exception of St. John Chrysostom (*De virg.* 19, 29, etc.–cf. M. Moulard, *Saint Jean Chrysostome, le défenseur du mariage et l'apôtre de la virginité* [Paris 1923] esp. 72 ff.), this opinion was held quite generally. Cf. D. Lindner, *Der usus matrimonii. Seine sittliche Bewertung in katholischer Moraltheologie alter und neuer Zeit* (Munich 1929) 57 ff. For a recent verdict on the Augustinian, traditional view in this particular matter, I may quote from an earlier contributor to the present series—L. A. Arand, *Saint Augustine: Faith, Hope, and Charity,* ACW 3 (1947) 135 n. 259: 'The interpretation of all these authors is incorrect. *Secundum veniam,* the version we have here [*Enchir.* 78], or *secundum indulgentiam,* as the Vulgate translates it, means a concession of something *less perfect,* but *not sinful,* since sin cannot be conceded or permitted.'

On the present subject, cf. Mausbach, *op. cit.* 1. 250, 321 f., 2. 240-53, for whom (1. 321) Augustine's strict view amounts to 'rigorism'; Pereira, *op. cit.* 87-99, who (89) finds that Augustine is 'intransigeant, rigoureux, peut-être même rigoriste, dans cette question'; A. Reuter, *Sancti Aurelii Augustini doctrina de bonis matrimonii* (Analecta Gregoriana 27, Rome 1942) 115-18 (n. 20: 'Severior haec Augustini de concubitu incontinentiae sententia'), 174-80; N. Ladomérszky, *Saint Augustin, docteur du mariage chrétien*: *Etude dogmatique sur les biens du mariage* (Urbaniana 5, Rome 1942) 43-45, 66, 84, who ignores the present difficulty almost entirely.

[66] 1 Cor. 7. 6. Augustine here has *secundum veniam*—cf. the note immediately preceding.

[67] *Ibid.* 7. 5.

[68] *Ibid.* 7. 6, 7.

[69] Cf. Ecclus. 14. 18 f.

[70] The aphorism that we eat to live, not conversely, is found, in one form or another, in many ancient writers; e.g. the author of *Rhetorica ad Herennium* 4. 28. 39: 'Esse oportet ut vivas, non vivere ut edas.' Plutarch and other writers credit Socrates with having formulated this principle. Cf. A. Otto, *Die Sprichwörter und sprichwörtlichen Redensarten der Römer* (Leipzig 1890) 123.

[71] Phil. 3. 19.

[72] Cf. 3 Kings 19. 6-8.

[73] In adoption the adopted passed from the *patria potestas* of his natural father into the *patria potestas* of his adopter. Up to the time of Justinian his severance from his former family and absorption by the new was quite complete. Cf. R. W. Leage, *Roman Private Law* (2nd ed. by C. H. Ziegler, London 1948) 83-85.

[74] Since the marriage legislation of the early Empire concubinage 'was a recognized connexion short of marriage.' Children born of such a union were not legally related to the father. As soldiers in service and others were not permitted to marry, concubinage was very common, though legislation in the Christian Empire was hostile to it. Cf. W. W. Buckland, *A Text-Book of Roman Law from Augustus to Justinian* (2nd ed. Cambridge 1932) 128 f.

[75] Regarding the apparent contradiction between the Evangelist Matthew who (1. 16) makes Jacob the father of St. Joseph, and Luke who (3. 23) mentions Heli: Augustine's suggestion that Joseph had two fathers, the one his natural father, the other his adoptive father, is also stated elsewhere, e.g. *C. Faust. Man.* 3. 3, *De cons. Evang.* 2. 3. By the time he wrote his *Retractationes*, he rejected this theory of adoption and accepted the celebrated solution of Julius Africanus, contemporary of Origen, in his *Letter to Aristides* (cf. Eusebius, *Hist. Eccl.* 1. 7): Joseph was the natural son of Jacob, but the legal son of Heli; that is, his mother had been married to Heli, who died without issue, whereupon by the levirate law (Deut. 25. 5) his brother (actually, half-brother)

Jacob took her to wife and begot Joseph, counted as the levirate or legal son of Heli. See *Retract.* 2. 7. 2 and 2. 12 for Augustine's adoption of this explanation. For Africanus and his theory, cf. P. Vogt, *Der Stammbaum Christi* (Bibl. Studien 12. 3, Freiburg i. Br.) 1-34; A. J. Maas, 'Genealogy of Christ,' CE 6 (1909) 411; D. Buzy, *Evangile selon Saint Matthieu* (La Sainte Bible 9, Paris 1946) 3; etc.

[76] *in ipsis eloquiis ecclesiasticis*: for *eloquia* = 'Sacred Scripture,' cf. J. P. Christopher, ACW 2 (1946) 113 n. 97.

[77] *gratia voluntatis;* Macmullen translates, 'the free choice of the will.'

[78] Cf. Gen. 16. 1-4 and 30. 1-13.

[79] 1 Cor. 7. 4. St. Paul certainly had no intention of extending the Old Testament privilege of simultaneous polygamy to the New Testament. But the present instance is not the only one in which this Pauline passage gave rise to difficulties for Augustine. See, for example, in his *De sermone Domini in monte* (1. 49 f.) the account of the peculiar case of a woman giving herself, with the permission of her husband—'the conjugal master of her body'—to a wealthy man in order to ransom her husband from prison: Augustine is quite uncertain as to the moral issues involved and remarks, 'Let each pass judgment as he wishes.' Regarding this case, cf. J. Peters, *Die Ehe nach der Lehre des hl. Augustinus* (Görres Ges. z. Pflege d. Wiss., Sekt. f. Rechts- u. Sozialwiss. 32, Paderborn 1918) 26, and the extract made from the same in ACW 5. 189 n. 129: 'Peters makes the point that at this time Augustine obviously was not clear on the contractual nature of marriage; that in the marriage contract the parties are not free to give up or transfer their rights, because these rights have been fixed by God *ab initio*.' For further discussion of this and similar passages, cf. Pereira, *op. cit.* 81-84.

[80] Cf. Exod. 2.
[81] Rom. 2. 14.
[82] Gen. 48. 5 f., quoted freely.
[83] *et in magno sacramento.*
[84] Gal. 4. 4 f.
[85] Rom. 8. 23.
[86] Ibid. 9. 3-5.
[87] Cf. Deut. 25. 5 f.; exemplified in Ruth 4. 1-13; cf. also Matt. 22. 24, Mark 12. 19, Luke 20. 28. The levirate (from the Latin

levir, 'husband's brother') law obliged the brother of a man who had died without leaving male issue, to marry the widow. The first-born son of this union became the legal son and heir of the deceased. See above, n. 75.

[88] Matt. 1. 16.
[89] Luke 3. 23.
[90] Cf. above, n. 75.
[91] Luke 2. 48.
[92] Matt. 1. 19.
[93] Cf. Luke 1. 60-63.
[94] *Ibid.* 1. 31.
[95] Matt. 1. 20 f.
[96] Luke 2. 7. Augustine leaves out 'her first-born' which modifies 'Son' in the Greek and in the Vulgate. Particularly striking, however, is his addition of the pronoun *ei*, 'to him,' after *peperit*, 'she brought forth.' As Macmullen remarked *ad loc.* more than a hundred years ago, 'there seems to be no trace of any such reading anywhere else.'
[97] Luke 3. 23. Augustine has *qui putabatur esse pater Iesu;* the Vulgate reads, *ut putabatur* ('as was supposed') *filius Ioseph.*
[98] That is, the prophecy given to Abraham—'In thy seed shall all the nations of the earth be blessed' (Gen. 22. 18; cf. also *ibid.* 12. 3, 18. 18, 26. 4, 28. 14).
[99] This confusion of David's son Nathan (2 Kings 5. 14) with the Prophet of the same name is corrected by Augustine in *Retract.* 2. 16, with reference to the same error in *De cons. Evang.* 2. 4. 12.
[100] Cf. 2 Kings 12.
[101] Cf. Gen. 15. 13; Acts 7. 6.
[102] Cf. Exod. 12. 40. Concerning the chronological difficulties involved in the numbers 400 and 430 (e.g. are we to begin this period with Abraham's immigration into Canaan—about 1920 B.C.?), cf. E. Mangenot, 'Chronologie Biblique,' in F. Vigouroux, *Dictionnaire de la Bible* 2 (Paris 1899) 727 f.; E. Kalt, 'Chronologie,' *Biblisches Reallexikon* (Paderborn 1931) 1. 333 f. Cf. also Augustine himself, *Quaest. in Hept.* 2. 47.
[103] 2 Cor. 5. 6. On the number '40' as signifying our life here on earth, see especially the exposition in *Serm.* 252. 11: 'Thus, too, is it by the temporal dispensation that we are led through a desert, as it were—through this life with its ceaseless cares, its fears, its dangers and trials. But if we bear the number forty well, that is,

if we lead good lives in this temporal dispensation, if our conduct follows God's commandments, we shall receive the reward of that denarius (ten—cf. Matt. 20. 1-10) which is given to the faithful; etc.' See also *Serm.* 125. 9, where Augustine shows that when we receive this reward of the perfect number '10,' it is added to the number standing for our earthly existence, '40'; we shall then be in the number '50'—the beatific vision, having God's praise as our sole occupation.

[104] For the number '10' as the perfect and sacred number in St. Augustine's writings, cf. A. Schmitt, 'Mathematik und Zahlenmystik,' in M. Grabmann-J. Mausbach, *Aurelius Augustinus: Die Festschrift der Görres-Gesellschaft zum 1500. Todestage des hl. Augustinus* (Cologne 1930) 262 f. For further literature on the mystical significance attributed by pagan and Christian writers to certain numbers, see the note by Dr. Plumpe in ACW 5. 203 f.

[105] Cf. Deut. 9. 9.
[106] Cf. 3 Kings 19. 8.
[107] Cf. Matt. 4. 2.
[108] Cf. Num. 32. 13.
[109] Cf. Gen. 7. 17.
[110] Cf. Acts 1. 3.
[111] Cf. 1 Cor. 11. 26.
[112] John 1. 14 and Rom. 4. 25.
[113] John 1. 14.
[114] Cf. Matt. 3. 16.
[115] *Transgressio* = 'transgression,' is lit. a 'going across, beyond set limits,' an 'overstepping' of such limits.
[116] Cf. 1 Tim. 6. 10; *avaritia*, 'avarice,' from *avere*, to 'desire eagerly,' to 'crave' (for more).
[117] *a Deo fornicanti*—cf. Ps. 72. 27.
[118] Phil. 2. 21.
[119] 1 Cor. 13. 5.
[120] See also *Serm.* 83. 7 for an exposition of the theory that the totality of sin is signified by the number '77,' which is the product of '11,' the number of transgression, multiplied by '7,' the number of fullness or completion (here, in *Serm.* 51. 34, the number of man); cf. Schmitt, *art. cit.* 365.
[121] In *De Trin.* 10. 19 Augustine says that in the faculties of memory (*memoria*), understanding (*intelligentia*), and volition

(*voluntas*) man's soul was created after the image of God. See also *Enarr. in Ps.* 6. 2.

[122] *quatuor primordia*, the four 'roots of all things'—fire, air, earth, and water—as first propounded in the fifth century B.C. by Empedocles; cf. M. J. McKeough, *The Meaning of the rationes seminales in St. Augustine* (Washington 1926) 18. The four elements account for the four fundamental physical qualities—dry (*aridum*), moist (*humidum*), hot (*calidum*), cold (*frigidum*)—cf. Augustine, e.g. *Enarr. in Ps.* 6. 2. The soul does not consist of any of the four elements or any combination of them—cf. *De quant. an.* 1. 2, and J. M. Colleran's observations, ACW 9. 195 n. 3.

[123] *In tribus et quatuor impietatibus non aversabor*—cf. Amos 1 and 2. Augustine's version is closer to the Septuagint than to the Vulgate, which reads, e.g. in 1. 3, . . . *Super tribus sceleribus Damasci, et super quatuor non convertam eum* . . . .

[124] Matt. 18. 22. Both Augustine and Jerome (Vulgate) read *septuagies septies* for the Greek numerals used. But while the latter interprets this as 'seventy times seven times' (it is thus rendered in the Douai-Rheims translation), Augustine (with Origen), as also appears from the present context, understood 'seventy-seven times.' Elsewhere, in *Serm.* 83. 3, Augustine, dicussing the same passage, requires that we forgive even seventy-eight times, a hundred times, an unlimited number of times—*omnino quoties peccaverit, ignosce*. Concerning the disagreement, ancient and modern, on the interpretation of the multiplicative found in the passage, cf. J. H. Moulton-W. F. Howard, *A Grammar of New Testament Greek* 2 (Edinburgh 1929) 175.

SERMON 2 (184)

[1] Also listed as *De diversis* 56. A new edition of the Latin text for this sermon appears in D. C. Lambot, *op. cit.* 74-76. This is followed here. From doctrinal elements in the sermon—mention of the misconceptions that certain heretics have concerning the Incarnation, emphasis on Mary's lasting virginity—Kunzelmann, *art. cit.* 503, deduces that the sermon was held after 411 or 412.

[2] Cf. Ps. 84. 12.

[3] 'Day of Day' in Augustine is equivalent to the more familiar and more frequently used 'Light of Light,' or 'God of God'; note *Deum de Deo, lumen de lumine, Deum verum de Deo vero* in the

Credo of the Ordinary of the Mass. Regarding the probable origin of this phrase with Augustine, see below, n. 2 to *Serm.* 7(189).

[4] Cf. Ps. 117. 24.

[5] Matt. 11. 25.

[6] Note the inimitable wordplay, 'tanto *adiumento*, tamquam infirmitatis suae *iumento* . . . .'

[7] *apud Patrem* (Lambot), *id eum* (Maurists).

[8] *quam virgo ante conceptum, tam virgo post partum.* All the early Fathers attest that Mary was and remained a virgin when she conceived. But they are not in complete agreement on her virginity as continuing during and after the birth of her Son. Origen and Tertullian both denied her *virginitas in partu*. Augustine, of course, was not the first to affirm Mary's perpetual virginity; but he is a frequent witness to it, and he speaks in no uncertain terms. Besides the present passage, there is his well-known *Concipiens virgo, pariens virgo, virgo gravida, virgo feta, virgo perpetua* (*Serm.* 186. 1); also, *Sanctae quippe Matri omnipotens Filius nullo modo virginitatem natus abstulit* (*Serm.* 188. 4); *Concipit, et virgo est; parit, et virgo est* (*Serm.* 189. 2); *Ipsa virtus (Spiritus Sancti) per inviolata matris virginea viscera membra infantis eduxit* (*Ep.* 137. 8); and similar passages. Regarding the apparent diffidence of the earlier Fathers in discussing Mary's virginity in her childbearing, and for earlier witnesses to Mary's virginity *in partu* and *post partum*, see J. C. Plumpe, 'Some Little-Known Early Witnesses to Mary's *Virginitas in Partu*,' *Theol. Studies* 9 (1948) 567 f.

[9] *gravida masculo, sine masculo.*

[10] Cf. 1 Cor. 15. 45-47.

[11] Cf. Rom. 8. 3.

[12] *pueri sancti.*

[13] It is impossible to determine here for certain whether Augustine means that those who are called to 'spiritual marriage' are enabled to reject 'carnal marriage,' or whether he means that even those who have a vocation to the married state are able to lead a life of celibacy. It is probable that he meant both. Here and in the preceding he regularly uses *nuptiae* for 'marriage.'

[14] *quae nec concipiendo, nec pariendo potestis perdere quod amatis.* Regarding Christ as the Spouse of virgins, see also in this volume *Serm.* 10(192). 2, where Augustine exhorts, '. . . conceive Him by faith, give birth to Him through your works . . . .'

15 The Maurists add *saeculis*—'to the ages.'
16 Isa. 53. 8.
17 The heavens, that is, the star, announced the birth of Christ to the Magi; the angels announced the birth to the shepherds. See in this volume the Epiphany sermons, nos. 18-23.
18 . . . *et infans erat et Verbum*: Augustine makes frequent use of the original sense of the Latin word *infans* as 'speechless,' or 'not yet able to speak' (Cf. Plautus, *Persa* 174 = *fans atque infans*.). Unfortunately, the idea of an *infans Verbum* loses its paradoxical flavor when translated. See below, *Serm.* 8(190). 3; 18(199). 2, 3.

SERMON 3 (185)

1 Also listed as *De diversis* 62. Because a number of Scriptural passages are found that might well have been present to St. Augustine's mind at the time of his difficulties with the Pelagians, Kunzelmann (*art. cit.* 466) dates this sermon A.D. 412-416.
2 'speechless Babe' is a rendering of the single Latin word *infantem,* which Augustine has obviously used here in a twofold sense. See above, n. 18 to *Serm.* 2(184).
3 Ps. 84. 12.
4 Eph. 5. 14.
5 'magnus et aeternus *dies ex* magno et aeterno *die*': The concept of the timeless *dies* applied to both God the Father and God the Son recurs elsewhere in Augustine's preaching. See below, n. 2 to *Serm.* 7(189); also n. 3 to *Serm.* 2(184).
6 1 Cor. 1. 30 f., with a reminiscence of Jer. 9. 23 f.
7 Rom. 10. 3. Augustine has *suam volentes constituere,* the Vulgate, *suam quaerentes statuere.*
8 John 14. 6.
9 *Ibid.* 1. 14.
10 James 1. 17.
11 John 3. 27.
12 Rom. 5. 1 f. Departing from the Vulgate, Augustine here drops 'through faith' before 'into this grace,' and 'of the sons' before 'of God.'
13 Ps. 84. 11.
14 Although the Vulgate, as stated in n. 12, reads 'of the glory *of the sons* of God,' Augustine's version agrees with the Greek, ἐπ' ἐλπίδι τῆς δόξης τοῦ θεοῦ.

15 Luke 2. 14.
16 Eph. 2. 14; 'both,' that is, Jew and Gentile.
17 Cf. 2 Cor. 1. 12.
18 Ps. 3. 4.
19 This conclusion is also referred to by Kunzelmann, *loc. cit.*, as indicating the time when St. Augustine was involved in the Pelagian controversies.

SERMON 4 (186)

1 Also listed as *De tempore* 19. Kunzelmann (*art. cit.* 502) places this sermon in the winter of 411/412. He points out that in § 3 the reference to certain people who have false opinions concerning the Incarnation of Christ, is very close to passages in Augustine's letters to Volusianus (*Ep.* 137) and Honoratus (*Ep.* 140), both of which were written in that winter in answer to requests for clarification of certain problems.

2 *visceribus fecundis et genitalibus integris.*

3 The verb used here by Augustine, *effudit*, lit. 'poured forth,' further intimates the idea that Mary gave birth to Christ without labor pains, without injury or change to herself. For earlier and more direct evidence of this belief, see J. C. Plumpe, *art. cit.* 569 f.

4 *pariens virgo.* The manuscripts have *permanens virgo.*

5 *caro ad Verbum . . . accessit.* Some manuscripts read, *carni Verbum . . . accessit*, others, *caro Verbum . . . accepit.*

6 John 1. 14.

7 *Ibid.* 1. 1. The close resemblance in thought and expression of this section to passages in Augustine's letters to Volusianus (*Ep.* 137. 8) and Honoratus (*Ep.* 140. 12) has already been referred to above, n. 1. For a good conspectus of Augustine's teaching on the Incarnation, cf. E. Portalié, 'Augustin (Saint),' DTC 1. 2 (1903) 2361-66; see also J. Riviére, *Le dogme de rédemption chez saint Augustin* (Paris 1928).

8 Matt. 26. 38.

9 Phil. 2. 6 f.

10 *Ibid.* 2. 8.

11 Rom. 1. 1-3.

12 Gal. 4. 4.

13 Here St. Augustine of course refers to a Hebrew word rendered by St. Paul in Greek. The Greek text uses γυνή for 'woman';

and this word in all periods of Greek, in both the Septuagint and the New Testament, designates primarily the female being as distinguished from man—see A. Oepke, ' γυνή,' TWNT 1 (1933) 776. Augustine seems to think it necessary to explain to his hearers that the use of the Latin word *mulier*, 'woman,' a word frequently used to designate a married woman or wife, does not mean that Mary was not a virgin. For a Latin definition of *mulier* in Augustine's sense, note in the *Digests* (34. 2. 26); 'mulieres omnes dicuntur, quaecumque sexus femini sunt.' For further remarks by Augustine on this passage in Galatians, see in this volume § 18 of *Serm.* 1(51); see also n. 48 to the same.

14 Augustine here as in other passages (e.g. *Serm.* 8[190] .1 and 10[192] .3) indicates that at his time Christmas was celebrated on the winter solstice; see above, the Introduction.

15 Cf. 2 Cor. 4. 16.

SERMON 5 (187)

1 Also listed as *De tempore* 27. Kunzelmann (*art. cit.* 504) places this sermon before Christmas, 411/412; cf. below, n. 10.

2 Cf. Ps. 50. 17.

3 See below, n. 2 to *Serm.* 7(189).

4 Cf. Phil. 2. 6 f.

5 Cf. Wisd. 8. 1.

6 Retaining—at the suggestion of Dr. Plumpe—*coelos excedere* (Maurists: *extendere*) of the MSS.

7 '*non consumpta* divina et perfecta *assumpta* humana substantia': the wordplay defies imitation.

8 John 1. 1 and 14.

9 Cf. Matt. 1. 23, quoting Isa. 7. 14; '*and they shall call His name Emmanuel, which being interpreted is, God with us.*'

10 Ps. 18. 16. Kunzelmann, *loc. cit.*, who argues from mention of the Virgin Birth that certain sermons of Augustine were delivered in the years 411 or 412, takes the fact that Augustine does not here refer to the virginity of Mary as he does elsewhere when quoting Ps. 18. 6, that the present sermon antedates those years. But does the context call for such reference or interpretation? Obviously, here the argument from silence proves nothing.

11 Phil. 2. 6 f.

12 'habit' (*habitus*), that is, '(human) form' (Knox, Confraternity Version).
13 John 14. 28.
14 *Ibid.* 10. 30.
15 Isa. 9. 6.
16 Cf. Luke 1. 26-35.
17 The Latin text here reads, 'ut . . . recte vocetur "Nobiscum Deus": non "alter Deus, alter homo." '
18 Ps. 117. 24.
19 Cf. Cant. 3. 11.

SERMON 6 (188)

1 Also listed as *De tempore* 25. Kunzelmann, *art. cit.* 427, finds no clues in the sermon to determine the year in which it was held.
2 The 'eye of the heart,' *oculus cordis* (cf. Eph. 1. 18), the obligation of cleansing it, clearing its vision, is a favorite theme in Augustine's sermons and treatises: note *Serm.* 53. 6; 88. 5; 159. 3; 9. 2 Morin; *Enarr. in Ps. 118 serm.* 18. 3; *Enchir.* 2. 76; *C. epist. Manich.* 2. 2; etc.
3 Matt. 5. 8.
4 John 1. 1.
5 *Ibid.* 1. 14.
6 Isa. 53. 8.
7 Ps. 18. 6.
8 Cf. Gen. 2. 19 f.
9 See above, n. 8 to *Serm.* 2(184).
10 . . . *bonum quod coniuges diligunt.* Augustine writes more fully of this 'good' in his treatise *De bono coniugali*, which was written about the year 401. In his *De Genesi ad litteram*, 9. 7. 12, Augustine summarizes his views on the threefold blessings of marriage—*fides, proles, sacramentum* (cf. also *De bono coni.* 19; *C. Iul. Pelag.* 5. 12. 46): a) *fides:* 'fidelity, providing against one of the parties violating the conjugal bond and seeking intercourse with a third person'; b) *proles:* 'offspring, which is to be lovingly received, brought up with kindness, and given a religious training'; c) *sacramentum:* 'a sacrament, preventing separation of the marriage, . . . even when this is sought for the purpose of having offspring.' On the subject, cf. especially A.

Reuter, *Sancti Aurelii Augustini doctrina de bonis matrimonii* (Analecta Gregoriana 27, Rome 1942).

[11] 2 Cor. 11. 2. Augustine has *aptavi* = 'I have prepared' (cf. below, Serm. 13[195]. 2 and n. 4) for the Vulgate *despondi* = 'I have espoused.' The Greek has ἡρμοσάμην which normally = 'I have set in order, fitted, prepared,' but also = 'I have taken to wife'; 'I have given in marriage, have espoused.' Augustine, who quotes the passage very often, within the same works uses both versions—*aptavi* and *desponsavi* (for Vulg. *despondi*, which Cyprian has—*Ep.* 75. 14): e.g. *In Ioan. Ev. tract.* 8. 4 (*aptavi*), 13. 12 (*desponsavi*); *Enarr. in Ps.* 39. 1 and 118 *serm.* 28. 2 (*aptavi*), 13. 12, 49. 9, and 90 *serm.* 2. 9 (*desponsavi*).

In the concluding part of the present sermon Augustine treats of the concept of the mystical marriage of Christ and His Church. In a sermon on the words of the Gospel in Matthew 22. 1-14, Augustine states that the wedding garment (*vestis nuptialis*) is charity (*caritas*). He says: 'For *the wedding garment* is taken in honor of the union, that is, of the Bridegroom and the bride. You know the Bridegroom—it is Christ. You know the bride—it is the Church' (*Serm.* 90.6). It is said that 'with St. Augustine nuptial Christology reaches its zenith' (cf. C. Chavasse, *The Bride of Christ* [London 1939] 135). For a collection of patristic passages on this subject, see S. Tromp, 'Ecclesia Sponsa Virgo Mater,' *Gregorianum* 28 (1937) 3-29.

[12] The concept that contaminated faith—heresy—debauches the faith and attacks the Church's virginity, is very common among the early Fathers: cf. J. C. Plumpe, *Mater Ecclesia. An Inquiry into the Concept of the Church as Mother in Early Christianity* (SCA 5, Washington 1943) 23-28, 60, 82, *passim*.

SERMON 7 (189)

[1] This sermon, also listed as *De diversis* 55, is no. 4 in the collection Frangipane, and is found in two places in ML: 38. 1005-1007 and 46. 981-83. Kunzelmann, *art. cit.* 452 f., believes that it was delivered before the year 410.

[2] Ps. 95. 1 f. Augustine's text for the last clause as restored by Morin, following the well-supported suggestion of the Maurists, reads: 'bene nuntiate diem de die salutare eius.' The Vulgate has:

SERMONS: CHRISTMAS

'annuntiate de die in diem salutare eius.' Augustine's use of *dies* as a name for God has already been noted in n. 3 to *Serm.* 2(184) and n. 5 to *Serm.* 3(185). In *Enarr. in Ps.* 105. 36 he also quotes Ps. 95. 2 as offering the Scriptural basis for such nomenclature: 'Cantate Domino et benedicite nomini eius: annuntiate *de die in diem* salutare eius.' Augustine comments that the Greek (Septuagint) text here has *evangelizate*—'give the good news of'—for *annuntiate*—'announce,' 'declare'—of the Latin version; and, he adds, 'for this reason was the Gospel (= *Evangelium*, 'good news') called Gospel, because in it there is announced *the Day that came from the Day,* the Lord Christ, the Light of Light, the Son of the Father.'

It is interesting to note ancient parallels of the personification or deification of 'day.' *Diespiter,* older form of *Iuppiter,* was explained by Varro (*De lingua latina* 5. 66) as being composed of *dies* and *pater* = 'Day Father.' Used in the feminine gender, following the Greek counterpart, *Hemera, Dies* is the daughter of Erebus and Night (Cicero, *De nat. deor.* 3. 17. 44); or she is a child of Chaos and Darkness (Hyginus, *Fab. praef.*). For further examples, see O. Waser, 'Dies,' RE 5 (1905) 476 f.; O. Jessen, 'Hemera,' *ibid.* 8 (1913) 230-32.

³ Ps. 5. 5. For 'will contemplate Thee,' *contemplabor,* the Vulgate (so also Augustine, *Enarr. in Ps.* 5. 5) has 'will see,' *videbo.*

⁴ Ps. 84. 12.

⁵ Rom. 10. 3.

⁶ *Ibid.* 1. 17.

⁷ Augustine's wordplay is—*dignatio, indignatio.*

⁸ 'Noli quaerere *prophetantem*': probably in reference to the statement just made and to what Job had said on the same subject (14. 1) 'Homo natus de muliere, brevi vivens tempore, repletur multis miseriis.' The abbé Raulx, *op. cit.* 7. 161, thinks of another meaning: 'Pourquoi chercher des tireurs d'horoscopes?'

⁹ 'Erat ante tempora, signavit tempora.'

¹⁰ The place of the sermon or homily in the liturgy of the Mass, following the reading of the Gospel, goes back to the earliest Christian times; cf. J. A. Jungmann, *Missarum sollemnia* (Vienna 1948) 1. 562 ff. = tr. from rev. German ed. by F. A. Brunner, *The Mass of the Roman Rite* (New York 1951) 1. 456-61.

¹¹ *cibaria,* fem., which is extremely rare; cf. note by Morin.

¹² Isa. 1. 3.

¹³ Cf. John 14. 6: '*I am the way* and the truth and the life.'

14 Cf. Mark 11. 7; Luke 19. 35.

15 The 'two peoples' referred to above in the bold application of the 'two animals' in Isaias, are the Jews (= ox) and the Gentiles (= ass), to which latter Augustine's hearers belong. In *Enarr. in Ps.* 126. 11 this application is made in great detail. Note also § 3 of the sermon to follow.

16 '. . . quo vocet,' that is, 'direct by calling.'

17 That is, the heavenly Jerusalem; cf. Heb. 12. 22.

SERMON 8 (190)

1 Also listed as *De diversis* 61. Kunzelmann, *art. cit.* 431 f., dates the sermon 391-400; see below nn. 7, 9.

2 See also *De civ. Dei* 5. 7.

3 Referring, of course, to the virgin from whom He was born and the day on which He was born.

4 Augustine was not always so firmly opposed to astrology. From his own writings (cf. *Conf.* 4. 3. 4-6; 7. 6. 8-10) we know that as a young man, notably when he was a Manichaean, he was intensely interested in this pseudo-science. The many cases of twins who are born under the same astrological conditions but who fare quite differently in life, finally convinced Augustine that astrologers were only charlatans (cf. Augustine's *De Gen. ad litt.* 2. 17. 35-37; also *De civ. Dei*, 5. 1 ff.). See L. J. de Vreese, *Augustinus en de Astrologie* (diss. Amsterdam 1933). Regarding the tremendous influence exerted by astrologers—the *Chaldaei* and *mathematici*—on all classes in Roman Imperial times, see especially F. Cumont, *Les religions orientales dans le paganisme romain* (4th ed. Paris 1929) 151-79; for briefer orientation, see B. Farrington, 'Astrology,' OCD 110.

5 Rom. 13. 12 f.

6 Augustine here gives a mystical significance to Christ's birth at the time of the winter solstice; however, see above, Intro. 8 f.

7 Kunzelmann, *loc. cit.*, sees in this bit of anti-pagan polemics an indication of early composition of the present sermon.

8 John 1. 14.

9 Kunzelmann, *loc. cit.*, sees an allusion to the Manichaeans who worshipped the sun. Most of Augustine's sermons and treaties against this sect date from the last decade of the fourth century and the first five years of the fifth.

SERMONS: CHRISTMAS

[10] The Mithraic festival *Natalis Solis Invicti* was also celebrated on December 25; see above, Intro. 9.

[11] *Ideo ut non possemus mortem nostram in femina velut motu iusti doloris horrere* . . . . This is in accordance with the early Christian tradition that we were redeemed through a woman that man might not disparage woman for being the cause of his fall; cf. Irenaeus, *Adv. haer.* 5. 19. 1; *Dem. praed. apost.* 33; Epiphanius, *Haer.* 78. 18; etc. In a sermon delivered during Easter Week, *Serm.* 232. 2, Augustine draws a similar argument from the fact that Christ after His Resurrection first appeared to a woman, Mary Magdalen.

[12] Cf. Matt. 18. 12; Luke 19. 10.
[13] See above, n. 18 to *Serm.* 2(184).
[14] Isa. 1. 3. See the previous sermon, 7(189), § 4 and n. 15.
[15] Cf. Matt. 21. 1-9.
[16] See above, n. 2 to *Serm.* 7(189).
[17] Ps. 95. 1 f.
[18] *Ibid.* 66. 2. This passage as quoted by Augustine lacks the repeated plea for mercy, *et misereatur nostri*, which the Vulgate carries at the end of v. 2, but which is absent in the Hebrew and the Septuagint.
[19] John 14. 6.
[20] See above, n. 10 to *Serm.* 7(189).
[21] Cf. Luke 2. 26.
[22] *Ibid.* 2. 29.
[23] Cf. Ps. 95. 2.
[24] Ps. 95. 3.

SERMON 9 (191)

[1] Also listed as *De diversis* 60. Kunzelmann, *art. cit.* 503, would place this sermon into the same time, 411 or 412, as no. 186; cf. above, n. 1 to *Serm.* 4(186).

[2] Augustine uses the word *botrus*, which is here metonymically translated as 'Vine.' *Botrus* is a loan word from the Greek, meaning a 'cluster' or 'bunch of grapes.' It occurs in the Vulgate (Mich. 7. 1, Apoc. 14. 18, etc.); cf. also the fragment of Papias preserved in the old Latin version of Irenaeus, *Adv. haer.* 5. 33. 3 (= ACW 6. 114).

[3] Ps. 84. 12.
[4] Luke 24. 39.
[5] Cf. John 20. 19.

⁶ Compare the similar passage in Augustine's letter to Volusianus on the Incarnation (*Ep.* 137. 8): 'Ipsa virtus per inviolata matris virginea viscera membra infantis eduxit, quae postea per clausa ostia membra iuvenis introduxit.'

⁷ Cf. Ps. 18. 6. 'Bridal chamber,' of course, refers here to the spiritual nuptials of Christ's divinity and humanity in His Incarnation. Cf. in § 3 of the sermon immediately following: '. . . de thalamo suo, id est, de utero virginali, ubi Verbum Dei creaturae humanae quodam ineffabili coniugio copulatum est.'

⁸ 2 Cor. 11. 2. See above, n. 11 to *Serm.* 6(188).

⁹ . . . *et mater est et virgo.* The concept of the Church as a mother was developed long before the time of Augustine. For a monograph on this subject for the first three centuries, see J. C. Plumpe, *Mater Ecclesia, An Inquiry into the Concept of the Church as Mother in Early Christianity* (SCA 5, Washington 1943); for the concept in Augustine, cf. F. Hofmann, *Der Kirchenbegriff des Hl. Augustinus* (Munich 1933) 262-68; P. Batiffol, *Le catholicisme de saint Augustin* (5th ed. Paris 1929) 271-76.

¹⁰ Except that he addresses the full congregation in the last brief paragraph, the rest of the sermon is given to the *virgines sacrae* (here, *virgines sanctae*), 'holy virgins.' These, along with the virgins of the other sex—*confessores*—constituted a very important group among the members of a local church. They were ascetics who remained within a Christian community, without practicing segregation or isolation from the world as did the solitaries or the cenobites. The *virgines* and the *confessores,* and a third group, the *viduae*—widows who remained in the state of widowhood—were highly honored in the community of the faithful. A reception of the virgins (*consecratio, benedictio virginum*), finding a place in the solemn liturgy in Rome, is mentioned as existing at the time of Pope Damasus (cf. his decree, ML 13. 1182), or in the latter half of the fourth century. This reception took place on Christmas, Epiphany, Easter Monday, and the feast of St. Peter (June 29). It consisted of the *velatio,* imposition of the veil by the bishops, and other ceremonies. The function signified the virgin's mystical marriage with Christ. The bishop also made an address to the candidates; and in the present sermon, so it would appear, we have a specimen of such an address surviving the centuries. There is a Roman counterpart in the sermon which Pope Liberius delivered 'on the birthday of the Savior' in A.D. 353, when Marcel-

lina, sister of St. Ambrose, took the veil. It is preserved in Ambrose's *De virginibus* 1. 3. See B. Botte, *op. cit.* 34-37; cf. J. Quasten, *Theol. Revue* 33 (1934) 142-44. On the subject, see Duchesne, *op. cit.* ch. 13; Eisenhofer, *op. cit.* 304 f.

[11] Cf. 1 Cor. 7. 32-34.
[12] Cf. Rom. 10. 10.

SERMON 10 (192)

[1] Also listed as *De tempore* 16. Kunzelmann, *art. cit.* 503 f., thinks this sermon was delivered after the years 411/412.
[2] Ps. 84. 12.
[3] Cf. John 1. 12.
[4] *Deos facturus qui homines erant, homo factus est qui Deus erat.*
[5] Matt. 12. 50.
[6] From Apostolic times widows were not only cared for by the Christian community (cf. Acts 6. 1 ff., James 1. 27), but, provided they fulfilled certain conditions, were admitted to a certain order or society—*viduae, viduatus*—with definite duties to perform (1 Tim. 5. 9 f.). They seem to have been, in good part, the female counterpart of the deacons in executing certain duties of the bishop: they took care of the women among the sick, assisted in the care of the poor, etc. Cf. J. Viteau, 'L'institution des diacres et des veuves,' *Rev. d'hist. ecclés.* 22 (1926) 513-37; also ACW 13. 121 f., where further literature is cited.
[7] See above, n. 12 to *Serm.* 6(188). See also some sentences farther on: '(Ecclesia) virgo integritate fidei et pietatis.'
[8] On Augustine's thoughts on the Church as the mystical body of Christ, see Hofmann, *op. cit.* 120-23, 193-212, 478 ff., *passim.*
[9] That is, in baptism.
[10] 'unity'—*unitas*—understood as 'oneness.'
[11] Cf. John 3. 31.
[12] John 16. 8-10.
[13] Ps. 18. 7.
[14] *Ibid.* 18. 6 f.

SERMON 11 (193)

[1] Also listed as *De diversis* 58. Kunzelmann, *art. cit.* 461, assigns this sermon to the year 410. The section headings appearing in the translation have been added by the translator.

² Luke 2. 14. Regarding the reading of the Gospel, see above, n. 10 to *Serm.* 7(189).

³ Augustine's use of the words *feta, fetum,* and *fetalia* within a single sentence results in a wordplay that cannot be reproduced in translation. This is apparently the only occurence of *fetalia* ('feast for a delivery or birth') in ancient Latin literature: cf. TLL 6. 1. 632. 80-82.

⁴ Ps. 33. 13-15, quoted freely and in the third person, as in 1 Peter 3. 10 f.

⁵ Rom. 7. 18.

⁶ *Ibid.* 7. 22 f., adapted to the second person.

⁷ *Ibid.* 7. 24 f.

⁸ Gal. 5. 17.

⁹ Eph. 2. 14, where 'both' refers to Jews and Gentiles.

¹⁰ John 8. 31.

¹¹ Ps. 84. 12.

¹² *Ibid.* 118. 106.

¹³ Rom. 7. 23.

¹⁴ Ps. 118. 107.

¹⁵ Rom. 7. 18.

¹⁶ Ps. 118. 108.

¹⁷ Rom. 5. 5.

SERMON 12 (194)

¹ Also listed as *De tempore* 23. Kunzelmann, *art. cit.* 504, assumes that this sermon, like no. 5(187), was delivered before 411/412; cf. above, n. 1 to *Serm.* 5(187).

² Ps. 32. 1.

³ John the Baptist was born six months before Jesus (cf. Luke 1. 26); therefore, following ancient tradition, on June 24, the Julian summer solstice. Cf. below, n. 18 to *Serm.* 14(196).

⁴ John 3. 30, quoting John the Baptist.

⁵ 2 Cor. 5. 15. The Vulgate has 'for them': Augustine's 'for all' (cf. also *Enarr. in Ps.* 55. 14) is found also in some of the Greek MSS.

⁶ Gal. 2. 20.

⁷ Ps. 94. 7. The Vulgate has, 'and we are the people of His pasture and the sheep of His hand,' which is also Augustine's reading in *Enarr. in Ps.* 94. 11.

⁸ Luke 2. 14.
⁹ John 1. 1.
¹⁰ *Ibid.* 1. 14.
¹¹ 2 Cor. 8. 9, adapted from the second person to the first.
¹² Ps. 30.20, adapted from the second person to the third.
¹³ Freely, from 1 Cor. 13. 9 f.
¹⁴ Cf. Phil. 2. 6 f.
¹⁵ Cf. *ibid.* 3. 21.
¹⁶ 1 John 3. 2.
¹⁷ John 14. 8.
¹⁸ Ps. 16. 15.
¹⁹ Cf. John 10. 30.
²⁰ Cf. *ibid.* 14. 9.
²¹ Ps. 23. 10.
²² Cf. *ibid.* 79. 4.
²³ *Ibid.* 26. 8 f. The Vulgate has 'My face hath sought Thee' for 'I have sought Thy face.'
²⁴ John 14. 21. The Vulgate reads, 'He that hath my commandments and keepeth them, he it is that loveth me . . . .'
²⁵ Cf. 1 Cor. 2. 9.
²⁶ Cf. 2 Cor. 5. 7.
²⁷ Cf. *ibid.* 5. 6.
²⁸ Cf. Matt. 5. 6.
²⁹ Ps. 109. 3.
³⁰ *Ibid.* 71. 17.
³¹ Cf. *ibid.* 18. 6.

SERMON 13 (195)

¹ Also listed as *De tempore* 12. Kunzelmann, *art. cit.* 503, thinks that this sermon should be dated after 411/412.

² Isa. 53. 8.

³ Ps. 44. 3.

⁴ 2 Cor. 11. 2. Augustine has *aptavi* for *despondi*—see above, n. 11 to *Serm.* 6(188).

⁵ Cf. Gal. 4. 22 f., 26 f. For this and other Scriptural passages in the history of the concept, Mother Church, cf. Plumpe, *Mater Ecclesia* 1-9.

⁶ 'in mente': Augustine's use of the terms *mens* and *animus* often leaves little room for distinction; regarding these and related terms (*anima, spiritus, ratio, intelligentia, intellectus*), cf. E. Gil-

son, *Introduction a l'étude de saint Augustin* (2nd ed. Paris 1943) 56 f., n. 1.

[7] Cf. John 1. 10, 11, 5.

[8] This difficult text reads in Latin: 'Venit in medicinali terra, unde curaret interiores oculos nostros, quos exterior nostra excaecaverat terra.' Regarding the 'inner eyes,' see above n. 2 to *Serm.* 6(188). Christ in the role of a doctor, Christ as our Physician, was always a popular concept with the early Fathers. Cf. J. C. Plumpe's observations, ACW 5 (1948) 190 f.

[9] Cf. Eph. 5. 8.

[10] Cf. Ps. 18. 6.

[11] Cf. John 1. 14.

SERMON 14 (196)

[1] Also listed as *De diversis* 59. Kunzelmann, *art. cit.* 491, finds that as to the time of its delivery, nothing more can be said than that the sermon was given after Augustine became a bishop, that is, after the year 394.

[2] See above, n. 14 to *Serm.* 4(186).

[3] Isa. 53. 8.

[4] John 1. 1.

[5] Phil. 2. 7, 6.

[6] *Ibid.* 2. 7.

[7] On Mary's perpetual virginity—*ante partum, in partu, post partum*—cf. above, n. 8 to *Serm.* 2(184).

[8] See above, n. 10 to *Serm.* 9(191) and n. 6 to *Serm.* 10(192).

[9] Cf. Luke 1. 39-56.

[10] See above, n. 10 to *Serm.* 7(189).

[11] See above, n. 8 to *Serm.* 2(184); regarding the way virgins are to imitate the life of Mary, cf. in particular § 4 of *Serm.* 9(191).

[12] Ecclus. 3. 20. Elsewhere, in *Enarr. in Ps.* 99.13, Augustine states: 'Melius est humile coniugium quam superba virginitas.'

[13] *Caritati vestrae*: see above, n. 2 to *Serm.* 1(51).

[14] *Christiani estis omnes; Deo propitio, Christiana est civitas;* the sole manuscript available to the Maurists reads: *Christiani estis; omnis, Deo propitio, Christiana est civitas.* Because of this sweeping statement it was doubted that this sermon should be credited to St. Augustine (cf. the note to the Maurist text). It was pointed out that surely Hippo Regius, Augustine's episcopal see, counted a goodly number of heretics, e.g. Manichaeans. Moreover, before

Augustine's time Hippo had been one of the strongholds of the schismatic Donatists; that they were still there in formidable numbers, can be gathered from a protest filed by Augustine in 405 with the civil magistrate, Caecilianus, against their *haeretica audacia* in Hippo and vicinity (cf. *Ep.* 86). See the interesting and valuable account by Pope, *op. cit.* 5 f. It should be observed, however, that Augustine does not speak of Hippo as a *Catholic*, but a Christian city. The dissident groups, especially the schismatic Donatists, were still Christians.

[15] Hippo seems to have had Jews in no small numbers, and they particularly may be meant when in the following Augustine alludes to reprehensible practices taking place on New Year's Day (cf. the following note). Cf. Pope, *op. cit.* 6 f.

[16] The kalends of January—the first day of the new year—had been kept by the pagans from time immemorial as a civil and religious feast day, dedicated to Janus (hence, January), god of openings and beginnings. It was a most popular holiday and notorious as an occasion for riotous and dissolute conduct in theaters, games, etc. Tertullian, *De idol.* 14, complains bitterly of Christian participation in the pagan festivities and accompanying excesses. Following Tertullian, the Fathers, especially those of the West (Augustine, Maximus of Turin, Peter Chrysologus, Martin of Bracara, etc.), through the centuries constantly warn against and condemn the obstinately surviving evils of this pagan festival and the equally obstinate insistence of Christians to take part in them. This struggle for Christian discipline is also reflected in a number of sacramentaries which provide for a Mass to be said on the octave of Christmas—*ad prohibendum ab idolis*—and in the prescription by bishops and councils of penitential fasts, litanies, and processions to atone for the superstitious and licentious practices rampant on this day.

The second council of Tours in 567 gave certain directions (c. 17) for the Mass to be celebrated on the feast of the Circumcision, January 1, to propitiate God and *ad calcandam gentilium consuetudinem;* cf. C. J. Hefele—H. Leclercq, *Histoire des conciles* 3. 1 (1909) 17. The earliest mention of the feast occurs in southern Italy (Capua) in the year 546. Prior to its introduction, New Year's Day went unnoticed in the liturgy except as the octave day of Christmas—*Octava Domini.* In Rome as late as the ninth century this was still the only liturgical commemoration of the day. Cf. F. Cabrol, 'Circoncision (fête de la),' DACL 3. 2 (1914) 1717-28; Duchesne, *op. cit.* 273 f.; K. A. H. Kellner, *Heortology, a History of the Christian Church Festivals from their Origin to the Present Day* (tr. from the German, London 1908) 163-65; J. J. Tierney, 'Circumcision, Feast of the,' CE 3 (1908) 779 f.; the same, 'New Year's Day,' *ibid.* 11 (1911) 19 f.

As to the games (*lusus*) to which Augustine refers in the present passage, dice may be mentioned, and as types of amusement (*iocus*), drinking, dancing, frequenting the theaters; all of which pastimes are mentioned in *Serm.* 16(198) to follow below.

[17] *Non sibi faciant homines iudices*: the meaning seems to be that they should not by their riotous conduct make themselves subject to prosecution and sentencing by the civil authorities—'Do not call the courts upon yourselves.' Raulx renders: 'Gardez-vous d'appeler la vengeance des juges.'

[18] Following the suggestion of the Gospel (Luke 1. 26) that the Baptist was born six months earlier than Jesus, the feast of his birth was kept on the Roman summer solstice, June 24; cf. above, n. 3 to *Serm.* 12(194). The date is mentioned again by Augustine in *Serm.* 287.4. In the same sermon (1) he states also that the Church celebrates two birthdays only, that of Christ and that of John (hence 'Summer Christmas'). Cf. Kellner, *op. cit.* 217-23; Duchesne, *op. cit.* 271.

[19] Not, 'baptized themselves,' as Pope, *op. cit.* 8, appears to have understood the Latin, *se baptizabant;* and Augustine is referring to a pagan, not a Donatist, practice kept by some of his Christian people. This practice consisted in taking purificatory baths at or before dawn on the day of the summer solstice (see the preceding note). Obviously, John's baptism of Christ served the accommodation of the ancient pagan religious custom to Christian usage. More than a century after St. Augustine the practice still persisted in southern Gaul, where we find St. Caesarius of Arles castigating some of his subjects for bathing in fountains, streams, and even swamps on St. John's Day; cf. J. Zellinger, *Bad und Bäder in der altchristlichen Kirche* (Munich 1928) 118 f.

SERMON 15 (140)

[1] The Maurists state that in the codices seen by them the present sermon is grouped with the *Sermones de Christi natali,* and is listed

under that title. They remark, however, that they do not believe that this means that Augustine himself gave the sermon on Christmas, but only that it was to be read on that day. They suggest also that to adapt this sermon for reading on Christmas Day, the word 'to-day' (*hodie*) was added in § 2 and again in § 6, near the end. Kunzelmann, *art. cit.* 489, is certain that the discourse was given on Christmas Day A.D. 427 or 428; see the following note.

[2] In the year 427 (428?) an army of Visigoth mercenaries, under the command of a German, Sigisvult, had been hired by the Roman government to put down a civil war in Africa arising from the contumacy of its governor, the *comes* (count) Boniface (cf. Prosper of Aquitaine, *Chronicum* = ML 51. 594AB; E. Barker, in *The Cambridge Medieval History* 1 [New York 1911] 408 f.). With Sigisvult came an Arian bishop named Maximinus. The latter, at the suggestion of his civil superior, left Carthage for Hippo to engage in a public debate with the aged Augustine on the Holy Trinity. Possidius reports (*S. Augustini vita* 17) that the heretic managed to take for himself by far the greatest part of the time allotted for the debate, so as to make it necessary for Augustine to limit himself to making only a few remarks. Returning to Carthage, Maximinus claimed that he had quite decisively worsted Augustine in a discussion on the focal point of difference between Catholicism and Arianism—the Trinity. The official record of the debate has been preserved: *S. Augustini collatio cum Maximino Arianorum episcopo*: ML 42. 709-742. To rectify the account given of the debate by Maximinus at Carthage and to give himself the opportunity denied him by the crafty Arian at the time of the debate, Augustine later composed a reply: *Contra Maximinum haereticum Arianorum episcopum libri duo*: ML 42. 743-814.

The present sermon enters the lists with Maximinus on a point also recorded in the longer *Contra Maximinum* (2. 22), a misinterpretation of the unity of the will of the Father and the Son.

At the time the sermon was given, Arianism had been condemned long since in general councils at Nicaea (325) and Constantinople (381); also, Augustine had long before (399-416) written his fifteen books *De Trinitate,* books 5-7 of which are directed against the Arian heresy. On Maximinus, cf. also H. W. Phillott, 'Maximinus (6),' in W. Smith-H. Wace, *A Dictionary of Christian Biography* 3 (1882) 873 f.; O. Bardenhewer, *op. cit.* 4. 479 f.

³ John 12. 44.
⁴ Cf. *ibid.* 12. 46 and 8. 12.
⁵ *Ibid.* 12. 49 f.
⁶ 1 John 5. 20, freely adapted; though 'Jesus Christ,' absent in the Vulgate, is found in the original Greek.
⁷ John 10. 30.
⁸ Augustine uses *minor* here and frequently in the present discussion. The word 'complete' in the following renders the Latin *perfectus*.

Regarding Augustine's teaching on the equality of the Persons in the Holy Trinity, see his earlier (399-416) treatise *De Trinitate*, especially book 1. Augustine notes (*De Trin.* 1. 11. 22) that there are some Biblical passages which seem to say that the Son is less than the Father, and some which stress the Son's equality with the Father. The rule by which these apparently incongruous passages may be harmonized is: When the Son is spoken of under the form of God, He is coequal with the Father; when the Son is spoken of under the form of the servant, He is not only less than the Father, He is less than Himself. Regarding Augustine's theology on the doctrine of the Trinity, see J. Lebreton, 'Saint Augustin théologien de la Trinité—son exégèse des théophanies,' *Miscellanea Agostiniana* 2 (Rome 1931) 821-36; M. Schmaus, *Die psychologische Trinitätslehre des hl. Augustinus* (Münster i. W. 1927).

⁹ Isa. 7. 9, according to the Septuagint. The Vulgate reads 'continue' for 'understand.'

¹⁰ 2 Cor. 6. 13 f. I owe 'open your hearts' for *dilatamini* to Knox's translation.

¹¹ In the opening sentence of his *De Trinitate* (1. 1) Augustine had warned against those who are led astray by 'an immature and perverse love of reason'—*qui fidei contemnentes initium, immaturo et perverso rationis amore falluntur*. Now he is telling his listeners that unless they believe, they will not understand. It is interesting to note here that the fifteen books of the *De Trinitate* may be divided into two groups, the *first* (1-8) offering the Scriptural basis for the doctrine of the Trinity, the second (9-15) presenting a rational explanation to the extent that such is possible. Not long after the date of the present sermon, in 428 or 429, Augustine wrote that 'faith resides in the believer's will,' which is again prepared by God (*De praed. sanct.* 5). On the subject, cf. E. Gilson, *Introduction à l'étude de saint Augustin* (2nd ed. Paris 1943) 31-47; M.

C. D'Arcy, in *A Monument to Saint Augustine* (repr. London 1945) 159-62; P. Batiffol, *Le catholicisme de saint Augustin* (5th ed. Paris 1929) 21-64; etc.

SERMON 16 (197)

[1] This sermon exists only in fragments. These were gathered from two unique sources, two immense collections of Augustinian texts containing passages from St. Paul along with St. Augustine's explanation or application of the same. These collections are by the Venerable Bede (673/4-735) and Florus the Deacon of Lyons (d. ab. 860). The work of Florus was ascribed early to Bede, while the authentic work of Bede was lost for a long time. The excerpts of Bede still await publication, those of Florus are given in abbreviated form in ML 119. 279-420. The difficult problem of distinguishing the two works from each other has received the attention of A. Wilmart, 'La collection de Bède le Vénérable sur l'Apôtre,' *Rev. Ben.* 38 (1926) 16-52; cf. the same, 'Sommaire de l'exposition de Florus sur les Epîtres,' *ibid.* 205-216.

Kunzelmann, *art. cit.* 450, finds that no further approximation of date is possible than that the sermon was delivered on the first of January of some year antedating 420. In § 4 there is mention of the Donatists, who disappear from Augustine's writings beginning with approximately the year 420.—Regarding the observance, or lack of such, of New Year's Day in the liturgy of the early Church, see the Intro. (14) and n. 16 to *Serm.* 14(196).

The section headings found in the translation are the translator's.

[2] Rom. 1. 18.
[3] *Ibid.*
[4] *Ibid.* 1. 19.
[5] *Ibid.* 1. 20.
[6] How the soul of man and its characteristics can be known although it itself cannot be seen, was discussed by Augustine in his earlier (387 or 388) *De quantitate animae*, written in the form of a dialogue between himself and Evodius, one of his closest friends. See J. M. Colleran's translation of this work, *The Greatness of the Soul*, in ACW 9 (1950) 13-112.
[7] The argument from the order in the universe had been developed centuries before Christ by the Greek philosophers: for Socrates, cf. Xenophon, *Mem.* 1. 4. 4-10, 4. 3. 3-9; Plato, *De leg.*

bks. 10 and 11 *passim*. It is, of course, taken up many times by the Fathers; cf. Minucius Felix, *Oct*. 17 ff.; Theophilus of Antioch, *Ad Autol*. 1. 5 f.; Athanasius, *C. gent*. 27, 43; etc. For Augustine, cf. also *Conf*. 11. 4. 6; *De civ. Dei* 11. 4; *Enarr. in Ps*. 73. 25; etc.

[8] Rom. 1. 21.

[9] *Ibid*. 1. 22.

[10] On purification (*purgatio, lustratio*) in Mithraism and other mystery cults, see Cumont, *op. cit*. 35-38, 145 f., 310 n. 61.

[11] Rom. 1. 23.

[12] *Ibid*. 1. 23 f.

[13] *Ibid*. 1. 25.

[14] *Ibid*.

[15] Neptune was the god of the sea only after he had been identified with the Greek sea-god Poseidon; in primitive Roman religion he was the god of water presiding over springs and streams and thus preventing droughts. Cf. H. J. Rose, 'Neptunus,' OCD 603.

[16] Augustine was very fond and proud of his countryman, quoting Cyprian (c. 200-258) more than one hundred times in his writings; see especially the five sermons, 309-313, delivered on the anniversary of his martyrdom. In one of these, 312. 4, he gives a glowing account of how the orator Cyprian after his conversion deserted the *forensium mendaciorum certamina* and diverted his talents *in aedificationem Ecclesiae*.

[17] 'Nisi fideliter praecederet piscator, non humiliter sequeretur orator'—most appositely quoted by F. J. Sheen, *Philosophy of Religion* (New York 1948) 314, in a discussion of Christ's injunction to His followers that they should go out to the masses, and of the Fathers insisting that it is not dialectics or philosophy that makes converts.

[18] Cf. Acts 8. 18 f.

[19] 1 Cor. 3. 7.

[20] *Ibid*. 3. 6.

[21] *Ibid*. 1. 13.

[22] Paul had stated *ibid*. 2. 2 f.: 'For I judged not myself to know anything among you, but Jesus Christ and Him crucified. And *I was* with you in weakness, and *in fear,* and in much trembling.'

[23] Gal. 1. 8.

[24] Regarding the Donatists, see above, n. 14 to *Serm*. 14(196), and below, n. 4 to *Serm*. 21(202).

SERMONS: NEW YEAR'S DAY

[25] 2 Cor. 13. 3.
[26] Gal. 4. 14.
[27] Matt. 25. 35.
[28] Cf. also *De civ. Dei* 4. 10 f.; *De cons. Evang.* 1. 45. Juno appears to have been originally a deity of light and the sky and a moon-goddess. Cf. J. H. Rose, 'Juno,' OCD 471 f.
[29] Col. 2. 8.

SERMON 17 (198)

[1] No year can be given for the delivery of this sermon—cf. Kunzelmann, *art. cit.* 427.
[2] Ps. 105. 47.
[3] *Strenae* were originally branches or boughs, later coins or other gifts, exchanged on the first day of the new year. The word itself means 'omen' and the gift served as an omen of the new year. At Rome the practice also evoked a goddess—Strenia. Cf. M. P. Nilsson, 'Strena,' RE 2. R. 4 (1932) 351-53.
[4] Cf. John 1. 29.
[5] Prov. 28. 27.
[6] Matt. 25. 34.
[7] *Ibid.* 25. 41. The Vulgate reads, 'Depart from me, you cursed, into everlasting fire . . . .'
[8] *stant*—the people stood while the preacher sat; cf. Pope, *op. cit.* 141.
[9] 2 Cor. 6. 14-16.
[10] 1 Cor. 10. 20.
[11] Eph. 4. 20 f.
[12] *Ibid.* 5. 7 f.

SERMON 18 (199)

[1] Also listed as *De tempore* 34. The year in which this sermon was given is not known; cf. Kunzelmann, *art. cit.* 427.
[2] John 4. 22.
[3] Isa. 49. 6, quoted in Acts 13. 47.
[4] Epiphany seems to have been received in the West from the East at about the same time, the fourth century, that the East received Christmas from the West; see above, the Intro. 10 f.
[5] Luke 2. 14.

6 Eph. 2. 14.
7 Cf. Isa. 28. 16.
8 Eph. 2. 15, 17, freely adapted.
9 Matt. 2. 2.
10 Cf. 2 Cor. 5. 7.
11 *infantem—loquentem* (see in the first sentence of § 3 below, *Verbum infans*): cf. above, n. 18 to *Serm.* 2(184).
12 In *Contra Faustum Manichaeum* 2. 5, Augustine states: 'Non ex illis erat haec stellis, quae ab initio creaturae itinerum suorum ordinem sub Creatoris lege custodiunt; sed novo Virginis partu novum sidus apparuit . . . .'
13 Cf. Matt. 2. 1-12. The actual date of the adoration of the Magi is of course unknown, as is also the age of the Child Jesus when they came. Augustine believed that they came twelve days after the Nativity; cf. below, *Serm.* 22(203). 1. It is more likely that they came when the Lord was a year or more old. The word *Magi* seems to indicate that they were members of a priestly caste. Their number is also unknown. The number frequently accepted, three, is as likely false as true. Oriental tradition favors the number twelve. Early Christian art shows two, three, four, and eight Magi. Cf. W. Drum, 'Magi,' CE 9 (1910) 527-30; H. Leclercq, 'Mages,' DACL 10. 1 (1931) 980-1067 (with numerous illustrations).
14 Cf. Luke 2. 8-20.

SERMON 19 (200)

1 Also listed as *De tempore* 30. The sermon belongs to the first period, 393-405, of Augustine's struggles with the Donatists—so Kunzelmann, *art. cit.* 436 f. It is used in the Roman Breviary, in the second nocturn of the second and third days within the octave of Epiphany.
2 Cf. Ps. 18. 2.
3 Cf. Wisd. 9. 4.
4 Ps. 2. 10 f.
5 Cf. John 18. 36.
6 Matt. 2. 5 f.
7 *iustis*. Of course, Augustine is not stating here that the Magi (whether the Magi who came to Bethlehem are referred to or the priestly caste to which they belonged, is not entirely clear)

were *iniusti* in the sense of 'unjust men,' 'men with characters contrary to right and justice'; rather that they were not 'just' inasmuch as they were not keepers of God's law as set down in the commandments. For a discussion of this notoriously difficult concept, *iustus—iustitia*, as occurring in the Gospels, see R. Knox, *The Trials of a Translator* (New York 1949) 59-66.
[8] 1 Cor. 1. 27.
[9] Matt. 9. 13.
[10] Ps. 117. 22.
[11] Rom. 11. 5.
[12] Cf. Eph. 2. 11-22.
[13] Cf. Rom. 11. 17-24. See § 2 of the sermon to follow.

SERMON 20 (201)

[1] Also listed as *De tempore* 31. Kunzelmann, *art. cit.* 427, finds no clues to the year in which this sermon was delivered.
[2] Cf. Eph. 2. 11-22.
[3] Matt. 2. 2.
[4] John 19. 19.
[5] *Ibid.* 19. 22.
[6] Ps. 56. 1.
[7] Matt. 8. 11 f.
[8] The Latin here (*illi orienti, hoc est nascenti; ille autem occidenti, hoc est morienti*) can scarcely be rendered satisfactorily in English. Augustine uses *Oriens* and *Occidens* in the preceding sentence as 'East' and 'West.' In this sentence he uses the same words as adjectives modifying *Regi*, 'King.' *Oriens* is originally a participle meaning 'springing forth,' 'becoming visible,' 'rising'—hence, East is where the sun rises; the participle *occidens* means 'going down,' 'falling down,' 'dying,' 'setting'—hence, West is where the sun sets.
[9] Cf. Rom. 11. 24. See the conclusion of the preceding sermon.
[10] Matt. 2. 5.
[11] *Ibid.* 27. 24.
[12] Cf. Gen. 4. 1-15.
[13] Ps. 58. 12; the Vulgate reads: *Deus ostendet mihi super inimicos meos; ne occidas eos, nequando obliviscantur populi mei.*
[14] Cf. Prov. 2. 22.

SERMON 21 (202)

[1] Also listed as *De tempore* 32. According to Kunzelmann, *art. cit.* 442, this sermon must have been delivered before the year 412. In § 2 Augustine writes: 'Merito istum diem numquam nobiscum haeretici Donatistae celebrare voluerunt.' For Kunzelmann this is evidence that the Donatists celebrated Epiphany, which was made impossible for them by the legislation of 412 (*Cod. Theod.* 16. 5. 52). I fail to see, however, why we need to read into Augustine's statement that the Donatists did celebrate Epiphany; cf. below, n. 4.

[2] Cf. Matt. 2. 1-12.

[3] Cf. Eph. 2. 17, 14-16.

[4] The schism of Donatism as it occupied St. Augustine's best efforts for more than thirty years, has recently been made the subject of a monograph: G. G. Willis, *Saint Augustine and the Donatist Controversy* (SPCK, London 1950). The roots of the schism reached back into the third century, to the purist-extremist views of the Cyprianic Anabaptists, especially that the Church consists of the *cathari*—the pure and the saints—and that the validity of the sacraments, notably baptism, is conditioned by the worthiness of the minister.

Donatism as an organized sect took its rise in late A.D. 311 or early 312 when the archdeacon Caecilian was elected bishop of Carthage. An influential widow, Lucilla, who was a personal enemy of Caecilian, prevailed upon a goodly percentage of the Carthaginian clergy to refuse obedience on the ground that Caecilian had been invalidly consecrated (because his consecrator, Bishop Felix of Aptunga, was charged with being a *traditor,* that is, with having delivered over sacred books or vessels during the persecution of Diocletian). Bishop Donatus of Casae Nigrae consecrated the lector Majorinus as the antibishop of Carthage. The name 'Donatiani' or 'Donatistae' is due either to Donatus of Casae Nigrae or to Donatus the Great, successor to Majorinus as schismatic bishop of Carthage. The schism spread through Africa with such speed that within less than two decades the Donatists could hold a synod attended by 270 bishops. They were especially strong in Augustine's own native Numidia.

The liturgy of the Donatists remained quite the same as that of the Catholics. They tended to be conservative, ignoring feasts of recent Catholic institution. I think that Willis (28) is right in interpreting the present passage as indicating that Epiphany, universally celebrated in the Catholic Church of the West since the close of the fourth century, was ignored by the Donatists. On the other hand, they introduced numerous feasts of martyrs of their own sect. These they often celebrated with riotous merriment.

For further information on Donatism, see especially the contemporary work of Optatus of Mileve, *Contra Parmenianum Donatistam* (6 bks.—cf. the annotated translation by O. R. Vassall-Philipps: *The Work of St. Optatus Against the Donatists* [Paris 1912-1922]). See also P. Monceaux, *Histoire littéraire de l'Afrique chrétienne* (Paris 1912-1922) vols. 4, 5, 6; G. Bareille, 'Donat,' DTC 4. 2 (1910) 1687-92; 'Donatisme,' *ibid.* 1701-28; for the archaeological and liturgical material, H. Leclercq, 'Donatisme,' DACL 4. 2 (1921) 1457-1505.

[5] Cf. Isa. 8. 4.
[6] Cf. Matt. 10. 23.
[7] Cf. Matt. 22. 37-40. The two precepts referred to are, of course, 'Thou shalt love the Lord thy God with thy whole heart . . . ,' and, 'Thou shalt love thy neighbor as thyself.' Augustine here attaches a mystical significance to the number '2.' His works abound with passages of this nature in which he attaches such significance to various numbers. See above, nn. 103 f. to *Serm.* 1(51). For evidence of the fascination of numbers for Augustine, see also in this volume *Serm.* 1(51). 32-35, where he treats of the numbers '3,' '4,' '7,' '10,' '11,' '40,' and '77'; *Serm.* 22(203). 3, where he considers the numbers '3,' '4,' and '12.'
[8] Cf. Exod. 12. 9-11.
[9] Cf. Rom. 11. 25.
[10] Ps. 18. 2.

SERMON 22 (203)

[1] Also listed as *De diversis* 64. Because Augustine refers so often to the operation of grace, Kunzelmann, *art. cit.* 461, assigns this sermon to the anti-Pelagian period; and because all such allusions are quite brief, the first stage of this period, 410-412, is taken as the time of delivery.

² *ante dies tredecim natus*: Regarding the actual date of the Magi's coming, see above, n. 13 to *Serm.* 18(199).
³ Cf. Matt. 2. 1-12.
⁴ Luke 2. 14.
⁵ Ps. 18. 2.
⁶ Cf. Eph. 2. 11-22.
⁷ Cf. Luke 2. 20: 'Et reversi sunt pastores glorificantes et laudantes Deum . . . .'
⁸ Cf. Matt. 2. 11: 'Et intrantes domum . . . procidentes *adoraverunt eum*.'
⁹ Cf. Matt. 8. 5-10.
¹⁰ Matt. 15. 28.
¹¹ Cf. Rom. 11. 17.
¹² Jer. 16. 19.
¹³ Cf. Luke 13. 29.
¹⁴ The Latin word *trinitas*, 'Trinity,' 'threeness,' apart from its theological connotation, apparently first found in Tertullian, of course also means the number '3.'
¹⁵ On '12' as a sacred number, cf. also Augustine's *In Ioan. Ev. tract.* 27. 10; *Enarr. in Ps.* 86. 4. It is the perfect number: *ibid.* 59. 2.
¹⁶ Cf. Acts 10. 11 f.

SERMON 23 (204)

¹ Kunzelmann, *art. cit.* 427, finds no approximation of date for this sermon. Cf. below, n. 10.
² 1 Tim. 3. 16.
³ Ps. 18. 2.
⁴ Eph. 2. 15 f. The Vulgate has *reconciliet* ('might reconcile') for *commutaret* ('change,' 'make over').
⁵ *Ibid.* 2. 16 f.
⁶ Ps. 33. 6.
⁷ 1 Peter 2. 6.
⁸ Cf. Isa. 1. 3.
⁹ Ps. 17. 45.
¹⁰ Do we have an indication here that at the time the present sermon was delivered, Epiphany was a very recent institution in Africa?
¹¹ Cf. Eph. 4. 3.

[12] Cf. Matt. 21. 42; Acts 4. 11.
[13] 1 Tim. 1. 7.
[14] Cf. Ps. 117. 22.
[15] Cf. Gen. 32. 24-32. Augustine also has this interpretation elsewhere: *Enarr. in Ps.* 44. 20; *Serm. Guelferb.* 10. 3 (473 Morin).
[16] Matt. 21. 9.
[17] Cf. Augustine's sermon on St. Stephen—314. 2, and K. Baus, *Der Kranz in Antike und Christentum* (Theophaneia 2, Bonn 1940) 181 f.
[18] Gal. 1. 22-24.

INDEX

INDEX

Abraham, 27, 31 ff., 37 f., 40, 64 ff., 166, 176, 202
actor, 153
Adam, 56, 68, 97; whole human race descended from him, 65
adoption, 57 f., 200; referred to in Scripture, 59, 61; through divine grace, 61
adulter, adulterium, etymology of, 196
adultery, 12, 34, 51, 60; is mortal sin, 196
Africa, Africans, 10 f., 16, 195, 221, 230
air, Juno, 148
alliteration, in St. Augustine's sermons, 16
alms, 151; almsgiving wipes away lesser sins, 196
Ambrose, St., 4, 215; influence of his sermons on St. Augustine, 4, 186, 193
Amos, 69
amphitheater, 23 f., 153
angel, angels, 23, 42, 44, 63, 74, 76, 79, 85, 87, 96, 104 f., 117, 122 f., 130, 132, 147, 154, 170 f., 178
anima, animus, 217
Anna, 114, 131 f.
Annunciation, 90
antithesis, in St. Augustine's sermons, 16
Apollo, 146
Apparitio, the feast of Epiphany, 11
Arand, L. A., 199
arena, 22, 153

Arian heresy, 13, 221
ass, symbol for the Gentiles, 212
Artisan, God, 150
Ascension, 9
astrology, astrologers, 15, 164, 212
Athanasius, *C. gent.* 27, 43: 224
Augustine, St., early life foreshadowed success as orator, 4; interest in astrology, 212; difficulties with the Scriptures, 30 f., 192 f.; influenced by sermons of St. Ambrose, 4, 186, 193; ordination, 186; popularity as an orator, 4 f.; fascination with numbers, 12, 202 f., 229 f.; doctrine on Trinity, 222; doctrine on marriage, 196-201, 209 f.; witness to Mary's perpetual virginity, 13, 205; reluctant to accept St. Jerome's translation of the Bible, 17; exchange of letters with St. Jerome, 190

Collatio cum Max. Arian. episc., 221; *Conf.,* 192; 1. 26 f.: 186; 3. 4. 7 f.: 192; 3. 4. 9: 192; 4. 3. 4-6: 212; 5. 23: 186; 5. 24: 186; 6. 3. 3 ff.: 193; 6. 6: 186; 7. 6. 8-10: 212; 9. 19: 195; 11. 4. 6: 224; *C. epist. Manich.* 2. 2: 209; *C. Faust. Man.* 2. 5: 226; 3. 3: 200; 15. 7: 195, 197, 199; 20. 6-8: 188; 30. 5: 197; *C. Iul. Pel.* 3. 43: 195 ff.; 5. 12. 46: 209; 5.62: 199; *C. Max. haer. Arian. episc.* 2. 22: 221; *De bono*

235

coni., 209; 6: 196; 10 f.: 198; 11: 197; 15: 195; 19: 209; *De bono vid.* 5: 196 f.; *De cant. novo*, 188; *De catech. rud.*, 15; *De civ. Dei* 4. 10 f.: 225; 5. 1 ff.: 189, 212; 5. 7: 212; 11. 4: 224; 14. 18: 195; *De cons. Evang.* 1. 45: 225; 2. 3: 200; 2. 4. 12: 202; *De cont.* 27: 198; *De div. quaest.* 1. 56: 188; *De doct. christ.*, 189; 3. 26 f.: 195; *De Gen. ad litt.* 2. 17. 35-37: 212; 9. 7. 12: 209; 11. 56: 195; *De grat. Christi et de pecc. orig.* 2. 43: 195, 197; *De nupt. et conc.* 1. 16: 196, 197, 198; *De pat.*, 188; *De praed. sanct.* 5: 222; *De quant. an.*, 223; 1. 2: 204; *De serm. Dom. in monte* 1. 49 f.: 201; *De Trin.*, 221 f.; 1. 1: 222; 1. 11. 22: 222; 4. 5. 9: 188; 10. 19: 203; *Enarr. in Ps.*, 7; 5. 5: 211; 6. 2: 204; 13. 12: 210; 39. 1: 210; 44. 20: 231; 49.9: 210; 51. 7: 187; 55. 14: 216; 59. 2: 230; 73. 25: 224; 80. 21: 195; 86. 4: 230; 90 *serm.* 2. 9: 210; 94. 11: 216; 99. 13: 218; 105. 36: 211; 118 *serm.* 18. 3: 209; *serm.* 28. 2: 210; 126. 11: 212; 147. 7: 192; *Enchir.* 2. 76: 209; 78: 196, 199; *Ep.* 21. 2: 186; 28: 190; 40: 190; 41.1: 186; 86: 219; 102: 190; 137. 8: 205, 207, 214; 140. 12: 207; *In Epist. Ioan. tract.*, 7; *In Ioan. Ev. tract.*, 7; 8. 4: 210; 27. 10: 230; 34. 2: 188; *Quaest. in Hept.* 2. 90: 188; 2. 47: 202; *Retract.*, 200; 2. 12: 201; 2. 16: 202; 2. 7. 2: 201; *Serm.* 9. 18: 195 f., 198; 19: 191; 37. 7: 195; 53. 6: 209; 82. 10: 193; 83. 3: 204; 83. 7: 203; 88. 5: 209; 90. 6: 210; 125. 9: 203; 150. 1: 190; 159. 3: 209; 232. 2: 213; 252. 11: 202; 278. 9: 195, 197; 278. 9 f.: 198; 287. 4: 220; 314. 2: 231; 332. 4: 195; 351. 5: 197; 355. 2: 186; 9. 2 Morin: 209; Caillau 2. 19. 7 (270 Morin): 191; Mai 158. 2 (382 Morin): 191; Guelferb. 10. 3 (473 Morin): 231

Aurelian, emperor, 9
Author, God, 135, 143
avarice, root of all evils, 69
avaritia, avere, 203

Babylon, 33, 37, 39-42, 193. See transmigration
Babylonians, 40
baptism, remission of all sins in, 68; of John, 65, 68
Bardenhewer, O., 15, 189, 221
Bareille, G., 229
Barker, E., 221
Barry, M. I., 186
baths, purificatory, on summer solstice, 220
Batiffol, P., 214, 223
Baumgartner, W., 194
Baus, K., 231
beast of burden, we are Christ's, 100, 104
Bede, Venerable, 223
belief, necessary for understanding, 140 f.
Benedictines of St. Maur, 18;

Index

edited sermons of St. Augustine, 6 f. See Maurists
benedictio virginum, 214
Benjamin, 40
Bethlehem, 156, 161 f., 166, 169, 226
Bible, quarry for St. Augustine's doctrine, 17; St. Jerome's translation of, 17 f., 190
Blood, of Christ, 167; of the Immaculate Lamb, 151
body, 89, 108; composed of four elements, 69; number four stands for nature of, 70; of man cannot live forever, 53
Boniface, count, 221
bonum matrimonii, 198, 209
botrus, 213
Botte, B., 189, 215
bread, of the children, 176; name for Christ, 75, 107; of the angels, 122, 132
bridal chamber, 88, 93, 116, 125, 128, 214; is womb of the Virgin, 109, 115
Bridegroom, Christ, 88, 93, 115 f., 125, 127 f., 210
Brunner, F. A., 211
Buckland, W. W., 200
Bute, J. Marquess of, 190
Buzy, D., 201

Cabrol, F., 220
Caecilian, 228
Caecilianus, 219
Caesarius of Arles, 220
Cain, 168
Cana, 11
Canaan, 202
Canaanite woman, the, 175
Caritas vestra, 191, 218

Carthage, 4 f., 189, 221, 228
cathari, 228
Catholics, 4, 33, 135, 229; Catholic faith, 102, 139; Catholic Church, 229
centurion, the, in the Gospel, 175
Chaldaei, 212
chamber, of the heart, 88; of the soul, 111
charioteer, 153
charity, 41, 69, 94, 117, 120, 150, 152; wedding garment is, 210
Chastiser of wicked kings, 160
chastity, 198; conjugal, 114, 132; nuptial, 114
Chavasse, C., 210
children, born in wedlock preferred to others, 57; may be begotten (adopted) by benevolent act of will, 59; should be subject to parents, 46; of God, 75; of the kingdom, 166; and heirs of grace, 162; of light, adopted into kingdom of God, 121
Christ, 8 f., 11-14, 22, 24, 28 ff., 35, 37 ff., 41 ff., etc.; had two births, 74, 99, 102, 121, 126 f., 129 f., 135 ff.; genealogy of, 31 ff.; not born of seed of Joseph, 43, 64; why born of a woman, 25 ff.; regarded Mary and Joseph as His parents, 44; was subject to His parents, 46; could have been born without woman, 25 f. See Bread, Bridegroom, Chastiser of wicked kings, Christ, Cornerstone, Day, Day of Day, Deliverer, Dweller of the heav-

ens, Food, Head, *Imperator*, Infant Spouse, Jesus, King, Lamb, Life, Light, Lord of David, Lord of Hosts, Master, Mediator, Peace, Physician, Power, Priest, Prince, Redeemer, Revealer of the Father, Ruler, Savior, Second Man, Shepherd of shepherds, *Sol Iustitiae*, Son of Abraham, Son of David, Son of God, Son of man, Son of the Most High, Spouse, Sun of Justice, Supreme Commander, 'true' Son of God, Wisdom, Word

Christian, Christians, 15, 35, 38, 40 ff., 49, 68, 74, 82, 102, 133, 152, 168, 172, 219; how they should live, 14

Christian faith, 71, 168

Christmas, history of feast, 8-11; sermons for, 71-141

Christopher, J. P., 189, 201

Chrysostom, St. John, 15
  De virg. 19, 29: 199

Church, 9, 26, 28, 41, 49, 57, 59, 67, 94 f., 109, 114, 127, 131, 134, 180, 186, 193, 210, 223, 228; mystical body of Christ, 215; bride of Christ, 94 f., 127, 210; as a virgin, 94 f., 127, 210; both mother and virgin, 109, 114, 127 f.; as a mother, 36, 214, 217; mother of unity, 114; Western, 4, 229; of Africa, 11; of Carthage, 189; Oriental, Eastern, 10 f., 170; of the Gentiles, 170

cibaria, 211

Cicero, 192 f.

Circumcision, history of the feast, 14, 219 f.

circus, 153

Colleran, J. M., 204, 223

Comeau, M., 186, 190

concubinage, 200

conjugal debt, 49, 51, 60. See marriage

conjugal fidelity, 197

conjugal love, 48; grows stronger the more concupiscence is restrained, 49

confessores, 214

consecratio virginum, 214

Constantinople, council of, 221

Cornerstone, Christ, 14, 41 f., 154, 162 ff., 170, 175, 178, 180 ff.

Creator, 27, 74, 84 f., 90, 93 f., 112, 122, 145, 164; recognized from government of universe and directing of souls, 143

creature, not of itself bad, 26; signified by the number seven, 68 f.

Cross, 24, 83, 179 f.

'Crown,' that is, Stephen, 181

Cumont, F., 212, 224

curtains, sign of honor, 29 f.

Cyprian, St., 145, 192, 224

Damasus, pope, 214

dances, dancing, 149, 220

Daniel, 39

D'Arcy, M. C., 223

David, 31 ff., 37 f., 47 f., 66, 83, 202

Day, Day of Day, God of God, 71, 77, 85, 92 f., 96, 104 f., 112, 204, 211

day of our heart, 90

daystar, 125

INDEX 239

deacons, 215
De Bruyne, D., 190
Decalogue, 68
Deceiver, Satan, 144
Declaratio, the feast of Epiphany, 11
Degert, A., 185
Deliverer, Christ, 27
demon-worshippers, 144
demons, 153
Dengler, A., 189
Deogratias, 189
devil, devils, 24, 153
dice, 220
dies, dies ex die, 206, 211
Diespiter, 211
Diocletian, emperor, 10
divine nature, cannot be made less good, 81
divinity, hidden, 76
Dix, G., 189
Dölger, F. J., 185, 188
Donatism, Donatists, 4, 10, 15, 147, 170, 219, 223 f., 228 f.
Donatus, 147, 228
Drum, W., 226
drunkards, 54
Duchesne, L., 188, 215, 220
Dux, Christ, 192
Dweller of the heavens, Christ, 159

Egypt, Egyptians, 144, 171
Eisenhofer, L., 189, 215
eleven, signifies transgression or sin, 68 f., 203
Elias, 54, 67
Elizabeth, 114, 131
Emmanuel, 87, 90, 208
Empedocles, 204
eloquia, 201

Epiphania, 167, 169, 174, 178
Epiphanius, *Haer.* 78. 18: 213
Epiphany, history of feast, 8, 10 f.; sermons for, 154-182
Eusebius, *Hist. Eccl.* 1. 7: 200
Eve, 109
Evilmerodach, 193
Evodius, 223
eye, eyes, of the heart, 23, 91, 209; of the body cannot see soul, 143
Ezechiel the Prophet, 39

faith, 23, 29, 36, 41, 45, 78, 94, 97 ff., 108, 114, 117, 124, 130, 135, 146, 150, 152, 155, 165, 175 f., 181 f., 193; Catholic, 102, 139; Christian, 71, 168; importance of, 13; nest of, 3, 31; resides in believer's will, 222; comprehends what reason cannot solve, 103; contaminated faith—heresy—attacks Church's virginity, 210; we were night when living without, 102; first fruits of, 174; thousands of martyrs have died for, 33
fans, fari, 104, 206
Farrington, B., 212
Father, God the, 13, 44, 46, 68, 72, 74, 76, 80-83, 85, 87, 89, 91, 96, 98 f., 101, 104 f., 107 f., 113, 115, 121, 123-128, 135-141, 152, 158, 177 f., 206, 211, 221 f.
Felix of Aptunga, 228
femina, 194
fertility, in marriage, inferior to virginity in life of piety, 94
Festus, 196

feta, fetum, fetalia, 216
fides, in marriage, 198, 209
fifty, number for beatific vision, 203
Finaert, J., 186
first man, not made of woman, 25
first fruits, 173, 179; of the Gentiles, 159, 170, 174, 177, 180; of the faith, 174
Florus, deacon of Lyons, 223
Food, eternal, of the angels, 122; and Bread of the angels, 132; of wisdom, 86; of incorruption, 76; Christ became our, 100; of the faithful beasts of burden, 104
food, spiritual, 31
fornication, 146, 198; a mortal sin, 196
forty, signifies life on earth, 66, 202 f.; in Scripture, 66 f.
Fountain, Christ, 107; of life, 124, 156
four, stands for the nature of the body, 70
Frank, H., 188 f.
Freese, J. H., 191
Friedländer, K., 191

Gabriel, 90
games, 133, 220
Gaul, 6, 220
genealogy of Christ, 12, 191; why traced through St. Joseph, 42 f., 62 ff.
Gentiles, 11, 14, 39-42, 60, 105, 142, 149 f., 152, 154, 158 f., 162-168, 170, 172-175, 177, 179 f., 182, 212, 216
Getty, M. M., 185

gift, of the Holy Spirit, 146; which the married cherish, 94
Gilson, E., 217 f., 222
gladiatorial shows, 21, 191
gluttons, 54
God, 3, 9, 13, 17, 21-24, 26, 33, 36 f., 41, 43-48, etc.; argument for existence of, 142 f., 223 f.; praise of, sole occupation in the beatific vision, 203; nature of, 81; begot Son as an equal, 136 f.; number of, not increased when God was born of God, 126; has many sons, 138
gold, 169, 171, 173; of honor, 172
good will, 79, 118 ff., 122
gormandizers, 54
Gospel, 27, 33, 37, 40 ff., 47, 81, 83, 99, 105, 117, 131 f., 157, 165, 173 f., 176, 211, 216, 227; is 'good news,' 211; of John, 137, 141; Gospels not in disagreement, 29
Grabmann, M., 187, 203
grace, 49, 61, 78 f., 103, 114, 118 f., 138, 155, 162 f., 175 f., 229
Gundel, W., 189
γυνή, 207 f.

habitus, 209
Head, Christ, 114, 147; of the Church, immaculate, 109
heathens, 153
heaven, heavens, 74, 76, 116, 147, 154 f., 158 f., 173, 177 f., 182, 206
Hefele, C. J., 219

INDEX

happiness, signified by the number ten, 68
Heli, 59, 62, 200
Helios, 188. See sun
Hemera, 211
Herald, John the Baptist, 131, 133
heresy, attacks the Church's virginity, 210
heretics, 139, 163; usefulness of, 36
Herod, 11, 156, 160, 169, 172
Hippo, 4, 5, 186, 218 f., 221
Hofmann, J. B., 194, 196, 214 f.
Holy Spirit, 12, 33, 35, 40, 43, 45, 63 f., 68, 115, 120, 146, 181; gift of, 146
homily, in the liturgy of the Mass, 211
homoeoteleuton, in St. Augustine's sermons, 16
Honoratus, 207
hope, 41, 94, 117, 146, 150, 152; of salvation, 103
Howard, W. F., 204
Humeau, G., 19
humility, of God, 28, 71 f., 75, 93 f., 99, 159
Hummel, E. L., 192
husband, conjugal love and relations of, 49; conjugal master of wife's body, 201
husbandry, of God, 41
Hyginus, *Fab. praef.*: 211

idols, idolatry, 14, 144, 148, 171
image, images, 144 f., 148
image-worshippers, 148
Imperator, Christ, 192
Incarnation, 40, 98, 107, 204, 214; all sins of the human race assumed in, 65
incense, 153, 169, 173; of adoration, 172
infans, 104, 206
infans Verbum, 13, 206, 226
Infant Spouse, 109
inner chamber of soul, 111
inner eyes, 218
inner man, 84
intellect, 88
intellectus, 217
intelligentia, 203, 217
interpreters, of what images represent, 148
Irenaeus, *Adv. haer.* 5. 19. 1: 213; 5. 33. 3: 213; *Dem. praed. apost.* 33: 213
Isaac, 31, 166, 176
Isaias, 129, 212
Israel, 38, 40 f., 163, 171, 173, 175, 182
Iuppiter, 211
iustus, iustitia, 226 f.

Jacob, son of Isaac, 31, 60, 166, 176, 181
Jacob, father of St. Joseph, 32, 58, 62, 200 f.
Janus, 219
Jechonias, 32, 37 ff., 41 f., 193
Jeremias, 39 f., 176
Jerome, St., 18, 204; exchange of letters with St. Augustine, 190
Jerusalem, 43, 100, 104, 193, 212
Jessen, O., 211
Jesus, 22, 25, 29, 31 ff., etc.; means 'Savior,' 35. See Christ
Jews, 16, 39, 40 ff., 47, 61, 77, 97, 133, 142, 154 ff., 160, 165 f., 174 f., 179 f., 212, 216; in Hippo, 219; their Scriptures

bear witness to Christ and instruct the Gentiles, 14, 161 f., 167 f., 172 f., 181
Job, 211
John the Baptist, 65, 68, 121, 216, 220; Herald of the Judge, 131, 133
John Chrysostom, St., 15, 199
John the Evangelist, 140 f.; Epistle of, 137; Gospel of, 137, 141
Joseph, St., 32 f., 35, 44, 46 ff., 56 f., 68, 202; paternity of, 12, 63 f., 189; why Christ's genealogy is traced through him, 42 f., 62 ff.; two fathers of, 58-62, 200 f.; witness of Mary's virginity, 34
Joseph, son of Patriarch Jacob, 60
Judas, the traitor, 36
Judea, 154 f., 158, 182
Judge, Christ, 107, 131, 133
Judgment, 132, 160
Julian of Eclanum, 199
Julian Calendar, 9
Julius Africanus, 200 f.
Jungmann, J. A., 211
Juno, 148, 225
justice, 63, 69, 76 ff., 97, 107, 114 f., 119, 124
Justinian, 200

Kalt, E., 202
Kellner, K. A. H., 220
King, Christ, 173; of the ages, 165; of glory, 124; of heaven, 154; of the Jews, 14, 155, 165 ff.; of all nations, 57
kingdom, 38 f., 152, 160; of God, 121; of heaven, 176; of the devil, 171
kings, 24, 28, 40, 145, 160, 165
kiss of peace, 179
Knox, R. A., 194, 209, 222, 227
Koehler, L., 194
Kübler, B., 195
Kunzelmann, A., 18, 186, 190 f., 204, 206-210, 212 f., 215-218, 221, 223, 225-230

Ladomérszky, N., 199
Lamb, Immaculate, 151
Lambot, D. C., 18, 187 f., 204
Lauer, P., 186 f.
laurel, 53
Law, the, 142, 172, 180 f.; giving of, 61
Leage, R. W., 200
Lebreton, J., 222
Leclercq, H., 189, 219, 226, 229
levir, levirate law, 200 ff.
Lia, 60
Liar, Satan, 144
Liberius, pope, 214
lie, 145
Life, Christ, 107; of men, 91; and Light of men, 92
Light, Christ, 107; of the world, 154; of men, 92; and Life of men, 91; of Light, 96, 126, 204, 211
Lindner, D., 199
lineage, of Christ, 31 f.
Lord of David, Christ, 47 f., 90
Lord of Hosts, Christ, 124
Lucilla, 228
Luke, St., 12, 58, 62, 64 f., 68, 70, 176, 200
lust, 34, 50, 52-57; does not make a wife, 48 f.
lustratio, 224

INDEX 243

Maas, A. J., 201
Macmullen, R. G., 18, 202
Magi, 8, 11, 14, 16, 76, 154, 156 ff., 160-164, 166 f., 170-176, 178 f., 206, 226, 230
Magnus, L. A., 191
Majorinus, 228
male sex, shown preference in the Incarnation, 26
man, consists of body and soul, 70, 81; made after image of God in his soul, 69, 203 f.; signified by the number seven, 203; cannot see soul, 143; to be given precedence over woman, 63; wanted to be God, 93; needs God's salvation and mercy, 142
Mangenot, E., 202
manger, Christ in the, 75 f., 85, 93, 99 f., 104 f., 122, 125, 132 f., 171
Manichaeans, 188, 193, 198, 212, 218
Manifestatio, Manifestation, the feast of Epiphany, 11, 159, 164, 167, 169, 174, 178
Marcellina, sister of St. Ambrose, 214 f.
marriage, 12, 49, 51, 56 f., 73, 109, 114, 195; of Word of God and human creation, 115; of Christ and the Church, 210; spiritual, 205; mystical, of virgins, 214 f.; threefold blessings of, 209; St. Augustine's doctrine on, 196-201, 209 f.
marriage contract, 50 f., 195, 201
married life, 54, 58, 131
Martin of Bracara, 219
Martindale, C., 189

martyrs, made a spectacle, 23; thousands died for faith, 33
Mary, 8, 12 f., 25, 31 ff., 35, 42 f., 47 f., 62 ff., 78, 82, 109, 114, 127, 131 f., 204, 208; ever a virgin, 45, 94-97, 108, 113, 127, 130, 205, 218, *passim*; her virginity to be imitated, 110 f.; bore Christ without labor, 207; modesty and humility of, 44 f., 63
Mary Magdalen, 213
mas, 194
Master, 74, 109
mathematici, 212
Matthew, St., 12, 30 f., 33, 36, 58, 62, 64-67, 200
Maurists, 187, 190, 206, 208, 210, 218, 220. See Benedictines of St. Maur
Mausbach, J. 187, 196, 199, 203
Maximinus, Arian bishop, 221
Maximus of Turin, 219
McClure, M. L., 188
McKeough, M. J., 204
Mediator, Christ, 67, 127
Megalius, primate of Numidia, 186
members of Christ, 114, 131, 133, 172
memoria, memory, 203
mens, 217
Migne, P. J., 18, 185
Milan, 4, 186, 193
Milne, C. H., 190
mimic, 153
Minucius Felix, *Oct.* 17 ff.: 224
Mithraism, 224
Mohrmann, C., 19, 187 f., 190
Mommsen, T., 191
Monceaux, P., 229

Morin, G., 18, 188, 210 f.
Moses, 60, 67
Moulard, M. 199
Moulton, J. H., 204
mulier, 194, 208
Müller, J., 189
munus, munera, 191 f.
myrrh, 169, 173; of burial, 172
mysterium, 193
mystery, mysteries, 13, 25, 35-38, 61, 70, 101, 159, 166

Nabuchodonosor, 193
natalis Solis Invicti, 9, 213
natalis Christi, 9
Nathan, 66, 202
nature, divine and human, mutability in, 81
Nazareth, 46
Neptune, 145, 224
New Year's Day, 8; pagan celebrations and festivities on, 13, 219; Circumcision probably not celebrated before sixth century, 14; sermons for, 142-153
New Year's presents, 150 ff., 225
Nicaea, council of, 221
night, when living without faith we were, 102
Nilsson, M. P., 225
Noe, 65
number, numbers, St. Augustine's fascination with and mystical significance attached to, 12, 202 f., 229 f.
Numidia, 228

O'Brien, M. B., 191
occidens, 227
oculus cordis, 209

Oepke, A., 208
olive, 53, 163, 166, 176
Optatus of Mileve, 11, 229
orators, 28, 145
oriens, 227
Origen, 200, 205
Otto, A., 200
ox, symbol for the Jews, 212

pagan, pagans, 4, 14 f., 144, 147, 150, 162
pantomime, 153
Papias, 213
Paradise, 26, 45, 93
parallelism, in St. Augustine's sermons, 16
Passion, 9, 36, 163, 165; Passiontide, 167
passover, 172
patria potestas, 200
Patriarchs, 52; allowed plurality of wives for sake of procreating children, 55 f.
Paul, St., 40, 61, 109, 138, 146, 148, 190, 196 f., 201, 223 f.
Paulus Diaconus, 196
paupers, 145
peace, 41, 78 f., 118 f., 154, 170, 179 f.; name for Christ, 114, 164, 175
Pelagians, 199, 206 f.
Pentecost, 9
Pereira, B. A., 195, 199, 201
Peter, St., 70, 138, 145, 177, 190, 214
Peter Chrysologus, 219
Peters, J., 201
Pharaoh's daughter, 60
Pharisees, 163
Phillott, H. W., 221

Index

Philocalus, Philocalian Calendar, 189, 191
philosophers, philosophy, 28, 145, 148
Physician, Christ, 128, 218
Pilate, 165 ff.
Plato, *De leg.* 10 f.: 223 f.
Plautus, *Persa* 174: 206
Plumpe, J. C., 203, 205, 207 f., 210, 214, 217 f.
Plutarch, 200
Pontet, M., 190
Pope, H., 17, 185 ff., 189 f., 219 f.
Portalié, E., 207
Poseidon, 224
Possidius, 3, 185, 190, 221
    Vita S. August. 4: 186; 5: 186; 7: 187; 8: 186; 17: 221; 31: 185; *Indiculus* 8: 190
Power, Christ, 46
presbyters, 133
pride, 94, 143 f., 146, 163; great evil of the human soul, 28; hinders understanding of the Scriptures, 30
Priest, Christ, 173
primordia, four elements, 204
Prince, Christ, of virgins, 94; and Shepherd of shepherds, 104
proles, 199, 209
prophecy, prophecies, 162, 168 f., 172 f.
Prosper of Aquitaine, 221
Providence, 162
pueri sancti, 205
purgatio, 224

Quasten, J., 215
quaternity, 81

Rachel, 60
Rahner, H., 10, 189
ratio, 217
Raulx, M., 18, 211, 220
Redeemer, Christ, 74, 110, 151
Resurrection, 9, 40, 107, 181, 213; announced to Apostles by women, 26; announced to the world by Apostles, 27
Reuter, A., 199, 210
Revealer of the Father, Christ, 85
Rhetorica ad Herennium 4. 28. 39: 200
rhyme, in St. Augustine's sermons, 16
rites, of the pagans, 144
Riviére, J., 207
Rome, Romans, 4, 9 f., 83, 219
Rose, H. J., 188, 224 f.
Rule of Faith, 81 f.
Ruler, Christ, 75; of stars, 85, 132, 158; of all days, 121; of pious kings, 160
Rush, A. C., 188

sacramentum, 193, 201, 209
saints, God speaks in, 147
salvation, 22, 28, 77, 96, 105, 111, 154; man needs God's, 142; of faith, hope, charity, the spirit, God's promises, 150; both man and woman have hope for, 103; announced by women, 26; first fruits of, 174; of all nations, 177
Samaria, 170 f.; synonymous with idolatry, 171
Sanctitas vestra, 193
Sara, 60
Satan, 51

Sauer, J., 187
Savior, 13, 35, 71, 94, 99, 117, 122, 127, 170, 173, 181, 214; is meaning of Jesus, 35
Schmaus, M., 222
Schmid, J., 190
Schmitt, A., 19, 203
Schneider, K., 191
Scribes, 163
Scriptures, 27, 30, 34, 36, 42 f., 45 f., 49 f., 53 f., 59 ff., 66, 70, 81, 83, 96, 151, 155 f., 160 ff., 167 ff., 172, 175; are lamps lit in the night of our life, 96; St. Augustine's first experience with, 192; to be approached with humility, 30; how to consider, 13, 70; as used in St. Augustine's sermons, 16 ff.
sea, 145, 148, 224
Second Man, Christ, 73
secundum veniam, in 1 Cor. 7. 6, 197, 200
sedatio concupiscentiae, 196 ff.
senators, 145
septuagies septies, in Matt. 18. 22, 204
sermon, in the liturgy of the Mass, 211
sermons of St. Augustine, how preserved, 5 ff.; number of, 7; length of, 15; language of, 15 f.; use of Scripture in, 16 ff.; reflect lives of early Christians, 3
serpent, used woman to cause downfall of man, 103
seven, signifies creature, 68 f., 203; number of fullness or completion, 203

seventy-seven, signifies remission of all sins, 68, 70
Sheen, F. J., 224
Shepherd of shepherds, Christ, 104
shepherds, of Bethlehem, 76, 117, 154, 158, 163 f., 170, 174 ff., 178 f., 206
shows, 22, 153; gladiatorial, 21, 191
Sigisvult, count, 135, 221
Simeon, 105
Simon Magus, 146
sin(s), signified by the number eleven, 68; committed in will alone or by works of the body, 69; derived from pride, 144; are also punishments, 144 f.; lesser, wiped away by almsgiving, 196; remission of all, signified by the number seventy-seven, 68, 70
Sion, 179
Smith, W., 221
Socrates, 200, 223
v. Soden, H., 193
Sol, equivalent to Helios, 188
Sol Invictus, 9, 11
Sol Iustitiae, Christ, 188
Solomon, 32, 37 f., 66
Son, Son of God, 13, 22, 25, 36, etc.; of Abraham, 31 ff., 66; of David, 31 ff., 47 f., 66, 90; of man, 13, 22, 25, 44, 46 f., 79, 81 ff., 85, 87, 90, 108, 113, 123, 126; of the Most High, 45
songs, 149
sons of God, 112, 123, 138, 206
soul(s), 17, 82, 89, 99, 111, 127, 130, 144, 146, 159, 223; number three stands for nature of,

INDEX

70; created after image of God, 204; in which there is a certain image of the Trinity, 69; cannot be seen by body's eyes, 143; does not consist of the four elements, 204; presence of, recognized from activity and government of the body, 143; separates itself from the Lord by fornication of sin, 69; not destroyed with the body, 23

spectacles, of truth and of flesh, 22; of truth seen with eyes of the heart, 23; for the mind, 37; Christ and martyrs made a, 22 f.

spectare, spectaculum, spectator, 192

spectators, sensual and spiritual, at Christian shows, 23

spirit, 108

spiritus, 217

Spouse, Christ, 109, 146; of the Church, 95; of virgins, 110, 205

star, of Bethlehem, 10, 14, 154-159, 161, 164 f., 169 ff., 174, 178, 206; a new, 158, 165; of the Magi, succeeded by the Gospel, 165

stars, do not affect men's lives, 101, 157 f. See astrology

Stephen, St., 181, 231

strenae, Strenia, 225

Strength, Christ, 107

'summer Christmas,' 220

summer solstice, 216, 220

sun, 9, 80, 85, 102, 145, 165, 188, 212. See Sol, *Sol Invictus*

Sun of Justice, Christ, 9, 13, 102, 188

Supreme Commander, Christ, 25

Susanna, 132

tabulae nuptiales, matrimoniales, 195

Teacher, Christ, 93, 107, 156

temple, Christ's in hearts of believers, 106

ten, signifies sum total of righteousness and happiness, 66-68; the perfect number, 203

Tertullian, 192, 205, 219, 230
  De idol. 14: 219

theaters, 151, 153, 220

Theophilus of Antioch, *Ad Autol.* 1. 5 f.: 224

three, stands for nature of the soul, 70

Tierney, J. J., 220

Tours, council of, 219

traditor, 228

transgressio, transgression, that is, sin, signified by the number eleven, 68 f., 203

transmigration, to Babylon, 32 f., 38, 41; prefigured passage of the Gospel to the Gentiles, 38 ff.

treasures, of wisdom and knowledge, 123; hidden not to deny, but to arouse desire, 29

trinitas, 230

Trinity, 81, 176, 221 f., 230; appeared at Lord's baptism by John, 68; image of, in man's soul, 69

Tromp, S., 210

'true' Son of God, 138

truth, 36, 75, 81, 128, 135 f.,

145 f., 165, 168, 171, 173; name for God, 13, 71, 76-79, 97 f., 107 f., 112, 114 ff., 119
twelve, sacred number, 176; perfect number, 230

unbelievers, will remain ignorant, 141
understanding, 203; faith necessary for, 140 f.
uxor, 194

Valerius, bishop of Hippo, 4, 186
Varro, *De lingua latina* 5. 66: 211
Vassall-Philipps, O. R., 229
Vega, A. C., 185
Verbum infans, 13, 206, 226
viduae, viduatus, 214 f.
Vigouroux, F., 202
Vine, Christ, 107
virgines sacrae, sanctae, 214
virginity, glory of, began with Mary, 57; of Mary to be imitated, 110; way of life, 131; leads to fruitfulness of the spirit, 110 f.; in life of piety is better than fertility in marriage, 94
virgins, why they pass over opportunity of being mothers, 94; may espouse selves to Christ without corruption, 73, 110; should not praise themselves, 132; reception of, 214 f.; how we should all be, 111, 114
virgo, 194
virtus, 194
Visigoth mercenaries, 221

Viteau, J., 215
Vogt, P., 201
volition, 203
voluntas, 204
Volusianus, 207, 214
de Vreese, L. J., 212

Wace, H., 221
Walde, A., 194, 196
Waser, O., 211
Way, Christ, 100, 107
wedding garment, charity as a, 210
wedlock, a way of life, 131. See marriage
Weiskotten, H. T., 185
widowhood, 114; a way of life, 131
widows, 114; position and duties of, 214 f.
Willis, G. G., 228 f.
Wilmart, A., 187, 189, 223
Wilpert, J., 187
winter solstice, 208, 212; date for *natalis Invicti* and for *natalis Christi,* 9
wisdom, true, is of and is God, 71 f.; food of, 86; name for Christ, 46, 76, 132
Wissowa, G., 188
woman, used by serpent to cause man's downfall, 103; has hope for salvation, 103; man deceived and saved through, 26; the word, as used in Scripture, 45, 83, **194, 207 f.**
Wood, the Cross, 24, 166
Word, Word of God, 9, 13, 43, 46, 67, 75 f., 78, 80 ff., 85, 89, 91 ff., 96, 98, 102 f., 107, 115,

122, 128 f., 132, 140, 157, 171, 174; remains forever and unchangeable, 88; is never silent, 43; compared with human words, 86 ff.
wordplay, in St. Augustine's sermons, 16
wrath of God, 142

Xenophon, *Mem.* 1. 4. 4-10, 4. 3. 3-9: 223

Zacharias, 63
Zachary, 131
Zarb, S. M., 192
Zellinger, J., 220
Ziegler, C. H., 200